D0162807

# A CONCISE GUIDE TO COMPOSITION

# A CONCISE GUIDE TO COMPOSITION

## THIRD EDITION

LOUISE E. RORABACHER

Harper & Row, Publishers
New York, Hagerstown, San Francisco, London

Sponsoring Editor: George A. Middendorf
Project Editor: Alice Solomon
Designer: Michel Craig
Production Supervisor: Francis X. Giordano
Compositor: American Book–Stratford Press, Inc.
Printer: The Murray Printing Company
Binder: Halliday Lithograph Corporation

A Concise Guide to Composition, Third Edition

Copyright © 1956 by Harper & Row, Publishers, Inc. Copyright © 1963 by
Louise E. Rorabacher. Copyright © 1976 by Louise E. Rorabacher.

All rights reserved. Printed in the United States of America. No part of this
book may be used or reproduced in any manner whatsoever without written
permission except in the case of brief quotations embodied in critical articles
and reviews. For information address Harper & Row, Publishers, Inc., 10
East 53rd Street, New York, N.Y. 10022.

Library of Congress Cataloging in Publication Data

Rorabacher, Louise Elizabeth, Date—
    A concise guide to composition.

    Includes index.
    1. English language—Rhetoric. I. Title.
PE1408.R67        1976        808′.042        75–34157
ISBN 0–06–045569–1

# CONTENTS

# 9 DOING LIBRARY RESEARCH   227

# 10 HANDLING THE BUSINESS LETTER   263

# APPENDIXES   291

# INDEX   319

# TO THE INSTRUCTOR

*The conciseness of the first edition of* A Concise Guide to Composition *was somewhat disturbed in the second by the addition, as a result of general demand, of chapters on the research paper and the business letter. Now, in the third, you will find that the book has been restored to approximately its original size with little loss of subject matter through a general streamlining. The exercises in particular have been reduced sharply on the recommendation of users who recognize that no models in this book could be as valuable to you and your class for analysis and correction as your students' own themes. If other prepared exercises are desired, however, they are available in the practice pages designed for use with this text.*

*The handbook sections of dictionaries are usually devoted to the mechanics of writing: punctuation, capitalization, etc. So is* A Concise Guide. *But it goes farther, becoming a small rhetoric by concentrating also on such matters as the organization and writing of themes, the development of paragraphs, and the choosing of words. Its omissions are the necessary price of conciseness.*

*Many college courses can be laid out neatly from simple beginnings to complex ends. In writing, unfortunately, the student needs to know everything at once. As instructor you* will of course feel free to present the material here in any order you see fit or to omit any for which you lack time or inclination. The chapters on writing the theme and the paragraph have been placed first here in the belief that students of composition ought to start right in composing, for their own practice and for your diagnosis. The materials on the use of the word (dictionary, diction, spelling) come next for their interest and usefulness. A new chapter on building the sentence replaces the earlier chapter on traditional grammar, which has become an alphabetized Glossary of Grammatical Terms in the Appendix for ready reference as needed. But as before, the library research paper and the business letter are left until last, when the student will have gained the confidence and the competence necessary for undertaking these special types.

In this new edition the entire book has been updated, not only in models but in judgments. Language is a changing thing, and its custodians are having an increasingly difficult time in keeping up with it. The middle years of this century have seen the change from the authoritarianism of the prescriptionists to the permissiveness of the descriptionists, a change made vivid by the differences between the Second Edition of the unabridged Webster's New International Dictionary (1934) and the Third (1961).

From the flood of dictionaries published in recent years I have chosen the American Heritage Dictionary as my guide to usage in this book, as I find invaluable its percentage rendering of the acceptability of a debatable form by its Usage Panel— more than a hundred present, prestigious, and professional users of the language ranging from Walter Lippman to Gloria Steinem. How better to determine what English is ''standard''? My best advice throughout this book to students who aspire to master their language is to read the works of good users of it, watching how they employ words. The Heritage Panel's judgments are just a quicker way to learn the feeling of many writers about a particular use; I have invoked its majority rulings freely and frequently.

Where these have been lacking, I have reported my own impressions of commonly observed distinctions between standard and nonstandard, formal and informal English, while *recognizing that there are honest differences of opinion in these matters and that usage is changing so rapidly as to make any book such as this one out-of-date, in spots, before it gets into print. I have also tried to indicate, with labels, the really sour notes with which nonstandard English assaults the ears of standard English users, as apart from relatively minor differences. The labels* Right *and* Wrong *have been replaced by a variety of gentler and more discriminating notations.*

*This book is still intended for the student who is obliged to do some writing rather than for the writer who happens to be a student. For this reason it has been kept brief and simple in language and arrangement as well as in matter. It is written in direct, familiar English, its contents held to a few chapters. As before, the headings of the various topics discussed in some of these chapters have been given appropriate abbreviations (S i for Sentence—incomplete, etc.). Listed alphabetically inside the front cover, and in the order of their appearance inside the back, they make it easy for the users to find their way around in the book. They have also been used generously as cross references within the text itself and from the Glossary of Grammatical Terms to the text.*

*As instructor you may find them convenient to use as correction symbols in the margins of student papers, with a choice of levels: for example, P for punctuation in general, P d for dash, and even P d 2 for dash, rule number 2. Being logical abbreviations instead of the arbitrary numbers used in some handbooks, they will come readily to your mind at the first two levels, as well as being conveniently at hand. And on a theme they will guide the student writer to the sections of the text that need reviewing before the errors are corrected.*

*To snug up the material I have from the beginning taken the liberty of omitting the customary "Mechanics" section, and have included (logically, I think) capitals, numbers, and abbreviations in the spelling section, along with the usual apostrophes, plurals, and hyphens; and italics in the punctuation section, since they are sometimes interchangeable with quotation marks. I trust that these arrangements will not confuse but will, as intended, simplify.*

*L.E.R.*

**ACKNOWLEDGMENTS**

*The author and publisher are grateful for the aid of the following persons for their initial guidance relative to the direction that this present revision should take, and their subsequent careful review of the manuscript: George F. Estey of Boston University, Susan Waugh Allen of Meramac Community College, Georgia S. Dunbar of Hofstra University, David Hurt of General Motors Institute, and Nell Ann Pickett of Hinds Junior College*

*The author would like to acknowledge the assistance of Page Karling, West Lafayette, Indiana; Carol Lawrence, Sun City Center, Florida; Janet McNary, Orangeburg, South Carolina.*

# A
# CONCISE
# GUIDE
# TO
# COMPOSITION

# 1
# WRITING THE THEME

Just as in a speech course you do some talking, so in a composition course you do some writing. Your instructor will probably assign a number of themes—papers whose primary purpose is to give you writing practice. Many of the general suggestions for their preparation will also be useful in the writing of other compositions, now and later—term papers and essay-type examinations in college, letters and job and community project reports outside college.

## T S / THEME—SUBJECT

*In deciding on a subject, think first of yourself as writer, next, of your readers.*
(Exercises 1–2, p. 23)

For yourself, you will wish to choose something on which you can write competently and enjoyably; for your readers, something in which you can interest them. Your instructor may give you a particular subject to write about, or a group of subjects from which to choose one, or a large area within which to find a small one, or a particular type of composition such as a process, a comparison, an analysis. In any event you your-self will have to decide just what materials you will use for the assignment. And when you think of your readers in making your selection, think of them not just as your instructor and your class but as the general reading public. Only in technical writing will you be likely to need to appeal to a specialized group.

Your chief source of subject matter is your personal experience, which is inevitably a rich one. The college freshman who once complained that he would have to go out and get run over by a truck in order to have something to write about just hadn't learned how and where to look for worthwhile material. For considerably more than a decade you have been living, reading, thinking—perhaps living in various places and under various circumstances, certainly reading about various subjects and arriving at various conclusions. All of this is a rich lode of experience waiting to be mined for your writing. Let your thoughts run slowly over the areas listed below, and others they suggest, to see what a wealth of material emerges.

1.  Your family: background, members, relationships, home, business, customs, pets, relatives, vacations.
2.  Your community: type, location, interests, industries, special places, events.
3.  Your education: at home, kindergarten, grade school, high school, or other.
4.  Your courses: kinds—lectures, discussions, labs; subjects—history, mathematics, literature, band, shop.
5.  Your activities: gangs, clubs, sports, music, dramatics.
6.  Your recreation: radio, television, movies, hobbies.
7.  Your reading: books, magazines, newspapers.
8.  Your jobs: part-time, full-time, summer.
9.  Your travel: places, means, purposes.
10. Your attitudes: political, religious, educational, social; likes and dislikes; changes in attitude.
11. Your acquaintances: neighbors, teachers, odd characters, employers, friends (of both sexes).
12. Your future: hopes, plans, career, location, family.
13. Events and problems: campus, community, state, national, international.

14. Developments: agriculture, aviation, biology, education, journalism, law, business, engineering, home economics, medicine, politics, space program.
15. Customs: clothing, hair styles, entertainment, dating, manners.

A good rule to follow in your compositions is to write, as the specialist is said to learn, "more and more about less and less." This does not mean that you should pad or inflate a simple subject, but that you should develop a limited area thoroughly rather than a large one sketchily. Your instructor— or time, or interest, or other circumstances—will probably suggest an appropriate length for a given assignment. In choosing your material, take a subject that can be handled thoroughly within that length. You might write within a class period a successful account of your first train or plane ride, whereas the general subject of railroads or aviation would be far too large for you to attempt under any circumstances. Avoid the twin hazards of overcondensing your material to fit a large subject into a small space, and of padding it with excess words (**D w**) and unimportant or unrelated details (**Par u**) to make a small subject fill more pages.

Two examples of writing follow. The first, an account of a brief but significant personal experience, was written by a student in a freshman composition course. Note that she accomplished her purpose in well under the 500 words frequently suggested for such papers. The second is a longer published article by an educator. Read both carefully, for they will be referred to frequently throughout this chapter.

**Example I:** Out in the Cold
Martha Solomon

(1)  Another sharp, snow-filled gust of wind blew against my back, and practically pushed me around the corner of the block. Instinctively I drew my coat collar closer and shoved my hands deeper into my pockets although I did not really need to, for my coat was very warm and my gloves thick. With this reassuring thought of warmth flitting across

my mind, I was startled to notice a small boy huddled against the stone molding which projected from a store front.

(2)    The child was visibly shaking, and this was certainly understandable, for his coat was thin and patched, as were his pants, and his shoes showed evidence that other pairs of feet had walked and run in them, for they were worn and far too large for his feet. His shaggy hair, with no cap to cover it, fell into his eyes.

(3)    His face looked rather expressionless, but as I stooped down, his gaze focused on me, and a chill went up my spine to see the eyes, not of a child, but of one who had known suffering and the hard realities of the world about him.

(4)    Having taken my lunch hour, I was on my way back to the store where I worked, so I timidly asked him to come along. Trying to read his thoughts, I added, ''Loads of people stop in to warm up on days like this.'' He did come, but again that strange feeling came over me, for when he stood up, he didn't hesitate, yet he didn't do it with enthusiasm; he just came.

(5)    At the store we sat and munched on cookies left over from someone's lunch. He told me his name was Bob —not Bobbie, but Bob. In this and with each sentence he uttered, his apparent maturity appalled me. His solemnity never relaxed, although I tried and tried to make him smile.

(6)    As the afternoon wore on, I returned to him after each customer, for he was content to sit quietly and observe. However, when I started toward his chair once again, I found him gone, though no one had seen him leave. The independent and ragged little boy with the knowing eyes had once again stepped out into the cold.

**Example II:**    The Functions of the Community College
                   Sigurd Rislov

(1)    Since the turn of the century, a new educational institution has appeared in America. During the past fifty

years, it has grown at an accelerated pace until it has become standard equipment in the nation's public school program.

(2)   This institution is the public two-year college, sometimes called a junior college, a community college, or just plain college. The typical community college is a local organization, either district or county. Nine-tenths of its students live within a 35-mile radius. There are no fraternities or sororities and usually no dormitories. It boasts small classes, emphasis on teaching, a comprehensive advisory and counseling program for its students, and a personal student-teacher relationship. It undertakes three major functions.

(3)   First and paramount is its program of lower-division, freshman-sophomore courses paralleling the state university and other senior institutions. Students planning to specialize in any of the regular or academic professional areas, such as law, medicine, dentistry, engineering, teaching, business, psychology, physics, chemistry, botany, can begin college in their own community and transfer with comparable advanced standing to senior institutions for completion of their training without loss of time or credits. About 35 per cent of the full-time students in community colleges complete advanced work at a senior institution.

(4)   Second, it provides terminal training for students who are not going to be baccalaureate candidates but who want and need more education than high school provides. For these there are such alternatives as trade courses in airframe and aircraft engine mechanics, auto mechanics, radio and television servicing, metal shop, machine shop, or courses for the semiprofessional technician in the various branches of engineering or in laboratories. Some terminal students take business courses, secretarial training, or agriculture. Others take regular lower-division college courses in order to be more knowledgeable persons with broader intellectual and emotional horizons, whatever their occupations.

(5)   Besides these two services for the college-age

**5**

population, the community college attempts to be an educational and cultural reservoir for the adult population of the area. This is its third function and it does this in several ways. One is by providing evening courses for people already employed or in business. The content of such courses is determined by the nature of the group for which they are operated and by interests and wants of the population. There may be classes in modern world problems, history, psychology, philosophy, economics, or whatever interest and facilities warrant. Many of the adults in these classes are college graduates who either want to take those courses which their degree requirements excluded, or want to retake some they once had in order to renew acquaintance with an area of worth to them. Others are without academic degrees, but wish to drink deeper at the Pierian spring.

(6)   Another primarily adult service of the community college is to act as a focal point for cultural activities. Do those with musical ability wish to cultivate their talents? The college organizes a chorus, an orchestra, or produces an opera with a local cast. Are there people willing to put forth a concerted effort to make better sense out of current affairs? A college-community forum is organized and leading figures in contemporary problems are brought in to present their views and discuss possible solutions. Comparable assistance can be given to amateur thespians, writers, artists, both in performance and appreciation.

(7)   This triadic obligation—to the university-bound student, to the terminal student, and to the adult—is, of course, not assumed by every two-year institution. Some have a highly specialized objective to which all else is legitimately subordinate. What has been described is what appears to be the emerging pattern for the typical public two-year college.

(From Sigurd Rislov, "The Community College," *Atlantic Monthly*, June 1957, pp. 64–65.)

# T O  /  THEME—ORGANIZATION

***To organize your material, you must decide on its parts and their order.***

(Exercises 3–5, p. 24)

Once you have decided on a subject and its proper limits for your purpose, you must organize your material. First, analyze it into its few major parts—probably from two to a half dozen. You may decide that the subject of a typical college day falls naturally into three sections:

> morning
> afternoon
> evening

Second, determine the order in which you will present them. You will almost certainly treat these three parts of the day in the order listed, that of successive events in time. The order of Example I is similarly chronological. Having recognized the limits of her subject (she found no need to tell us what city she was in, why she was there, even where she was working), the author narrated the event as it happened. But her material fell into several parts which, on a simple plan sheet, she might have jotted down for guidance as

> meeting the boy
> taking him to the store
> his behavior there
> his silent departure

If your purpose suggests instead a topical order, the main parts of a paper on your college day may be four (list A below). Or on a closer look you may decide to combine study and classes as work, leaving three major parts (list B). Or you may omit food altogether, leaving only two (list C).

**7**

| A | B | C |
|---|---|---|
| classes | work | work |
| study | study | study |
| recreation | classes | classes |
| meals | recreation | recreation |
| | meals | |

The writer of Example II announces "three major functions" of the typical public two-year college, but these are the major academic contributions of the college, and he also discusses a fourth function:

preparatory courses
terminal courses
adult courses
community extracurriculars

These topical items raise a second question: what order should they appear in? The answer will depend, like the parts you include, on your purpose. Clarity and emphasis may be gained by proceeding according to one of the following patterns:

1. From the simple to the complex.
2. From the known to the unknown.
3. From the basic to the less basic.
4. From the ordinary to the unusual.
5. From the less important to the more important.
6. From the past to the present.
7. From the near to the far.

If you write about food, clothing, and shelter as the necessities of life, you may—in terms of people's most fundamental needs—arrange them from the most essential to the least: food, shelter, clothing. But if you are concerned with them as items in a year's budget, you may put them in the order of increasing expense: perhaps clothing, shelter, food.

If your subject involves a comparison of two things, such as makes of automobiles, you may find yourself with a two-part plan, one part devoted to each make. As for order, you will probably decide to place second the make that you conclude is the better.

But if you wish to emphasize the areas of comparison, you may emerge with a four-part plan with these headings: appearance, purchase price, comfort, operating economy. (The two makes will then become subheads under each area.) As for order, you may now decide that appearance should remain first, as the most immediate impression a car makes; comfort second, being unrelated to the other two; and purchase price and operating economy, both involving money, third and fourth (or, combined under a single heading, third). Your decision as to the order in which the parts are to be treated will depend in any event on your purpose, *the part you wish to emphasize coming logically last.*

Whatever type of subject you may be handling, these same logical processes are involved. Perhaps you want to classify some group into the types it includes: students, for instance (on the basis of their purpose in college), into those who come to work, those who come to play, and those who try to do both. Perhaps you want to analyze some machine into the parts of which it is made, or some problem into the issues of which it is composed. The two problems of *finding the parts* of your subject and *deciding on their order* will always be with you.

For a short paper such as you will write in a composition class, you may be able to form and hold your plan in your mind. But it is well to get into the habit of jotting down at least its main points as a guide, for this practice will help you both to clarify your thinking and to keep the results of it before you. The longer the theme (see Chapter 9), the more important a written outline becomes and the more detailed it should be.

### Main Idea

Make it a habit first of all to set down in a single clear, concise sentence the main idea of your paper, the basic thought that you intend to develop. Such a sentence should waste no time beginning "I am going to write about," a fact that may be taken for granted, but should devote its full wording to the subject matter itself.

Suppose you had been preparing to write Example I, for instance. You might have been tempted to state simply "I had an experience with a child." But on second thought you would have found this too general to be useful as a guide, and you might perhaps have arrived at a more satisfactorily detailed statement such as:

I once encountered a poorly clad, chilled little boy who consented to return with me to the warmth of the store where I worked, but he did everything without any childlike enthusiasm, and later disappeared without a word.

For Example II the main idea may be expressed as:

The two-year community college, a product of twentieth century America, provides preparatory and terminal courses for students and evening courses for adults, and also organizes cultural activities for the community.

Assigned a theme on the subject of how you spent your summer, you might first think of your main idea as "Last summer I worked." But on second thought you would conclude that something like the following would be a better guide:

I enjoyed my job as handy man at a summer resort because it gave me a vacation, an income, and valuable experience.

Notice that this sentence not only states the main topic, your summer job, but also makes clear that you are going to limit your attitude toward it to one of enjoyment. It also indicates that the development will fall into three parts:

vacation
income
experience

Your instructor may wish to see such a one-sentence summary of your material before you write your paper, in order to get an idea of what you are planning to say. You yourself will find that keeping such a main-idea sentence before you as you complete your plan will prevent any wandering from the subject.

## T I / THEME—INTRODUCTION

***Consider how you can capture your reader's attention with an interesting beginning.***
(Exercise 6, p. 25)

A good composition will not plunge abruptly into the subject. Rather, you can capture the interest of your readers by the use of one or more introductory devices:

1. A question (to set the readers thinking).
2. A startling statement (to catch their attention).
3. A narrative incident or a bit of dialogue (to arouse their interest).
4. An apt quotation (to illustrate what you are going to say with what others have said).
5. A comparison of contrast (with something the readers already know).
6. A brief history of the subject (to provide the perspective of background).
7. A mention of the points you are going to make, the problem you are going to discuss, or the fact you are going to establish (to show the readers what to expect).

Such an introduction may be only a sentence or two in length, or it may be a paragraph or more, depending on the requirements of your subject and the length you propose for your paper. The opening paragraph of Example I (p. 3) sets the stage for the ensuing narration: the warmth of the narrator, in this wintry weather, contrasted sharply with the chill of the child. The first two paragraphs of Example II (p. 4) give us the history and a definition—description—of the community college, ending with the announcement of the functions that will constitute the article. An introduction to the proposed theme on your summer's job might tell when and where the experience occurred, how you happened to get the job, what you enjoyed about it (a summary of the main points), or all of these.

# T C / THEME—CONCLUSION

***Consider how you can leave your reader with a sense of finality.***
(Exercise 6, p. 25)

A good theme should no more end abruptly with the last point than it should open abruptly with the first, but should finish with some kind of conclusion that will give your readers a sense of completion. Music lovers know how they would feel if someone stopped a melody short of that final key note; the reader of a theme would feel the same if you failed to provide a suitable ending. Like the introduction, the conclusion may vary in length from only a sentence that gives a feeling of finality, to a paragraph or more. It too may consist of various kinds of material:

1.  A summary of the material developed (to make certain the points are clear in the reader's mind).
2.  A conclusion drawn from it (to show why it was worth discussing).
3.  A prophecy concerning it (to give a glimpse into the future).
4.  An apt quotation.
5.  A restatement of the title or the introduction (to round out the subject).

Example I ends with a paragraph presenting the fact of the boy's quiet departure as final evidence of the maturity that he had displayed throughout; the closing words echo the title. Example II ends with a summary of the functions of the typical community college just discussed. Both papers therefore truly "conclude." The proposed theme about your summer's job might end with a summary of the benefits you derived from it or an expression of your hope of returning to the work another summer or a recommendation of it to others.

## OUTLINING

So much for the beginning and the end of your paper. The most important section is, of course, the middle, or body—the material itself. We have already looked at the main problems of organization: the determination of the major parts and of their order. The number of parts will probably run from two to a half-dozen. Eleven, say, is too many for a short paper, and one is no "part" at all, but the whole, the main idea. Example I, notice, has four parts: (1) meeting the boy, (2) taking him to the store, (3) his behavior there, (4) his silent departure. These major divisions follow one another in chronological order.

Example II also has four parts: (1) the preparatory courses for students, (2) the terminal courses for students, (3) the evening courses for adults, and (4) the cultural activities for the community. These do not follow the order of time, but follow a pattern equally logical. Three parts have been proposed as the number of divisions for your theme on your summer job, your enjoyment of it being due to its providing you with (1) vacation, (2) income, and (3) experience. Here again we depart from chronological order and use instead the order of increasing importance. (See #5 on p. 8.)

Now comes the problem of developing each part by deciding what subdivisions to include. In Example II the first part, the preparatory courses, divides into two advantages: (1) their being parallel to those in senior institutions and (2) their permitting transfer. The second part, the terminal courses, divides into three kinds according to content: (1) the technical courses, (2) the business and agriculture courses, and (3) the enrichment courses. The third part, the adult evening courses, divides into two kinds according to who takes them: (1) those taken by college graduates and (2) those taken by people without degrees. The fourth part, the cultural activities, divides into three major kinds of groups: (1) musical groups, (2) forums for discussion, and (3) groups interested in other cultural subjects. (See outline on pp. 16–17.)

The simplest way to indicate the plan of an essay (either by the writer before it is written, or by the reader afterwards) is to make an outline. This is a conventional arrangement of parts that has been called "the essay at a glance" because it shows so quickly and conveniently all the divisions of the material, their order, and their relationships. In the traditional system of labels used here, the main parts of the material are indicated by Roman numerals—I, II, etc.; their subdivisions, the second level, by capital letters—A, B, etc.; the third level by Arabic numerals—1, 2, etc.; the fourth level by lower-case letters—a, b, etc. Fifth and sixth levels may be indicated by Arabic numerals and lower-case letters, respectively, in parentheses—(1), (2), (a), (b)—but are seldom needed. (Another form of labeling uses only Arabic numerals, in a decimal system, the levels being designated by 1, 1.1, 1.11, 1.111, etc. Your instructor may indicate a preference.)

The main idea, the introduction, and the conclusion are assigned names instead of numbers or letters so that they will not be interpreted as major divisions of the material. An outline reading "I. Introduction, II. Body, III. Conclusion" is pointless, for every composition has these parts; the main divisions of the outline should indicate the parts of the body. Subdivisions of the introduction and conclusion, however, are numbered and lettered like those of the same level under the main parts. To make the relationships of the points at various levels visible "at a glance," those of the same value are always indented to the same point.

The two major kinds of outlines are the *topic outline* and the *sentence outline.* In the first, every item is expressed in a brief phrase or a word; in the second, in a complete sentence. In each, however, the main idea appears in sentence form, for clarity. A topic outline for the proposed theme on how you spent your summer might look like this:

TOPIC OUTLINE
Main idea. I enjoyed my job as handy man at a summer resort because it gave me a vacation, an income, and valuable experience.

Introduction. Ideal job
    A.   Needed vacation and income
    B.   Job provided both and more

I.   Vacation
    A.   Swimming every morning
    B.   Boating on afternoons off
    C.   Fishing on weekends
    D.   Dancing in the evening

II.   Income
    A.   Living provided
        1.   Room
        2.   Board
    B.   Small wages in addition
    C.   Generous tips from guests

III.   Experience
    A.   Keeping motors in running order
    B.   Operating all kinds of boats
    C.   Meeting all kinds of people

Conclusion. Hopes for returning next year

Such plans are invaluable in helping you to keep in mind what you have decided to include and the order in which you have decided to present it. Do not, however, make the mistake of regarding them as inflexible. If you wrote from the outline above, you might, for instance, decide to reverse the order of C and D under point I. At first thought you had fishing (C) following swimming (A) and boating (B) because they were all water activities, but as you wrote you found it more logical to round out the day by discussing evening (D) immediately after morning (A) and afternoon (B). You might even decide to eliminate fishing entirely because it was not directly connected with the resort, perhaps, or because describing your pleasure in it might dwarf your other activities. Feel free, as you write, to make any changes in material or order that seem to be advantageous, as long as you do not violate the essential purpose and logic of your plan.

A topic outline such as the one above is usually sufficient for your own use. But there are times (such as the writing of the research paper—see Chapter 9) when a sentence outline will be preferable. For one thing, preparing it will make you think through your material more thoroughly; for another, it will enable your instructor to see in advance exactly what you plan to include. The logic and labeling of the parts remain the same, the difference being that every item will be expressed in a sentence instead of in a phrase or a word. For this reason you will often have carry-over lines, and should note that these are always kept at a level with the beginning of the sentence so that they will not obscure the identifying number or letter. For Example II such a sentence outline would look like this:

SENTENCE OUTLINE
Main idea. The two-year community college, a product of twentieth century America, provides preparatory and terminal courses for students and evening courses for adults, and also organizes cultural activities for the community.

Introduction. The community, or junior, college has become a popular two-year educational institution.
  A.  It has developed in America during the twentieth century.
  B.  It is typically local and personal.
  C.  It has three major functions.

  I.  It provides for students who wish to graduate from senior colleges and universities.
  A.  Its professional courses parallel those of such institutions.
  B.  Its students can therefore transfer after two years without loss of credit.

 II.  It provides terminal training for students whose education will end in two years.

    A.   They may take a great variety of technical courses.
    B.   They may take courses in business and agriculture.
    C.   They may take regular lower-division college courses to broaden their outlooks.

III.  It offers evening courses for employed adults.
    A.   Many of these people are college graduates.
        1.   Some of them want courses their degrees did not include.
        2.   Others want to review courses taken earlier.
    B.   Some are without degrees and just want to learn.

IV.  In addition, it offers the community cultural activities in various fields.
    A.   It organizes musical groups.
    B.   It organizes forums in current problems.
    C.   It organizes groups interested in drama, writing, art.

Conclusion. These two-year institutions vary in their aims, but most follow the pattern described.

As you examine the sentence outline above, notice that the introduction, points I, II, III, and IV, and the conclusion are all parts of the main idea; that points A, B, etc., are of the same level of importance, being parts of the Roman-numeral point under which they appear; and that points 1 and 2 are similarly equal in weight, being divisions of point A under III.

Notice further that the sentences are kept as brief as possible; don't be tempted to rewrite the article under outline headings. They are also worded simply. Report the author's ideas but do not cling slavishly to his language. This is no place to repeat, for example, his allusion to the Pierian spring at the end of paragraph 5. In the article, this is an excellent metaphor; in the outline, just say what it means. The frequent use of parallel wording in the sentence outline to express points of the same level would be criticized as repetition in a theme; here it is a virtue, emphasizing their likeness.

Note particularly that there are *no single subpoints;* if an idea is divided, it inevitably has two or more parts. To write

I. Automobiles
   A. Ford

is simply to state

I. Ford automobiles

To write

I. Automobiles
   A. Ford
   B. Chrysler
   C. General Motors
   D. American Motors

is to outline.

You may be asked to make a sentence outline in preparation for writing a long paper of your own. You will also find it useful training as a reader to outline essays and chapters of textbooks; there is no surer way to get at an author's thought.

## T T / THEME—TITLE

***In choosing a title, decide what kind your material and your purpose call for.***
(Exercises 7–8, p. 25)

If you add a title to your finished theme to give it completeness and identity, give careful thought to its wording. A title may be a single word, a phrase, or even (though more rarely) a complete sentence. It may state, it may question, it may exclaim. It may be a simple straightforward description of your topic, as is customary in technical and other strictly informative papers. Such a title has the advantage of indicating clearly what the subject matter is.

How To Bowl
What Is Wrong with the American High School?
Working One's Way Through College

But in the more informal essays that many of your college themes are likely to be, you may wish to consider a title that will attract as well as describe, or that will provoke curiosity rather than satisfy it, or that will set the tone of the paper or have its own charm.

Beyond the Blue Horizon (For an essay about a long motorcycle trip)
So Help Me, God! (About being a witness in court)
The Muscle Grind (About a gymnastics exhibition)

The title of Example II, "The Functions of the Community College," is of the simple identifying sort; that of Example I, "Out in the Cold," arouses more interest. The suggested theme about your summer job might be called descriptively "My Job at a Summer Resort," but something like "Playing for Pay" will be more attractive to the reader. You may wish to choose your title before you write your paper and to use it as a kind of motif, with frequent references to it throughout. Or you may find that you don't wish to decide on its final wording until your paper is finished.

## PREPARING THE ROUGH DRAFT
If you are writing a theme in class, your first draft will be your final draft as well, for the class period is too short to permit rewriting. But themes written outside, with more time at your disposal, offer a chance for the best training you can get in effective composition.

After you have completed your plan to your initial satisfaction, start writing the theme, adding to the topics of your outline the material that will give it life as an essay. As you write this first rough draft, don't be too much concerned with polishing details. On the other hand, don't make a habit of postponing all the decencies of composition. Don't leave the punctuating, for instance, until you are finished, sprinkling in the commas like salt in a stew. Punctuation marks are an essential part of expression, as necessary to the writing of a sentence as legible letters to the spelling of a word. Train yourself to exercise on every writing occasion everything that you know about the mechanics of the job, and you will soon find that to write clearly will cease to distract you from your ideas because it will become largely automatic.

Try to choose for your writing a time and a place that will be free from interruption so that you can concentrate. Furthermore, write your rough draft as soon as possible after the theme has been assigned: first, so that you will clearly remember the assignment and any supporting material read or discussed in class; second, so that you will have time to put it away and forget about it for a while before writing the final copy. Such a lapse of time makes it possible for you to add ideas that have occurred to you in the meantime, to see new and better ways to express what you have already written, and to catch illogicalities or other errors that escaped you in the first writing. Now is the time for reading aloud to catch repetitious and otherwise awkward phrasings (**D s**); for eliminating unnecessary words and phrases and generally sharpening and tightening your style (**D r, D w**); and for cutting out or adding details or making any other changes that this later appraisal may suggest.

### PREPARING THE FINAL COPY

When you have finished revising it to the best of your ability, your theme is written; there remains only the mechanical task of making a clean copy to give to your instructor.

#### Paper and Ink

Unless a special kind of paper is prescribed, use the standard 8½ x 11 size—plain, if you type; ruled, if you write by hand. If you type, double space throughout. If you write by hand, write on every line, using a pen and making sure that your handwriting is legible.

#### Margins

If you write by hand, you will presumably use ruled paper on which the margins are already established. If they aren't, or if you type, leave about an inch and a half at the top and on the left side. The bottom and the right margins may be narrower, but keep the latter as even as possible by dividing words at the ends of lines (**Sp h 6**).

### Title

Center the title on the top line of the first page only. One line is usually enough; if it isn't, break the title at a logical point and center the second line under the first. Use any internal punctuation called for, but no terminal punctuation unless a question mark or an exclamation point is required. (Never use a terminal period, even though the title is a complete sentence.) Do not use quotation marks around your title or italicize (underscore) it, unless it is actually quoted from elsewhere or contains a title of something else; its position on the page is sufficient to indicate its function.

Avoid any confusion between the title and the beginning line of the theme by leaving a blank space between them. If you wish to refer to your title as you begin your theme, repeat it, in quotation marks; do not, even in the first sentence, refer to it with a pronoun, as the theme should be intelligible without it.

Capitalize the first word, the last word, and all other words in the title except for the small *and* unimportant words—articles, prepositions, and conjunctions. Words like *he* and *is* are small but important—capitalize them. Prepositions and conjunctions like *around* and *because* are unimportant but not small—capitalize them (the usual rule is "over five letters").

### Indentation

Indent each paragraph half an inch or more—enough so that the indentation can't be missed. Carry each line (except, of course, the last line of each paragraph) to the right margin, but do not crowd.

### Pagination

Number consecutively all pages, except the title page (though count it as page 1), at the top (center or right) with Arabic numerals.

### Folding and Endorsing

Your instructor will probably give you a particular pattern for folding your paper and for the arrangement of name, date, class, etc., on it. Follow it consistently.

### Proofreading

Presumably you made all major revisions in your paper before or during the preparation of your final copy, but you should never let it (nor anything else you have written, including class themes, examination answers, and personal and business letters) leave your hands until you have given it a final word-by-word proofreading. Make yourself forget on this final reading the wider sweep of your content and plan, which you have already revised, and concentrate on details. Whether you wrote by hand or machine, errors in copying have almost certainly slipped in; you may have omitted or repeated words, for example, or left off their endings. Check doubtful spellings or word divisions in your dictionary, and doubtful sentence constructions or punctuation in this handbook. Be sure that everything is in the best shape you can manage. Your instructors cannot always distinguish between ignorance and carelessness, but they can help you overcome the former, whereas only you can do anything about the latter. They will probably have no objections to your making minor last-minute changes on your finished copy, to avoid rewriting, but the paper you turn in should be neat and legible.

### CORRECTING THE THEME
(Exercises 11–12, pp. 25–26)

Even if you never saw your finished theme again, it would have been good writing practice for you. But the advantage of composition courses over other writing situations is that here experienced instructors will read your work—not just to grade it or even to correct it, but to point out to you its strengths and its weaknesses, as they see them, and to show you how to overcome the latter. If they write in your margins the symbols appearing inside the front cover of this book, you can quickly find out what your mistakes are and how to correct them, from the sections in which these are discussed. During the process you should come to an understanding of the errors involved that will keep you from repeating them.

Here is a sample paragraph with errors italicized and their nature indicated in the margin. Look up these symbols in the front cover of this book, study the sections to which they refer, and make the necessary corrections. Be prepared to explain your changes.

| | |
|---|---|
| WO | When <u>I and my brother</u> were little, we used to go down |
| Sp ab | to the <u>r. r.</u> tracks in the neighborhood and watch the big |
| D M | freight trains go by. <u>Sitting near the tracks</u>, their roar |
| A p | was scary, but sometimes an engineer waved. If <u>they</u> didn't |
| V ti | we would feel neglected. Sometimes we would just <u>lay</u> down |
| S i | there on the bank and shut our eyes. Pretending we were |
| Sp a | riding in the <u>engineers</u> cab. |

**EXERCISES**

T S / THEME—SUBJECT
(Discussion, pp. 1–6)

**1.** Make a list of a half-dozen areas (from those listed on p. 2 or any others they may suggest) in which you would like to do some writing. How well prepared are you to write on each? What appeal do you feel they would have for the general reader? Consider them as possibilities for development as part of the required writing of the course.

**2.** For each of the large subject areas you wrote down in Exercise 1, list at least five specific topics such as might be developed into a short theme (around 500 words).

*Example:* Subject area—my family
a. being an only child
b. a broken home
c. my big brother
d. my father's work
e. the "baby" of the family
f. second-generation Americans
g. a family custom
h. baby-sitting at home

T O / THEME—ORGANIZATION
(Discussion, pp. 7–11, 13–18)

**3.** Test your knowledge of the logic and the techniques of outlining by arranging in outline form, with each item properly labeled and spaced, the thirty-two scrambled items below, first noting that

a. Granted a common understanding of the terms, the grouping of parts and the relationships of main headings and subdivisions are a logical necessity, and will work out the same for everyone.

b. On the other hand, the order of the terms within any one group will depend on each individual's purpose. Be prepared to defend your own order at every point with the general rules suggested on p. 8.

c. What is the "main idea" covering the whole?

| | | | |
|---|---|---|---|
| caves | footwear | sandals | fruit |
| clothing | meat | oranges | shelter |
| sausage | tents | oxfords | hats |
| potatoes | vegetables | hamburger | beans |
| food | lemons | grapefruit | houses |
| cabins | suits | steak | beef |
| apples | cottages | boots | headgear |
| caps | bacon | pork | cabbage |

**4.** Jot down the names of several types of music, breeds of dogs, or makes of automobiles, motorcycles, radios, television sets, or refrigerators. If you were to write a theme about one of these groups, what order would you present them in? Why?

**5.** List several types of drivers, teachers, customers, musicians, or college students according to some one point of view (skill in driving, ability to teach, type of music played, etc.). Now arrange your choice in a logical order and justify your arrangement in terms of your purpose.

**6.** Study the effectiveness of the introductions and conclusions of several essays in a collection of readings or of several articles in an issue of a current magazine, as assigned.

### T T / THEME—TITLE
(Discussion, pp. 18–19)

**7.** Check through a current issue of a popular general magazine, studying the titles of the articles. Notice how many only name the topic, how many give an indication of how it is handled, how many have made an effort to attract, how many give no notion of the subject, how many are single words, how many are complete sentences: statements, commands, questions, or exclamations.

**8.** Write a half-dozen alternative titles for one of your themes, noticing the different effect of each.

### PREPARING THE ROUGH DRAFT
(Discussion, pp. 19–20)

**9.** Compare the first draft of one of your themes with your final copy. Which is longer? Why? Note the kinds of changes you have made, and your reasons for making them.

**10.** Turn in the rough draft and the final copy of one of the themes you write outside of class so that your instructor can compare the two.

### CORRECTING THE THEME
(Discussion, pp. 22–23)

**11.** Keep a careful and complete list of the errors that your instructor points out in your themes, noting the number of times that each kind appears. When you find one kind of error recurring in a later theme, make a special review of the section of this handbook in which it is discussed and a special effort to avoid making it again.

**12.** Keep a separate list of any words you misspell on your themes, reviewing it from time to time until you have mastered the words involved. If the misspelling was due to careless writing, train yourself to proofread more carefully.

# 2
# DEVELOPING THE PARAGRAPH

In the preceding chapter we looked at the larger problems posed by the whole theme; in this one we turn to examine in some detail the units of which a theme conspicuously consists, the paragraphs. The problems here consist of how much or how little material to include in each paragraph and of what methods to use in developing it.

A paragraph is a group of sentences that develops a thought —but so is a theme, or a book. Actually the paragraph is used not only as a logical unit but also as a psychological break to give the reader a sense of progress. (Chapter breaks in books serve either of the same two purposes: they may mark a change in subject, or they may be only a refreshing pause for the reader before the same thought is continued.)

There is no necessary connection between the number of points in an outline and the number of paragraphs used to develop them. It is entirely possible that in your short papers you may use one paragraph to develop each main point, but it is unlikely that you will do so regularly. Two such points may be developed so briefly that they can be suitably included in a single paragraph, while another point may require enough material to justify several.

However, since the main points in the outline and (usually)

the paragraphs are both logical parts of the main idea that the theme is developing, the treatment of a new point is likely to call for a new paragraph in all but very short papers, and a new paragraph is likely to mark the development of at least a new subpoint in all but very long ones. Going back to Example I (p. 3), we find the author using six paragraphs to narrate her four points (see **T o**), three of them being used to develop the first one. Told more briefly, her narrative might have appeared in a single paragraph; more fully, it could have run to dozens.

Example II (p. 4) uses one paragraph to develop each of its four major points, but two more are devoted to the introduction and one to the conclusion: seven in all. It is a fair guess that a theme developed from the topic outline on page 14 would require at least five paragraphs, likely more. The point is that the number of paragraphs you use will depend on the length of your development rather than on the size of your outline.

## PAR U  /  PARAGRAPH—UNITY

***Your paragraph, like the theme itself, should have unity of material.***
(Exercises 1–2, pp. 40–41)

However long or short a paragraph may be, it must stick to its subject. Don't let a paragraph on the education you received in a parochial elementary school wander off into a discussion of the relation between church and state or of the boy who sat beside you in the third grade. In expository writing a paragraph very often begins with a *topic sentence*—a sentence that announces what the subject of the paragraph is, thereby helping to keep both the reader and the writer from forgetting it. A paragraph with a topic sentence so located starts with a general statement which it goes on to develop with supporting material. A simple example designed to let you clearly see this pattern follows:

(1)    When I was a freshman in high school, I enjoyed most of my courses [topic sentence]. (2) Physical education, to be sure, I didn't like, probably because I was small for my age then, and rather frail. (3) But English was easy for me, as I had always been a great reader. (4) I found algebra mostly fun, even, as I am naturally good at figures and logical relationships. (5) It was biology, however, that I enjoyed most of all; this study of plants and animals opened a whole new world to me.

Paragraph unity is achieved here in that the writer sticks to the subject announced in the opening topic sentence, which is not just the courses taken as a freshman in high school but the writer's attitude toward them.

# PAR C / PARAGRAPH—COHERENCE

*Arrange your details in a logical sequence, and use transitional words and phrases among them.*
(Exercises 3–7, pp. 41–42)

The short model paragraph under **Par u,** above, also illustrates a second requirement of good paragraphing—coherence. A mere string of sentences, even on the same subject, may tend to remain so many isolated units; they must be made to "cohere"—to stick together. One convenient aid to coherence is the judicious use of words and phrases that serve as **transitional devices,** carrying the thought smoothly from one sentence to another by tying them together.

Notice in the model paragraph the phrase *to be sure* in sentence 2, indicating that the writer's attitude toward physical education is the exception to the general claim of enjoyment in the topic sentence. The word *but* at the beginning of sentence 3 shows that the attitude toward English is in contrast to that expressed about physical education in sentence 2. *Even* in the middle of sentence 4 stresses the fact that algebra is pleasurable too, despite what many students feel about it. In sentence 5 *however* indicates that the feeling toward biology is again in

DEVELOPING THE PARAGRAPH

contrast to that expressed in the preceding sentence, and *most of all* tells us that this subject is held in the highest regard.

None of these words and phrases would be present if the sentences stood by themselves; all are included to bind the sentences together into a meaningful paragraph. It is well to vary the positions of such transitional expressions as has been done here, putting them both at the beginning of the sentence and within it for variety and smoothness. Such devices are not needed in every sentence, but they should be used frequently.

Transitional words and phrases are even more necessary between paragraphs to show the relationship of these units to each other and to hold them together as a theme. They usually appear at the beginning of a paragraph, but occasionally at the end of one, leading to the next. Turn back to Example II (p. 4) and watch them at work:

> Paragraph 2: The opening "This institution" refers to paragraph 1. The closing "three major functions" prepares us for the paragraphs that follow.
> Paragraphs 3 and 4: "First" and "Second" note the sequence of points.
> Paragraph 5: "Besides these two services" refers to paragraphs 3 and 4, and "third" in the second sentence carries on the sequence.
> Paragraph 6: "Another" introduces a different kind of service, not quite worthy of being designated "fourth."
> Paragraph 7: "This triadic obligation" sums up paragraphs 3–6.

In long papers, an entire small paragraph may be used to express the transition from one large section to another:

> I have now completed my account of the early misunderstandings that divided my home town into its present bitterly rival factions. Now, before I go on to propose a program for community healing, let me relate some of the more regrettable incidents that have recently resulted from this state of affairs.

Books may occasionally have an entire small chapter devoted to making a transition from one section to another. But here we are concerned with the coherence of the small unit, the paragraph, for which some common **transitional expressions** and the kinds of relationships they indicate are these:

1.  Addition: *and, furthermore, moreover, besides, again, likewise, similarly, in addition*
2.  Contrast: *but, however, nevertheless, on the other hand, on the contrary*
3.  Result: *therefore, hence, thus, consequently*
4.  Enumeration: *first, second, third, etc.*
5.  Time: *then, in the meantime, later, soon, next*
6.  Space: *above, below, beside, behind, in front, next*
7.  Illustration: *namely, that is, for instance, for example*

All *conjunctions,* both within and between the sentences, help, in their role as connectives, to hold sentences together; even *pronouns,* by referring to their antecedents, have transitional value.

Useful as transitional devices are, they would be artificial by themselves; the logical progression of thought is what makes for real coherence. The paragraph, like the entire theme, must make the reader feel that he is being carried from a starting point through successive stages to a natural conclusion. This tight coherence may also contribute to emphasis. (And this last sentence, please note, is in itself a transitional device, leading you into the following section!)

## PAR E / PARAGRAPH—EMPHASIS

*Arrange the details within your paragraph toward a climax.*
(Exercises 8–10, p. 42)

The model paragraph on page 29 also illustrates emphasis, the third requirement of good paragraphing. The four subjects mentioned in support of the topic sentence are not just set down carelessly after it but are consciously arranged toward a kind of climax. Physical education is mentioned first because it

DEVELOPING THE PARAGRAPH

is the exception, the one that made the writer say, in the topic sentence, *most* instead of *all* about enjoying courses. English comes next because it is easy, therefore not unenjoyable, followed by algebra because though usually considered harder than English, it is relatively easy for the writer. And biology is carefully saved until last because it is the course that, offering the fullest measure of enjoyment, is to be emphasized. Notice too that it gets the longest sentence.

Another means of gaining emphasis is to recast the paragraph, keeping the topic sentence until the last as a kind of climax. Such a plan proceeds through the particulars to the general statement. Like the periodic sentence (**SV o**), it creates a measure of suspense, for not until the end is the reader aware of the full purpose of the accumulating details. Also like the periodic sentence, part of its strength lies in the fact that it is infrequently used. But it is a good device, worth experimenting with.

Rewritten for greater emphasis, the model paragraph would read like this:

> When I was a freshman in high school, I wasn't fond of physical education, probably because I was small for my age then, and rather frail. But English was easy for me, as I had always been a great reader. I found algebra mostly fun, even, as I am naturally good at figures and logical relationships. It was biology, however, that I liked most; this study of plants and animals opened a whole new world to me. All in all, I can say truthfully that I enjoyed most of my freshman courses.

## PAR D / PARAGRAPH— DEVELOPMENT

*Your topic and your purpose will determine what methods to use in developing a paragraph.*
(Exercises 11–12, pp. 42–43)

A topic sentence may appear, as we have seen, at the beginning of the paragraph (though not necessarily as the opening sentence) or at the end. Not every paragraph has a topic expressed in any one sentence, but it is sure to have a *topic idea* that it is required to develop.

Some common methods that can be profitably employed in developing paragraphs are the use of details, examples, causes, results, proof, definition, and comparison and contrast. These methods are explained and illustrated below. Notice that in every example the topic sentence has been placed, for convenience, at the beginning, and that the arrangement of the material within the paragraph follows the general principles laid down for the organization of the theme itself (p. 8).

### 1. Details

These are particulars, often descriptive, set down in support of the topic idea.

> The drought continues to plague the land. The August sun rises white-hot. There is no early morning chill to dispel, no mist to burn away. Only the parched, cracked earth awaits the sun's focus. A large cottonwood shudders as the hot, dry wind, searching for a lingering bit of moisture, rustles through its branches. The fields, neatly plowed and carefully planted, bear the stunted remains of springtime promise. Stalks of corn, grown to only half of their normal height, with tiny nubs where ears of grain should be, bear witness to the betrayal of this promise. A vineyard contains only leafless vines and a few pellet-like grapes. The land itself, though rich and black in the spring, is now bleached to a dismal gray. The richness of the soil has been beaten into a powdery aridity that is unable to provide sustenance for any living thing. The sun slowly rises higher, and its burning rays begin to reverberate from the earth and transform the entire landscape into a bizarre land of distortion and disillusion.

### 2. Examples

These are specific incidents illustrating the topic idea. The material used in support may be a number of short instances (paragraph A) or a single narrative event (paragraph B).

DEVELOPING THE PARAGRAPH

### A

A very definite relationship exists between the culture of a nation and that nation's language. Americans' love of brevity, for example, has initiated a general shortening of words. To say *automobile* seems foolish when the shortened form *auto,* or even the shorter synonym *car,* conveys the image in less time. The words *bicycle* and *tricycle* are rapidly being replaced by *bike* and *trike,* just as *omnibus* and *cabriolet* have been totally replaced in America by *bus* and *cab.* People do not care to take the time or the trouble to say *airplane, sidewalk, hoodlum,* or *photograph* when the derivatives *plane, walk, hood,* and *photo* serve just as well. Unaccented prefixes have been completely dropped from words such as *bestir, bestride, betake,* and *bethink,* so that today one hears the more concise forms *stir, stride, take* (as in the phrase, "Take to the boats"), and *think.* The word *motel* is derived from motorists' hotel: it has become so common that it is now used internationally and often designates establishments that were formerly referred to as hotels.

### B

Everybody seems to be agreed that honesty is the best policy, but that truism was only so many words to me until I was caught in dishonesty myself. I was employed last summer by a dairy company at the state fair. The employees where I worked received their lunches free by merely going through the kitchen and behind the counter to get the food. I had been eating in the back of the kitchen with a friend who was working at another part of the fairgrounds. With the original intention of paying for it, I got his lunch at the same time I got mine so that he wouldn't have to wait in the long line. However, when I couldn't get to the cashier, I didn't pay. The third time this incident occurred the manager called me aside, stated that he had seen me, and then fired me. My friends later comforted me that everyone "stole" a milkshake now and then, and that I just happened to get caught. Probably it seems ridiculous to suffer a guilty conscience over a couple of pilfered milkshakes, but then most people haven't been caught stealing. They haven't had their inflated opinions of their honesty pricked, as I have.

### 3. Causes

This method consists of giving the reasons why the condition stated in the topic sentence exists.

Americans are known throughout the world for their personal initiative. This national trait, which has impressed both visitors to our shores and people in other countries who have observed Americans abroad, may be first of all a matter of heredity. What is now the United States was largely developed as a nation by adventuresome spirits who had the aggressiveness to strike out for a new land, leaving the more passive natures at home. The initiative that these settlers brought with them was fostered by the circumstances under which they found themselves living in the new country—the demands of the lonely frontier life and the continual need for reaching out to develop new areas of the continent. It was further encouraged by the free-enterprise system, with the premium it put on individual aggressiveness; by the democratic form of government, with its demands on individual responsibility; and even, perhaps, by the Christian religion, with its emphasis on individual worth. Comparing these origins and ways of life with those of most older nations, one no longer marvels that the individuals they have produced are conspicuous among the world's peoples for their initiative.

### 4. Results

This method consists of giving the consequences of the condition or circumstances stated as the topic.

My brothers and I were brought up by a conscientious uncle who used to speak frequently of what might happen if he ''spared the rod.'' We were in no danger, however, for he often laid it on. One of our young neighbors, a boy named Gerald, however, was an orphan reared alone by doting grandparents, and he became a badly spoiled child. As a little fellow he was never able to play happily with us when we visited him, for his selfishness prevented him from making the necessary adjustments. When he went to school this kind of experience was repeated; he was admired by his fellows for his good looks, his fine clothes, and his steady supply of spending money, but he was never able to make close friends because of his inordinate demands upon others. In college the results of his upbringing were even more serious. Never having known the discipline of others, he was in continual trouble with the dean over infractions of campus rules; and never having been trained to discipline himself, he failed so utterly in the business of settling down to regular study that in spite of his good mind he was expelled in the middle of his second year. Now we learn that his subsequent marriage to a fine girl in our home town has failed—one more bit of testimony to the folly of the spared rod.

### 5. Proof

This method consists of giving evidence to prove the truth of the assertion in the topic sentence.

The grading system in use here is grievously unfair. In any class of twenty-five students there are twenty-five individuals, each with peculiar talents and abilities. But the grading system, with only five marks, forces those twenty-five human beings into five categories, labeling the students within each as though they were identical in performance with all others so labeled. This injustice is particularly conspicuous when percentage grades on tests (which have the virtue of offering twenty times as many categories as the letter grades given as finals) are converted into letter grades. Let us suppose that all the 90's get A's: the student with 100 is superior to the student with 90 by 10 points, yet gets the same grade; but the student with 89, who is inferior to the student with 90 by only 1 point, gets a B. In addition, students are graded not on what they actually know but on their performance on a given examination, which may have been seriously affected by entirely extraneous circumstances, such as misinterpretation of the directions, late arrival, or temporary physical unfitness. Until some more just and equable system of grading is devised, the thoughtful person must view grades with considerable skepticism.

### 6. Definition
This method is used when a term in the topic sentence needs to be explained at some length.

What is particleboard? Sawdust and glue, basically, but there's a bit more to it than that. Some producers prefer to call it hardboard. By any name, it's made of wood particles and adhesives run between heated rollers to get a hard, dense material that's usually smooth on both sides and available in thicknesses from ⅛ inch to 2 inches. "Peg board" is particleboard with holes. Without holes, it's used in the building trades as flooring and siding underlayment. The furniture industry sandwiches it between all sorts of veneers, from real wood to plastic laminates like Formica. Various grades are available. The density (and therefore the moisture-proofness) determines the quality of particleboard. Tempered grades are generally for exterior use in construction. What you find at your local lumber yard is "Standard" grade, and that's what the furniture makers use. It's easily worked with hand tools, takes paint (or glue) well, will hold nails or screws, and can be sanded—although that's not often necessary because of its smooth surface.*

### 7. Comparison and Contrast
This method is used when the topic idea deals with two subjects with a view to discovering their likenesses or their differences. If the two are presented separately, they are likely

* Reprinted with permission of and Copyright 1974 by Davis Publications, Inc.

DEVELOPING THE PARAGRAPH

to become two paragraphs. Those below are presented rather in alternating details, paragraph A, a personal subject, discovering mostly likenesses, and paragraph B, a scientific one, differences.

## A

When I first came to the Midwest from the East, people here seemed to think I was a Martian, or at least I might just as well be, for their money. I have been busy ever since, trying to explain that Massachusetts isn't different from Indiana, at least not in the things that count. We get up in the morning and see the same sun, believe it or not, if it's to be seen, and we go to our jobs or to school by the same methods of transportation, not by spaceships. Perhaps we plow through a bit more snow there, while here they slosh through more puddles. But we eat lunch at noon, as they do, work as hard as they do, and as we go home in the early evening, we see the same stars beginning to wink at us from the same darkening heavens. Maybe it gets dark a bit earlier for us, that's all. Oh, we may have a slightly different accent when we mumble in our sleep, or we may snore a little louder because of the colder air at times, but we're not really so different. Maybe the Martians are different, but I'm not a Martian. I'm only from Massachusetts, which makes me just another American like those in Indiana.

## B

Antarctica differs from the Arctic regions, which are better known to us and easier to reach. The North Pole is crossed daily by commercial airlines, whereas not a single commercial airliner operates over Antarctica. The Arctic is an ocean with drifting ice and hemmed in by the continents of North America, Asia, and Europe. The Antarctic, on the other hand, is a continent as large as Europe and the United States put together, and surrounded entirely by oceans—the Atlantic, the Indian, and the Pacific. More than a million persons live within 2,000 miles of the North

Pole, and the area is rich in forest and industry. There are animals and birds of many varieties. Within the same distance of the South Pole, there are no settlements apart from scientific stations, which are entirely dependent on outside supplies for every need. There is not a single tree and not a single animal. It takes 70 to 80 years to grow an inch of moss.

These methods of paragraph development are intended to suggest; they do not exhaust all the possibilities. Neither are they mutually exclusive; a paragraph may be developed by a combination of methods. Notice the use of details and examples, for instance, in the definition and the comparison and contrast paragraphs, and of examples in the proof paragraph. The best answer to the question of how to develop a paragraph is this: use any and all means that are congenial to your topic and suitable to your purpose, as long as they help you to produce a paragraph that is a unified, coherent, and emphatic whole.

## PAR L  /  PARAGRAPH—LENGTH

***In developing a paragraph, consider not only the nature of your material but the appearance of your page.***
(Exercises 13–16, p. 43)

Paragraphs may vary in length from a single brief sentence to a page or more—but rarely more, because of the forbidding appearance of an unbroken page. As we noted earlier, looks share with logic in determining paragraph length: paragraphs in newspapers and magazines are regularly shorter than those in books, for instance, one reason being that long paragraphs set in a narrow column of type fail to give the reader's eye the frequent breaks it has come to expect. But if too many long paragraphs are tiring, too many short ones violate the requirements of both looks and logic. They tend to give the page a nervous look and the reader a feeling that the writer is rushing on without properly developing his thought.

DEVELOPING THE PARAGRAPH

The lesson of all this is that if you find a paragraph filling more than a page, read it through to see if you can find a place where it can be logically divided. If, on the other hand, you find yourself with several paragraphs on a page, consider combining them or developing each more fully. An occasional short paragraph among longer ones is excellent, however; variety in length may be the spice of paragraphs as it is of sentences (**SV I**).

The subject matter of a paper and the style in which it is written also have their influence on paragraph length. Formal writing is likely to require longer paragraphs than informal, newspaper editorials longer ones than news stories, and expository articles longer ones than narrative accounts (notice in Chapter 1 that the paragraphs of Example II are longer than those of Example I). A sample check of paragraph lengths once revealed an average of about 40 words in newspaper stories, 90–120 in popular weekly and monthly magazines, and 300–400 in standard books of literary history and criticism, with single paragraphs in the latter as long as 1000. An author's material and purpose as well as his personal style and even the width of the columns in which his work is to appear—all may affect the length of the paragraphs he writes.

**EXERCISES**

**PAR U / PARAGRAPH—UNITY**
(Discussion, pp. 28–29)

**1.** Show at what points the following paragraph violates the principle of paragraph unity.

I have enjoyed stamp collecting ever since I was a child. When I was only six one of my uncles sent me a package of stamps from Japan. In the same package he sent a silk scarf to my sister and a can of green tea to my mother. Many of the stamps were beautiful pictures of Japanese scenery. I think the most beautiful mountain in the world is Mt. Fuji, which rises to a height of over 12,000 feet from almost sea level. My uncle says he climbed it twice while he was in Japan. At first I just enjoyed the pictures on the stamps, but as I grew older and got other stamps from other countries, I became curious about the stories behind them. Through them I learned a great deal of history and geography. History was my favorite subject in grade school. I didn't enjoy geography, probably because I didn't like the teacher. My stamp collection grew rapidly until I went to senior high school. Then I lost interest in it, and I haven't looked at it for years.

**2.** Rewrite the paragraph above, using the same opening sentence as a topic and carefully observing the principle of paragraph unity.

### PAR C / PARAGRAPH—COHERENCE
(Discussion, pp. 29–31)

**3.** List the transitional devices used in the nine paragraphs illustrating methods of development (pp. 33–39). Explain what each one does.

**4.** Read an article in a current magazine or a chapter in a textbook, including this one, noting the transitional devices used.

**5.** Look for transitional devices in one of your own themes. Should you have used them more frequently?

**6.** Supply any transitional words or phrases that will increase the coherence of the following paragraph.

My first overnight camping trip, taken with my older brother, was a mixed pleasure. We got our tent pitched all right in the evening. The sky was clear. We didn't take the trouble to dig a trench around our tent. During the night it rained violently. Our clothes stayed dry because we had them rolled up at the far end of our little pup tent. Our blankets got soaking wet from the rain that ran in under the tent flap. The next morning the sky was still overcast. The weather was warm. The humidity was high. Nothing got dry. The flies and mosquitoes

DEVELOPING THE PARAGRAPH

clung to everything, including us. The sun shone in the afternoon. We found an old boat and went fishing. The thrill of catching my first fish made me forget all the unpleasantness.

**7.** Rewrite the following paragraph, rearranging the ideas to achieve coherence.

John has always been interested in public speaking. When he was a senior in high school, he was a member of the debate team that won the state championship. Even before he entered the first grade, he was a familiar figure at PTA meetings, where he recited little poems his mother had taught him. He hopes to go into law as a career. Last year, as a freshman in college, he won fifty dollars in an all-college oratorical contest. When he was a sophomore in high school, he received a silver medal for placing second in a declamation contest. His friends predict a brilliant success for him as a lawyer.

## PAR E / PARAGRAPH—EMPHASIS
(Discussion, pp. 31–32)

**8.** Starting with a simple topic sentence, develop a good paragraph of approximately a hundred words.

**9.** Rewrite the paragraph, not expressing the topic idea until the end.

**10.** Compare the interest and the effectiveness of the two versions.

## PAR D / PARAGRAPH—DEVELOPMENT
(Discussion, pp. 32–39)

**11.** What method or methods do you feel would best serve in developing each of the following topic sentences into paragraphs?

1. When I first arrived on the campus, I heard several new slang words.

2. We Americans need to reexamine what we mean by democracy.
3. He was never able to live down his early reputation.
4. Johnson became known as a daring leader.
5. Botany and zoology are two phases of the same great subject.
6. At night during the Christmas season, the downtown district is beautiful.
7. A mortgage is a convenient source of cash for the property owner.

**12.** Write out three sentences that could be suitably developed by each of the following seven methods: details, examples, causes, results, proof, definition, comparison and contrast.

## PAR L / PARAGRAPH—LENGTH
(Discussion, pp. 39–40)

**13.** Look at a few pages in a magazine article or a book. How many magazine columns or book pages do you find with no paragraph breaks?

**14.** Look through some pages of your own writing with the same question. If any of your pages contain more than three paragraphs, can you justify the number, or do some of them need to be developed or combined?

**15.** In a newspaper story, a magazine article, a textbook, a novel (choose pages without dialogue), a book of essays— count the words in each of several successive paragraphs and then compute the average paragraph length. To what extent can you explain your results in terms of column width, material, purpose, style?

**16.** Find the average paragraph length of one of your own themes and compare it with your results in Exercise 15. Can you draw any conclusions of value to you as a writer?

# 3
# USING
# THE
# DICTIONARY

## DICT / DICTIONARY—CONSULT

***Consult your dictionary.***
(Exercises 1–2, p. 52)

In this guide the two most frequent pieces of advice to writers are "Read good books and magazines" and "Use your dictionary." The first is a long-term matter; you are already reaping the profits—or the losses—of your past reading habits. But the second is an immediate and constant help, if you will make it so.

### 1. Buy a good desk dictionary.
Dictionaries come in all sizes and at all prices. At one extreme are the many cheap little vest-pocket and paperback editions (conveniently portable for spelling purposes), but neither these nor the small high school editions are adequate for your college and adult needs. At the other extreme are the big unabridgeds, notably:

> *Webster's Third New International Dictionary of the English Language* (G. & C. Merriam, 1961), and the older second edition (1934), still preferred by many

USING THE DICTIONARY

> *Webster's New Twentieth Century Dictionary* (Collins-World, 1975)

These are valuable for the number of words listed and, more important, for the amount of information about each that their size permits; you should consult them when you are in the library, but they are cumbersome for everyday use.

What you should buy, choosing thoughtfully, is one of the several recent college editions, or desk dictionaries, on the market—modest in price, adequate in material, and convenient to handle. Among these, in alphabetical order, are the following:

> *Funk & Wagnalls Standard College Dictionary*
> *The Random House College Dictionary*
> *Webster's New Collegiate Dictionary* (G. & C. Merriam)
> *Webster's New World Dictionary of the American Language, Second College Edition* (Collins-World)

Special consideration should be given to a relative newcomer on the scene:

> *The American Heritage Dictionary of the English Language*

A couple of inches wider and taller than the collegiates and a couple of pounds heavier, the *American Heritage Dictionary* can't match them in portability, but being in the same price range it is definitely a "best buy" as a desk dictionary, for both quantity and quality of contents. Its extra size is devoted to printing in full all of the notations (save for the parts of speech) that are customarily and often frustratingly abbreviated; to wide margins containing generous illustrations, mostly photographic, instead of the usual scattering of line drawings through the text; and to a considerable use of illustrative quotations in definitions and of distinctions among listed synonyms. Especially welcome, in these changing times, are the reports of its Usage Panel, a group of professional users of standard English, on the relative acceptability of debatable items.

Each of these volumes has its own advantages: in material, or arrangement, or type size, or quality of paper, or ease of handling and using. Look at the table of contents to see what a given book has in the way of information other than the A–Z body, such as essays on language, lists of colleges and universities, sections on signs and symbols. A particularly useful addition may be a small handbook section containing information on grammar, punctuation, and other "mechanics" of writing.

A thumb-index is well worth in convenience the slight extra cost involved, but beware of a leather binding—it may tempt you to keep that copy too long. Language is a changing thing, and you should plan to get yourself a new dictionary every few years, at least every decade, to keep in touch both with new words and with the many changes occurring in old ones. For example, someone wishing to verify the new feminine title *Ms.* would look in vain for that use in the *American Heritage Dictionary* of 1969—but it appeared, complete with a choice of plurals, in the 1973 edition. The most important thing for you to look at before you buy is the copyright date on the back of the title page. Like some encyclopedias, dictionaries are now more often updated by frequent small changes than by great new editions. Between the 1972 and 1974 copyrights of *Webster's New World Dictionary,* for instance, hundreds of biographical and geographical entries were updated, and nearly a thousand new entries and new senses of established entries were added. Moral: watch those dates.

## 2. Know how to use your dictionary.

Different editors have different ways of indicating such things as preferred spellings or usage levels or the status of foreign words, so that one dictionary may prove confusing to a person accustomed to another. One college edition, for instance, used to enter all pronunciations in both the phonetic alphabet and diacritical marks, a practice that gave some uninformed readers the notion that a choice of pronunciation was given for every word. Another lists the various definitions of the same word in historical order, chronologically; others put the most commonly used definitions first, conveniently. Most now list everything in a single alphabetical arrangement, although some still have separate sections for such things as abbreviations, foreign phrases, and information about persons and places. You will save time and avoid misinformation if you will take a little while to learn from the editor's prefaces how to use your dictionary before you begin.

### 3. Know how much your dictionary can tell you about words.

When you think of a dictionary, you probably think chiefly of spelling, or pronunciation, or meaning—the things for which you go to it most frequently. But these are only part of the information about words—thousands upon thousands of them—that a good dictionary provides. Here is a typical entry to refer to as you go through the following discussion:

**stam·pede** (stam pēd′), n., v., **-ped·ed, -ped·ing.** —n. **1.** a sudden, frenzied rush or headlong flight of a herd of frightened animals, esp. cattle or horses. **2.** any headlong general flight or rush. **3.** *Western U.S., Canadian.* a celebration, including a rodeo, contests, exhibitions, dancing, etc. **4.** (in the Northwest U.S. and W. Canada) a rodeo.—*v.i.* **5.** to scatter or flee in a stampede. **6.** to make a general rush. —*v.t.* **7.** to cause to stampede. **8.** to rush or overrun (a place, exits, etc.). [AmerSp (*e*) *stampid*(*a*), Sp = *estamp*(*ar*) (to) stamp + *-ida* n. suffix]

### Spelling

The bold-faced main entry gives you the spelling of the word. But don't stop there; make certain that that spelling carries the meaning you want—*need* is not *knead,* nor *council, counsel.* This first entry shows whether the word is capitalized, spelled with an apostrophe, hyphenated or spelled as two words (modern dictionary entries include many phrases as well as single words). In addition it divides the word into all its syllables—useful information when you need to know where a word can be split at the end of a line (but don't confuse the mark that separates syllables with the hyphen, which in most dictionaries is conspicuously longer and heavier). All of this you can learn from the main entry alone.

### Pronunciation

Information about pronunciation may also begin with the main entry, accented syllables being indicated there in some dictionaries; know what kinds of marks mean heavy and light stress in yours. But the chief guide to pronunciation comes in the second entry, in parentheses, where the word is rewritten according to the sound. (Never mistake this entry for the spelling!) Letters not sounded are omitted, others are changed or added (*rough*—ruf), and vowel values are indicated (*knight-hood*—nīt'hood). Most American dictionaries use a system of diacritical marks for this purpose; consult the running band of familiar key words at the bottom of each pair of pages, or the list on the front or back inside cover of the book. These marks will vary somewhat from dictionary to dictionary—another reason for familiarizing yourself thoroughly with your own.

### Grammar

Many dictionary users are unaware of the extent of the grammatical information that a dictionary provides. Principally, it labels each definition or set of definitions with an abbreviation indicating the part of speech in which the word can be used in a particular sense (n., adj., etc.); observe these labels carefully. But in addition it includes the plurals of irregular nouns (*man, men*), the parts of irregular verbs (*know, knew, known*) and whether a verb is transitive or intransitive (v.t., v.i.), the degrees of irregular adjectives and adverbs (*well, better, best*) —and, by default, assurance that any forms not provided are regular.

### Etymology

Information about the origins of words is not only helpful to those who wish to use words exactly but also fascinating to the curious. (Who can forget the political term *gerrymander* after he has noticed the names of the governor and the animal that make it up?) Etymology is particularly interesting to those who

**49**

know some of the other languages from which so many of our English words have been borrowed. In some dictionaries the etymology precedes the definitions; in most, it is now placed at the end of the entry to get less frequently used information out of the way.

### Definition

Most of the space occupied by an entry is devoted to definitions, one or many. (For the word *cut,* for example, one desk dictionary lists some sixty meanings for its uses as noun, adjective, and two kinds of verbs, with another ten for phrases!) General definitions are usually given first, with the more specific ones following. Here the dictionary becomes a rich mine of information about usage, for it not only makes clear what part of speech a word may be used as, in a certain sense, but by numerous labels it also makes known if the word is not current (**D t**), or if it is restricted in use to one section of the English-speaking world (**D p**), or to one level of use or one special field of knowledge (**D o**), or is still regarded as foreign (**P i**). One of the many advantages of an unabridged dictionary over a collegiate is the space available for confirming and clarifying many definitions of words through quotations showing them in use.

### Synonyms and Antonyms

A collegiate dictionary includes lists of synonyms (words similar in meaning) for many words, of antonyms (words opposite in meaning) for a few. It may give only a brief note like this one under *fragrant:*

—*Syn.* **1.** odorous, aromatic. —*Ant.* **1.** malodorous, noisome.

Or it may pause to distinguish among them, by discussion and even example, as below; this subentry appears in a collegiate dictionary to expand the meaning of only one of its eight definitions of *proud:* ''4. inclined to excessive self-esteem.''

    **4.**    overbearing, disdainful, imperious. PROUD, ARROGANT, HAUGHTY imply a consciousness of, or a belief in, one's superiority in some respect. PROUD implies sensitiveness, lofty self-respect, or jealous preservation of one's dignity, station, and the like. It may refer to an affectionate admiration of or a justifiable pride concerning someone else: *proud of his son.* ARROGANT applies to insolent or overbearing behavior, arising from an exaggerated belief in one's importance: *arrogant rudeness.* HAUGHTY implies lofty reserve and confident, often disdainful assumption of superiority over others: *the haughty manner of a debutante.*

Cross references to other words related to those being defined are sometimes included also. And finally, explanatory illustrations—sketches, diagrams, maps—useful to the comprehension of certain words are scattered throughout. So much for the A–Z body.

### 4. Know how much information your dictionary contains outside the area of general word information.

A dictionary is almost encyclopedic in its range and can save you many trips to other reference works if you will learn to use its resources. Common features in many of them are essays on various phases of the English language, usually found in the prefatory material along with the most useful material of all—information on how to use the dictionary; a useful guide to punctuation and other mechanics of writing; a guide to letter writing, with forms of address; and lists of colleges and universities. Biographical and geographical information and a list of commonly used abbreviations may appear in separate sections, although most editors now alphabetize these into the body of the book. Other features sometimes included are sections of maps, lists of given names (and nicknames) for men and for women, and even a brief rhyming dictionary (words listed alphabetically by the sound of the final syllable) for versifiers.

All in all, a dictionary is the most useful—most indispensable —single tool you are likely to own. It may not be the most expensive book you are required to buy in college, but it certainly contains the most for the money. To get your full money's

worth, learn to use it with all its features—and use it frequently, and with care.

**EXERCISES**

DICT / DICTIONARY—CONSULT
(Discussion, pp. 45–52)

**1.** These questions are intended to help you familiarize
yourself with your own dictionary. If your instructor should have
you all bring your dictionaries to class on a given day, you
might enjoy talking these items over and comparing the
practices of different publishers.
   a. What dictionary do you own? Is it of college grade?
      Look at the publication date to see how recent it is.
   b. Read carefully any introductory material on the plan of
      the book, to familiarize yourself with its system.
   c. Glance through its illustrations. How frequent are they?
      Of what sorts? How useful?
   d. Where is the key to pronunciation—the list of marked
      words which serve as a guide to the sound values
      indicated in the pronunciation entries?
   e. Look at the main entries, in boldface. What information
      do these contain besides spelling? Notice the kind of
      mark used between syllables, and the one used to
      indicate a hyphen.
   f. Look up the word *genial.* Why are there two entries?
      Note the etymology and the pronunciation of each. List
      in the order of appearance the various kinds of
      information given in the first entry, explaining each item
      in detail.

**2.** For more extended practice in dictionary use, most
publishers of collegiate editions provide printed guides.
Consult your instructor, or write to the company that published
your own dictionary.

# —4—
# CHOOSING
# WORDS

One of the most important elements in your style as a writer is your choice of words—your diction—which should be both accurate and effective. The best route to a wide and discriminating vocabulary is through attentive reading of well-written prose, preferably aloud, to catch its rhythms. The next best, as we have detailed in the preceding chapter, is the regular use of a dictionary. A word is not necessarily good for your purpose just because it's "in the dictionary." But your dictionary does help your choice by labeling some words, or certain definitions of them, to indicate any peculiarities about their standing in time, in place, or in level of use. Words not labeled may be assumed to be in good general use as defined.

## D T / DICTION—TIME

*Choose words that are appropriate to the time
in which (or of which) you are writing.*

Language is a constantly changing thing. As time goes on, some words disappear from use, others change in meaning, and still others are created to cope with new concepts. The great *OED* (*The Oxford English Dictionary,* thirteen volumes

CHOOSING WORDS

including a supplement) is an invaluable record of English words, tracing their changes, with dates and illustrative quotations, throughout the history of the language. *The Dictionary of American English* (four volumes) is a similar historical record of words used in the United States.

Even your one-volume collegiate or desk dictionary is helpful in choosing words appropriate in time, for it designates those that are not in good current use. Commonly used time labels are *Arch.* for archaic, *Obs.* for obsolete, *Hist.* for historical. A word, or its use as one part of speech, or one of its meanings may be so labeled.

Archaic words were in common use long ago but are now antiquated, existing only in the literature of the past or surviving in idioms and proverbs or in the traditional uses of law and religion (*betwixt* for *between, to wit* for *namely*). Use them only in an effort to recapture the flavor of the past. Obsolete words or meanings (*henchman* for *groom, nice* for *coy*) have entirely disappeared from use and should of course be avoided in general writing, as should words in senses designated as historical, such as *hospital* as a place of shelter for travelers.

At the other extreme are neologisms, either new words or new uses of old ones. Words to express concepts in English have very often been adapted from Greek (*nemesis, photograph*) and Latin (*maternity, fragment*), as you will see if you check the etymological items accompanying dictionary definitions. But they also come in regularly from modern languages such as German (*blitz*) and French (*fiancé*). They are sometimes made up ("coined") by business (*Kodak, nylon*). Increasingly they are acronyms (a word which itself was borrowed recently from Greek)—words made up of the initial letters of phrases (*radar* from "radio detection and ranging," *WASP* from "white Anglo-Saxon Protestant"). In fact, more and more organizations deliberately choose names that will make pronounceable acronyms, as many older ones (YMCA, NAACP) do not. When the Cooperative for American Remittances to Europe enlarged its scope after the postwar period, it made sure that its new name, Cooperative for American Relief Everywhere, would still spell the well-established CARE.

New uses for old words are even more abundant than new words. Years ago, faced with the cover over an automobile engine, the British came up with *bonnet,* Americans with the comparable *hood.* More recently, names for two birds of differing temperaments, hawks and doves, took on a new meaning (thanks to columnist Stewart Alsop) in connection with American attitudes toward our involvement in Vietnam. The chief thing to remember about neologisms, as a writer, is this: if those you use are so new that they may not be generally understood, explain them.

## D P / DICTION—PLACE

**Choose words that are appropriate to the place in which (or of which) you are writing.**

English is widely spoken throughout the world, but there are differences in the language as spoken in England, in Australia, in the United States, etc., and even in that spoken in different sections of the United States. A dictionary indicates such differences with labels like *Brit.* (British), *Scot.* (Scottish). In England, gasoline is *petrol,* an elevator is a *lift. Corn* means wheat in England, oats in Scotland, whiskey in some parts of the United States.

Words limited to one section of the United States may be labeled *Prov.* (provincial), *Dial.* (dialectal), *Southern U.S.,* etc. The headline "Goober Crop Promising" in a farm paper published in the South is meaningless to many residents of the North. Such sectionalisms are tending to disappear in this age of movies, radio, and television. But you yourself, especially if you have traveled or are attending college outside of your own section of the country, have probably noticed certain words or meanings peculiar to an area: to a state, to a campus, even to your own family circle. You will of course try to avoid them in your writing, unless you are writing for an equally local audience, such as the readers of the college paper or the members of your family.

# D O / DICTION—OCCASION

**Choose words appropriate to the occasion for which you are writing.**
(Exercise 1, pp. 71–72)

There is a wide range of levels of use, as someone has pointed out in this series of phrases expressing the simple idea of *go:*

1. Leave us go. (Ungrammatical)
2. Let's scram. (Slang)
3. Let's go. (Colloquial)
4. Let us go. (Formal)
5. Let us depart. (More formal)
6. Let us hence. (Poetic)

Each may be "good English" on occasion—even the ungrammatical if the occasion calls for characterizing through conversation someone who is uneducated. But this much is certain: whatever level the occasion demands should be consistently observed. A patch of highly formal English in a casually chatty theme is as out of place as a slang expression in a serious research paper. Your instructor may insist that your themes (many of them, at least) be written at a reasonably formal level —not because other levels haven't their purposes but because most students, being already sufficiently familiar with slang and colloquial and dialectal English, need to have their attention directed to the richness and power of the more formal English vocabulary.

Your dictionary indicates levels of usage with such labels as *Illit., Slang, Colloq., Poetic, Rare.* Except for very special purposes the ungrammatical (*ain't, youse, I seen, that there*) should of course be avoided. Slang (*uptight, cool it, split, rap*) is often very vivid and effective, but being highly informal and vastly overused, it should be included only with conscious purpose. (It is a good diction experience to force yourself to translate as common a phrase as *I'm broke* into more formal English.) Colloquialisms (*dove* for *dived, enthuse*), contractions (*isn't*), and shortened forms (*lab, exam*) are dear to informal speech and writing. The colloquial tone is increasing even in public use—democratically, perhaps: compare the tone of Franklin Roosevelt's public utterances to "My Friends" with those of George Washington to "My Fellow Countrymen," and of this textbook with one written half a century earlier. But there are still many occasions where only a more formal level is appropriate—and where, consequently, "good English" is "formal English." English at the formal level has the advantage of being more permanent as to time (slang is particularly transitory: you may never have heard, even, the word *skiddoo,* popular in your grandparents' youth). Formal English is also more widely intelligible as to place. British stories of gangster life have to be "translated" for publication in the United States because of the national differences at the lower levels of usage, while formal English is an international medium.

Technical words present a special problem in appropriateness to the occasion. Again, your dictionary has numerous labels for words used only in special areas or for specialized meanings of general words. Under the word *axis,* for example, there may appear, besides general definitions, several labeled *Anat., Bot., Aeron., Math., Fine Arts.* As a student, you are rapidly acquiring a technical vocabulary for every specialized field in which you are taking a course, and you use it freely in writing in that area. But when the occasion is general, you must consider whether such special words should be omitted, or defined, or replaced with more common terms.

Good English, then, is appropriate English—appropriate not just to the time, the place, and the occasion, but also to the subject—and the anticipated reader. Children's books, for instance, are addressed in language as well as material to a particular age group.

# D E  /  DICTION—EXACT

***Choose the word that exactly suits your purpose.***
(Exercises 2–3, pp. 72–73)

The English language, because of its long history of borrowing from other languages, is particularly rich in vocabulary. This fact carries with it both a privilege and a responsibility: it

## CHOOSING WORDS

offers a wide choice of words suitable for your purpose, but it requires that you be careful to choose from among them the exact word. The habitual use of a dictionary, and better still, of a book of synonyms, will be a great help to you in your effort to use words precisely.

It has been said that there is no such thing as a synonym, and the statement is true in that few words, if any, have meanings so identical that they can be used interchangeably in all situations. *Big* and *large,* for example, are synonymous in many uses (a big room or a large room) but a large person will be big in size, while a big person may be important in position or magnanimous in spirit. *Famous* and *notorious* persons are both widely known, but the two words are in no sense interchangeable. The reason for the scarcity of exact synonyms is that while many words are alike in their basic meanings, **denotations,** they have come through association to differ in their suggested meanings, **connotations,** which often carry with them quite an emotional load. For many of us today, the word *apartment* denotes *home,* but it is unlikely that any latter-day Stephen Foster will move us with a song entitled "Apartment, Sweet Apartment."

The emotional element in connotations is a changing thing that we must keep abreast of. Take the word *Negro,* which came to us through Spanish and Portuguese from the Latin *niger,* meaning "black." Recently it has been swept out of American English with rare speed because of the denigratory (that's another, more recent, descendant from *niger*) connotations it has accumulated, to be replaced, in these days of rising racial pride, by the original *black.* Now the same situation is occurring in South Africa, where the original natives have long been called *Bantu,* a once innocent word meaning "people." But it has become so encrusted with emotion-rousing connotations that there is a strong movement there, officially as well as unofficially, to change it to *black people.*

At quieter levels, and for practical purposes, however, there *are* synonyms, and you will find lists of them invaluable, both when you wish to avoid repetition (**D s**), and when you are groping for a more exact word. We have noted earlier that a collegiate dictionary includes, in addition to definitions, limited lists of synonyms and occasionally devotes some space to distinguishing among them and even to giving examples of their use, while an unabridged dictionary has the space to carry such distinctions and illustrations much farther. A dictionary of synonyms, of which there are several, both small and big in size and price, goes farther still. But for the really discriminating writer, the favorite source of exact diction is Roget: not the *Roget's Thesaurus in Dictionary Form,* which merely arranges words alphabetically and lists their synonyms after them, but *Roget's International Thesaurus.*

This volume is slower to use, as it takes two operations: you must first look up the word you want to improve on in an alphabetical index, which will refer you to one or a number of pages in the body of the *Thesaurus.* Looking up *proud,* for instance, for which you saw dictionary synonyms on page 50, you will find page references to seven synonyms for the word (plus four more to phrases containing it): *pleased, magnificent, prideful, vain, conceited, boastful, arrogant.* It may be that one of these just suits your purpose, and you have found it in one operation. But you will be wise to look up one or more of these references in order to take advantage of the full richness of the *Thesaurus.*

For example, the word *knowledge* (with its antonym *ignorance* in adjoining columns) gets almost three pages, on which are listed synonymous nouns, verbs, adjectives, and adverbs, as single words and in phrases, with examples of their use drawn from numerous authors and several languages. The happy result may be that you will see, among all those possibilities, the very one you are looking for, the one that was on the tip of your tongue even if you didn't know it was there; or that you will be reminded of yet another; or that you will at least have a good time prowling. (A modern writer who loves the exact word claims to have worn out several copies of this *Thesaurus.*) Notice, however, that the book supplements rather than supplants the dictionary, for it gives no definitions.

**1. Distinguish between pairs of words that have similar basic meanings but different uses.**

*Bring* and *take* express movement, but in opposite directions. *Imply* and *infer* are both concerned with the process of suggestion, but carefully chosen, *imply* is used of the giver of the suggestion, *infer* of the receiver.

In his remarks he *implied* that he was willing, but from his actions I *inferred* that he was reluctant.

Compare these pairs: *disinterested, uninterested; few, less; between, among.*

**2. Avoid the malapropism, the misuse of one word for another similar in sound.**

Malapropisms are usually impressive words misused ignorantly, carelessly, or pretentiously with unintentionally amusing results. If you aren't sure of the right word, consult your dictionary.

That restaurant charges *exuberant* prices. (For *exorbitant*)
We all recognized him to be a child *progeny*. (For *prodigy*)

# D V / DICTION—VIVID

### Choose vivid words.
(Exercises 4–5, p. 73)

The words you choose should be not only exact but also vivid. To this end use specific rather than general words wherever possible: *dog* rather than *animal, collie* rather than *dog, Lassie* rather than *collie.* Look particularly for vivid verbs that carry the weight of several adverbs with them: compare *move* with *go; go* with *walk; walk* with *shamble, march, saunter, ramble, prowl, pace, plod, tread, wend, trudge,* and other equally specific verbs that a book of synonyms will supply.

The English language is particularly rich in adjectives; don't be content with using the same few over and over. Instead of *big,* consider *bulky, enormous, huge, vast, burly;* instead of *little,* try *minute, diminutive, puny, infinitesimal, petty.* But choose, of course, with due respect for connotations; and don't lightly overuse superlatives like *tremendous* and *magnificent* until they lose their force. (*Awful* and *terrific* have already been sacrificed to such overuse.)

# D F / DICTION—FIGURATIVE

**Use fresh and appropriate figures of speech.**
(Exercises 6–7, p. 74)

One of the best ways to gain vividness in your writing is to add a touch of imagination through occasional figures of speech. The most common of these are comparisons known as similes and metaphors. Do not confuse them with a literal comparison of two things of the same kind (your house and ours) or with an analogy, in which numerous points of comparison can be made between different things (the heart and a pump). The figurative comparison gains its force by comparing two things that are entirely different except for the one quality to be emphasized.

The **simile** expresses the comparison openly, with *like* or *as*.

> Her breath was as foul as a city sewer. (It stank.)
> He kept quiet while he counted to ten; then he let go like a time bomb. (A calculated explosion)

The **metaphor** is even more forceful, stating directly that something is something else, the comparison being only implied.

> Her hair was spun silk.
> He kept quiet while he counted to ten; then he blew a fuse.

The language is full of so-called "dead" metaphors—words that have been used figuratively for so long that they have lost their vividness by coming to be accepted literally.

> He sat on the *foot* of the bed.
> The river *ran* into the open sea.

**61**

CHOOSING WORDS

For vividness, think up fresh and original "live" ones.

**Hyperbole** is obvious exaggeration. To say a three-foot fish was five feet long is a lie; to say it was a mile long is hyperbole.

The sink was heaped with a mountain of dirty dishes.

**Litotes** is a kind of understatement that makes a point by denying its opposite.

Ten thousand dollars is no small price for an automobile. (It is a big one, actually.)
I get not a little satisfaction from playing chess. (That is, I get a lot of satisfaction.)

**Irony** expresses the opposite of one's meaning, or the unexpected.

When he gets up in the morning, he is a fine-looking sight. (*Bad,* actually)
He was so heart-broken that he didn't go to sleep that night for all of three minutes. (*Hours* was expected.)

**Personification** gives human attributes to things.

The engine wheezed, coughed, and died.

**Metonymy** designates a part by the whole, or the whole by a part.

We need three more hands to put up the scenery. (Three more people)
Detroit finally won the game. (The team did.)

In using figures of speech, be sure that they are appropriate to your occasion and your purpose and are in good taste.

**1. See that your figures of speech contribute to the effect you are striving for.**

The sun rose magnificently, glowing like a copper penny. (A penny is too small, in size and importance, to add any grandeur to our idea of the sun.)

**2. Be sure your figures attract attention to the point you are making rather than to themselves.**

As we ascended, the stairs in the old building groaned as though we had stepped on the stomach of a sick old man. (The writer is so repelled by the figure that he forgets the stairs.)

**3. Use figures for effectiveness, but avoid straining for effect with a clutter of them.**

He came up through the trap door like a jack-in-the-box. When he saw us, he smiled like a crescent moon and came rushing over to us like a tidal wave.

**4. Guard against the mixed metaphor, the result of changing your comparison in midstream.**

This offers more unintentional humor than illumination.

I've forgiven him, but I'm not going to run after him on bended knee.

To become a success you must dig deep—dig your way to the heights.

# D H / DICTION—HACKNEYED

*Avoid hackneyed, or trite, expressions.*
(Exercises 8–9, pp. 74–75)

Reaching for a forceful way of saying something, we are all too likely to get hold of a phrase that is echoing through our minds because of the numerous times we have heard or read it, and we feel comfortably secure in using words that have been used safely by so many before us. Trite expressions are loved by journalists in general and sports writers in particular, from *Time* to your college newspaper.

Train your ear to recognize such clichés as *broad daylight, colorful spectacle, burning shame, humanly possible, view with alarm, point with pride.* Search rather for fresh and original expressions or settle for simple and direct ones.

Above all, watch out for hackneyed figures of speech, which defeat their purpose of adding vividness and so are better omitted. Faced with "His face got as red as a beet," the reader has long since ceased to picture the beet; better to say only that it got red. In "College will help me to climb the ladder of success," the ladder too has disappeared from the reader's consciousness as a result of having been climbed too often. Let college just help you to succeed—unless you can find a vivid metaphor of your own.

# D I / DICTION—IDIOM

***Use idioms correctly.***
(Exercise 10, p. 75)

An idiom is a form of expression so peculiar to a single language that it doesn't make sense if translated literally into another. The English greeting *How do you do?* is no more logical —and no less useful—than the German *Wie geht's?* ("How does it go?") or the French *Comment-vous portez vous?* ("How do you carry yourself?") Idioms cannot be learned; they must be recognized by ear. There is no grammatical reason why *see* is followed directly by its object ("I see the house"), whereas its close synonym *look* requires the prepositional phrase ("I look *at* the house")—or why *enjoy* must be followed by a gerund ("I enjoy eating"), while its synonym *like* may be followed by an infinitive ("I like to eat"). Prepositions account for a good deal of idiom trouble in English, as foreigners will tell you while they struggle to master such distinctions as "Slacks for sale" and "Slacks on sale," or

I am pleased *with* the book.
I am fascinated *by* the book.
I am interested *in* the book.

To native-born Americans, fortunately, these expressions come naturally, for the most part. Careful writers still distinguish between *to* and *with* after *compare:*

Let me compare your answers *with* mine. (Literal comparison)
He is fond of comparing her *to* a kitten. (Figurative comparison)

But this distinction is seldom observed, informally.

*Different* raises another problem. Some British and the Australians follow it with the preposition *to;* Americans, traditionally, use the preposition *from,* still strongly preferred by careful writers here:

Your copy is different *from mine.* (Preposition and object)

That's the grammar of it; but an easier way to remember the connection is to think of the verb *differ:*

I certainly differ from you. (Never, by ear, *differ than.*)

Back to grammar, *than* is a conjunction, normally followed by a clause:

The Florida summer is hotter than I expected.

But informally the conjunction is now frequently used after *different:*

Your copy is different than mine.

Good reading and careful listening are the best ways to master idioms. When in doubt about a particular idiomatic pattern, consult the unabridged dictionary, which has more space than the college editions have to show words used in sentences.

## D S / DICTION—SOUND

***Avoid awkward sounds such as the repetition of the same word, syllable, or pattern.***
(Exercises 11–12, pp. 75–76)

Good writing should have euphony—it should appeal to the ear as well as to the mind. Words may be purposely repeated, for effect, as in Lincoln's famous "government of the people, by the people, and for the people'' and Steinbeck's ''the deep growl of the engines shook the air, shook the world, shook the future.'' But do not repeat a word pointlessly; such repetitions not only suggest a limited vocabulary but offend the ear.

**1. Read your writing aloud, whenever possible, to catch awkwardly repeated words.**

These can be replaced with synonyms or pronouns, or omitted by rephrasing the sentence.

Repetitious:   I have lived in my home town all my life. The Wabash River runs through my home town. My home town has a population of more than sixteen thousand people. Many people live in my home town and work in Fort Wayne.

Improved:   I have lived in *Huntington, which* is located on the Wabash River, all my life. *It* has a population of more than sixteen thousand. Many who live *here* work in Fort Wayne.

**2. Avoid the awkward repetition of the same word sound in the sentence, regardless of the spelling.**

I *mean* that the *mean* must first be determined.
Mr. *Luce* let *loose* a stream of profanity.

**3. Avoid the awkward repetition of the same syllable in different words.**

There are numerous <u>a</u>reas of <u>e</u>rror here.
Do you <u>pro</u>pose to report your <u>pro</u>gress on the <u>pro</u>ject?
I am only indicat<u>ing</u> the exist<u>ing</u> annoy<u>ing</u> conditions.

**4. Avoid the use of rhyme or regular rhythms.**

These are appropriate to poetry rather than to prose (although good prose has larger rhythms of its own).

And when I heard the *news,* I really got the *blues.*

**5. Avoid also the overuse of alliteration, the "Peter Piper" problem.**

The boss asked us to send the sixteen shipments as soon as
   possible.

**6. Avoid a long unbroken string of either one-syllabled or many-syllabled words.**

In my home town there is a man who likes to fish but not to work.
Universities frequently activate regulations penalizing under-
   graduates.

# D R / DICTION—REDUNDANCY

*Avoid the aimless repetition of ideas.*
(Exercise 13, p. 76)

Redundacy, or tautology, is the unintentional expression of
the same idea in different words. A thought may of course be
purposely stated in different ways to make it clear, just as a
word may be repeated time after time for emphasis. The first
sentence of the opening paragraph under **D s,** above, for
example, deliberately expresses the same idea twice, just as
the first sentence of this paragraph intentionally uses two different words meaning the same thing. But often such restatements, like repetitions, creep in aimlessly, giving a first impression that more than one thing is being said, as in the old
Southerner's remark: "It will do you good and help you, too,
besides the benefit you will derive from it." Prune your writing
rigorously of such purposeless restatements.

**1. An idea should not be aimlessly repeated in different words.**

He asked us to meet him at 4:30 p.m. this afternoon. (Use *4:30
   p.m. today* or *4:30 this afternoon.*)
The word *awful* has been so weakened by overuse that it has lost
   its strength. (Use *has been weakened by overuse* or *has lost
   its strength through overuse.*)

CHOOSING WORDS

### 2. Possession should not be indicated twice.

If a noun is followed by an adjective clause that shows possession, it should not be preceded by a possessive adjective.

Let me tell you about *my* experience that *I* had. (An experience)
He showed us *his* new motorbike that *he* had just won in a contest. (*The* new motorbike)

### 3. A double negative, once used for emphasis, is now unacceptable.

Let the idea of "no" appear once only.

People *don't hardly* think of walking any more. (Use *don't* or *hardly*.)
I *haven't never* had *no* education! (A triple! Cut out two; *any* can take the place of both *never* and *no*.)

### 4. A double comparative or superlative is also unacceptable.

One is enough (**Com 2**).

I am looking for a *more better* place to live, and this is the *most pleasantest* I have found. (Omit *more* and *most; better* and *pleasantest* are already the comparative and superlative of *good* and *pleasant.*)

### 5. A preposition or a conjunction should not be used twice as the same connective.

The repetition of such little words would not disturb the ear, but the structural redundancy offends the reason.

Of all the sports *in* which I have participated *in,* tennis is my favorite. (Omit either *in;* the use of the first is more formal than the second.)
We decided *that* since we didn't have to be in early *that* we could stay for the second show. (Omit the second *that;* the adverb clause should be within the noun clause.)

# D W / DICTION—WORDINESS

***Avoid the use of more words than are necessary to present your meaning effectively.***
(Exercise 14, pp. 76–77)

"I could have written you a shorter letter if I had had more time" has become a stylistic truism. Wordiness is likely to creep into your own first draft, when you are pouring out everything you have to say, but your final copy should be ruthlessly stripped of all excess. A famous writer has gone so far as to say that the most important part of revision is excision—the cutting out of superfluous words. Work toward simplicity and directness, and you will very likely attain effectiveness, a writer's chief goal.

### 1. Reduce predications wherever possible, never using two clauses if one will say the same thing better (SV c).

**Wordy:** Our puppy is very lively, and he is also very mischievous.
**Better:** Our puppy is very lively and mischievous.
**Wordy:** The town I live in is a place that is very pleasant.
**Better:** My home town is very pleasant.

### 2. Be on guard against the chief fault of fuzzy writing, sometimes called "jargon."
This includes the vague use of words like *nature, character, factor, aspect, line, capacity.*

Your problems and mine are *of a similar character.* (Are much alike)
We both like swimming and other sports *of that nature.* (And other such sports)

### 3. Shorten and tighten all overlong phrases.

*In the opinion of most people,* he is a failure. (Most people think . . .)

I wasn't aware of it *at that point in time.* (That point? That time? Or only then?)

We knew him *during the period that* he was in college. (We knew him while . . .)

### 4. Remove all unnecessary or redundant phrases (D r).

Detroit is the busiest city *to be found* in Michigan.

That chair is very comfortable *to sit in.*

The union is striking for higher wages *than are being paid at present.*

### 5. Avoid lengthy passive constructions (V v).

Make them active.

**Wordy:** He *was made* the recipient of a gold watch by the officials of his company.

**Better:** The officials of his company gave him a gold watch.

**Wordy:** The tree that *was blown* across the street by the hurricane has been cleared away by the maintenance men.

**Better:** The maintenance men have cleared away the tree that the hurricane blew across the street.

# D FW / DICTION—"FINE WRITING"

***Avoid flowery and euphemistic expressions known as "fine writing."***

(Exercise 15, p. 77)

"Fine writing" is a phrase used to describe writing that is *too* fine—that in a commendable effort to avoid being commonplace has become uncommendably ornate. Simple, direct wording is more effective because it sounds sincere.

### 1. Avoid elaborate and affected phrases.

**Affected:** When we departed thence, Mother Nature smiled on us.

| Simple: | When we left, the weather was fine. |
| Affected: | His overwhelming passion for her once knew no bounds, but now she is only a fragrant blossom in his garden of memories. |
| Simple: | He loved her passionately once, but now she is only a sweet memory. |

### 2. Avoid euphemisms.

A euphemism (not to be confused with *euphony*) is a mild and often roundabout way of expressing a harsh or unpleasant truth. *Roget's International Thesaurus* lists dozens of expressions, for instance, used to avoid the words *die* and *death*. Euphemistic writing has been very popular in the past; now, calling a spade a spade is generally preferred.

| Euphemistic: | My father passed away before I had attained the tender age of seven. |
| Direct: | My father died before I was seven. |
| Euphemistic: | The old wino wiped the perspiration from his brow, stretched out his limbs, and expectorated. |
| Direct: | The old wino wiped the sweat from his forehead, stretched out his legs, and spat. |

### EXERCISES

D O / DICTION—OCCASION
(Discussion, pp. 56–57)

1. In the following sentences,
    a. Identify any ungrammatical, slang, colloquial, poetic or technical expressions. (Consult your dictionary if necessary.)
    b. On what occasions, if any, might they be appropriate?
    c. Translate them into more formal English, preserving the meaning as accurately as possible. What is lost by the change? What gained?

CHOOSING WORDS

1. His first typhoid shot left him feeling woozy.
2. We came upon a snake in the process of exuviation.
3. Where'er thou goest, I shall go.
4. This here feller is smart compared to a lot of them dumb bunnies.
5. I think he really got a kick out of double-crossing me.

### D E / DICTION—EXACT
(Discussion, pp. 57–60)

**2.** Use each of the words in the following frequently confused sets in a sentence that clearly indicates its meaning. (Consult your dictionary if necessary.)

1. aggravate, irritate
2. amount, number
3. anxious, eager
4. apparent, evident
5. apt, liable, likely
6. beside, besides
7. credible, creditable
8. continual, continuous
9. deadly, deathly
10. emigrant, immigrant
11. farther, further
12. fatal, fateful
13. few, less
14. practical, practicable
15. if, whether
16. incredible, incredulous
17. intelligence, wisdom, knowledge
18. luxuriant, luxurious
19. respectfully, respectively
20. disinterested, uninterested

**3.** Supply a more exact word wherever advisable in the following sentences.

1. My cousin Joe has been a pupil at Coe College for two years.
2. I view my coming graduation with split feelings.
3. George told us some amusing antidotes about his life in the Navy.
4. Conditions were so bad that many Englishmen decided to immigrate to Australia.
5. I'm afraid there will be less people present tonight than last night.

D V / DICTION—VIVID
(Discussion, pp. 60–61)

**4.** Make the following bare statements vivid by replacing the general nouns and verbs in them with highly specific ones and by adding vivid adjectives and adverbs, phrases and clauses, as you see fit.

1. An automobile went past.
2. The bell rang.
3. The person looked at the skyscraper.
4. A boat was on the water.
5. The teacher lectured.

**5.** Replace the overworked words in the following sentences with words that are accurate and meaningful.

1. I felt terrible when I found I had shortchanged you.
2. How could you have made such a colossal mistake?
3. I think your new dress is absolutely magnificent.
4. Isn't the way the water drops over the falls cute?
5. Look at this tremendous mosquito bite!

## D F / DICTION—FIGURATIVE
(Discussion, pp. 61–63)

**6.** From what areas of experience are the metaphors in the following sentences taken? Correct the mixed ones by making them consistent.

1. Try to prune your writing of such excess baggage.
2. When I went through that pile of castoffs with a fine-toothed comb, I was rewarded with a good deal of pay dirt.
3. The consumer is being taken for a ride, but he doesn't know how to get off the hook.
4. We must put our shoulders to the wheel and bring this campaign in for a smooth landing.
5. Remember that the hand that feeds you usually has an eye for your best interests.

**7.** Watch for figures of speech in your reading, and jot down those that seem to you to be particularly successful.

## D H / DICTION—HACKNEYED
(Discussion, pp. 63–64)

**8.** Replace any hackneyed phrases in the following sentences with fresher or more direct words.

1. He has always had a weakness for the fair sex.
2. I'm going to discuss the matter with the powers that be this weekend.
3. I just met the blushing bride who is now Jim's better half.
4. The speaker of the evening needs no introduction.
5. We sat down to a sumptuous repast.

**9.** Eliminate the hackneyed figures of speech in the following sentences, replacing them wherever possible with fresh, original ones of your own.

1. His face got as white as a sheet.
2. When I was a freshman, I was as green as grass.
3. She is as pretty as a picture.
4. If you think you are overworked, remember I'm in the same boat.
5. Janice is always as busy as a bee.

## D I / DICTION—IDIOM
(Discussion, pp. 64–65)

**10.** Correct any faulty uses of idiom in the following sentences.

1. I have always found him as being a faithful friend.
2. Family life inevitably makes many demands from us.
3. I can't help to feel that we should have done something for him.
4. My friend Charley gets between five to ten letters every day.
5. I wonder whether you have really considered about the facts.

## D S / DICTION—SOUND
(Discussion, pp. 65–67)

**11.** Eliminate from the following sentences any awkward repetitions of the same word, replacing them with synonyms or pronouns if required.

1. When I am at home I like to work around the house and work in the garden.
2. At first very few families had television sets, but soon nearly every family had a television set.
3. After I had become familiar with all of the jobs around the mill, I was assigned permanently to one of the hardest jobs in the whole mill.
4. There are four classes open for technicians, and almost anyone interested in radio can qualify for one of the four classes for technicians.

CHOOSING WORDS

5.   These figures really prove that the Senator has really lost a good many of his followers.

**12.**   Eliminate any awkward repetitions of sound from the following sentences by rewording as necessary.

1.   Most of his income comes from his investments.
2.   I had applied for the job last spring, but I had not expected to be accepted.
3.   My mention of my suspension attracted his attention.
4.   The thing was out of tune when I played on it last June.
5.   My brother won't bother with another, either.

**D R  /  DICTION—REDUNDANCY**
(Discussion, pp. 67–68)

**13.**   Eliminate from the following sentences any needless repetitions of the same idea.

1.   We'll start as soon as we can get our clothes, food, and etc. together.
2.   The preface explains why and for what reason the book was written.
3.   In my opinion, it seems to me that a fifteen-hundred-dollar tuition fee is very high.
4.   My father promised that if we got the lawn mowed by noon that he would take us to the zoo.
5.   The modern world of today is a strenuous but exciting place to live in.

**D W  /  DICTION—WORDINESS**
(Discussion, pp. 69–70)

**14.**   Remove from the following sentences any words or phrases that can be eliminated without loss of meaning, rewriting as required.

1. Although I had had no previous experience along the line of selling, I applied for a job in a big department store.
2. Our white uniforms soon became a dirty gray in color.
3. My great-uncle was a brilliant man, but he was also a little on the eccentric side.
4. That company has long advertised watches of the finest character.
5. There are memories of occurrences that happened in my early life that I shall never forget as long as I live.

## D FW / DICTION—"FINE WRITING"
(Discussion, pp. 70–71)

**15.** Reword any flowery or euphemistic expressions in the following sentences into simple, straightforward English.

1. The eye of the day appeared in golden splendor over the horizon as our party gathered to explore the beauties of nature.
2. After he was called to his great reward, his mortal remains were brought home for the final obsequies.
3. The Senator had attained to manhood's estate among the economically underprivileged classes.
4. Sensing the sudden onslaught of an attack of *mal de mer,* Susie made a hurried departure in the direction of the little-girls' room.
5. Being conscious of a strong mutual regard for one another, they wish to enter into the bonds of holy matrimony.

# 5
# LEARNING TO SPELL

In the whole picture of handling the word, spelling is a minor but troublesome detail. Such importance as it has is entirely negative; unlike diction, which may show special strengths as well as weaknesses, spelling is either right or wrong, no merit being accorded a writer for correctness, only demerits for errors.

Unfortunately there are more wrong ways to spell a word than right ways, and nothing gives such an appearance of carelessness to a piece of writing as frequent misspelled words. Much misspelling is the result of haste and can be caught by a careful proofreading of the final draft. But a few people are naturally "poor spellers," not from a lack of intelligence or even of effort but from an apparently innate inability to visualize words. If you are one of these, you know it by now and should be particularly careful.

At your age the old-fashioned memorizing of a spelling list for spelling's sake hasn't much appeal; your best course is to concentrate on the words you actually use. Keep a list of the ones you misspell on themes and practice writing them. And most important of all, form the habit of having a dictionary always at hand and of consulting it whenever you are in doubt. Be sure that the spelling you choose coincides with the meaning you intend: *phase* is "in the dictionary" but is not a correct spelling if you mean *faze*.

Buy a cheap little vest-pocket or paperback edition of a dictionary for classroom use. This size isn't much good for most purposes but is very useful to the poor speller because it is easier to carry around and handier to consult than the much more valuable collegiate or unabridged editions. Make sure that your instructors are willing to have you use such a "crutch" in class, and don't spend too much of your limited time during examinations and class themes just looking up words. If you know you can't spell one word, use another. Learn from the student who turned in a class theme on "My Most Embarrassing Moment" with a sentence reading

I felt as out of place as a battleship in a fish ~~beal~~ ~~boul~~ ~~bowle~~ pond.

He weakened his simile, but he solved his problem.

## SP S / SPELLING—STANDARD

***Use the conventional spellings listed in a recent and reputable American dictionary.***
(Exercise 1, pp. 103–104)

English is a composite of borrowings from so many other languages that its spelling is sadly illogical (notice the five pronunciations of *ough* in the words *cough, rough, bough, though,* and *through,* and the three pronunciations of it in the word *slough* alone). But beware of reforms; they must come slowly, if at all. Some progress is being made, *medieval* now being accepted as well as *mediaeval, rime* as well as *rhyme* (but no change in *rhythm*), *sulfur* as well as *sulphur* (*sulfur* is now required in scientific writing, but *sulphur* continues to be used frequently elsewhere). *Encyclopedia* is now a generally preferred spelling, but we still have the *Encyclopaedia Britannica.* Study the prefatory guide to the use of your dictionary, whatever it is labeled, so that you will know how its editors indicate preferences among spelling choices.

Such phonetic spellings as *tho* and *thru,* convenient as they are for your own note-taking and other very informal writing situations, are not generally accepted. It doesn't help much to spell *night* "nite" unless you are willing to go the whole way and spell *light* "lite," *might* "mite," etc.; and the old unphonetic spellings do have the virtue of keeping homonyms (words with the same sounds but different meanings) conveniently distinct in phrases such as *the might of kings* and *the widow's mite.*

Much as there is to be said for spelling reform, the fact remains that a page of English completely transcribed according to phonetic principles will look like a foreign language. The headline "Frate Rates Lowered" in a newspaper that once adopted a few reformed spellings probably caused more concern to the average reader than it saved time and space for the printer. As a student, you will do well to follow standard practices, which will raise no question of taste or accuracy.

# SP R / SPELLING—RULE

*Know and follow common spelling rules.*

In spite of the illogicalities of our spelling, a few rules do apply to enough words to make them worth knowing, as they can save you many trips to the dictionary. Most of them have to do with the problems involved in adding letters.

## 1. Adding prefixes and suffixes.
These are syllables put at the beginning or the end of a word to qualify its meaning.

**a.** Do not drop the beginning letter of a word because a prefix ends with the same one.

mis + spelling = misspelling     un + necessary = unnecessary

**b.** Similarly, do not drop a final letter because a suffix begins with it.

final + ly = finally     green + ness = greenness

**81**

**c.** Conversely, do not add letters between a word and its prefix or its suffix (but see rule 3 below).

dis + appear = disappear    ski + ing = skiing

## 2. Dropping final e.

**a.** Drop the final *e* before a suffix beginning with a vowel (*a, e, i, o, u*).

quote + ing = quoting          brute + al = brutal
quote + ed = quoted            prime + ary = primary
quote + able = quotable        fame + ous = famous
quote + ation = quotation      precede + ence = precedence

Exceptions:  (1)  dyeing (Compare *dying*), singeing (Compare *singing*), hingeing
(2)  Words ending in *oe:* canoeing, shoeing, hoeing, toeing
(3)  Words adding suffixes beginning with *a* or *o,* when the *e* is preceded by *c* or *g* (the *e* keeps the sound of those consonants soft): notice + able = noticeable (But *noticing*); courage + ous = courageous (But *encouraging*); practice + able = practicable (The *c* becomes hard.)

A few words are spelled either with or without the final *e* (*like—likable* or *likeable, sale—salable* or *saleable*). You will be safe if you follow the rule.

**b.** Do not drop the final *e* before a suffix beginning with a consonant.

appease—appeasement (But *appeasing*)
crude—crudeness, crudely
state—stately (But *stating*)
safe—safety, safely

Exceptions:   duly, truly, awful, ninth, acknowledgment, judgment (*Acknowledgement* and *judgement* are primarily British spellings.)

### 3. Doubling final consonant.
Double the final consonant if the word

a.   has only one syllable or has the accent on the last syllable;
b.   ends in a single consonant preceded by a single vowel; and
c.   takes a suffix beginning with a vowel.

This rule isn't as difficult as it sounds; study these illustrations and get a picture of how it works.

din—dinning, dinned (Compare *dine—dining, dined* under rule 2 above.)
rap—rapping (Compare *rape—raping*.)

Double:

rub—rubbing, rubbed (One syllable)
prefer—preferring, preferred (Accent is on last syllable.)

Do not double:

prefer—preference (Accent is not on last syllable.)
prefer—preferment (Suffix begins with a consonant.)
hold—holding (Ends in two final consonants.)
boat—boating (Consonant preceded by two vowels.)

A few words ending in *l* may be spelled either way (*travel—traveler* or *traveller*). You may safely follow the rule. In doubling the final consonant of words ending in *c,* the second letter becomes a *k.*

picnic—picnicking    panic—panicky

LEARNING TO SPELL

## 4. Changing *y* to *i*.

If a word ends in *y* preceded by a consonant, change the *y* to *i* unless the added suffix begins with *i*.

silly—silliness          try—tries, tried (But *trying*)
merry—merriment     study—studious (But *studying*)
lady—ladies             pity—pitiful (But *pitying*)
valley—valleys          monkey—monkeys (*y* preceded by a vowel)

**Exceptions:**  lay—laid, pay—paid, say—said

## 5. Forming plurals.

The plural of English nouns is regularly formed by adding *s*.

dog—dogs     tree—trees     trick—tricks

Nouns already ending in *s*, or in any other sound after which the plural ending must be pronounced as an extra syllable, add *es*.

glass—glasses     box—boxes     church—churches

**Exceptions:**

**a.**  Some nouns borrowed from Latin retain their original Latin plurals.

alumna—alumnae     stratum—strata
alumnus—alumni     datum—data

Some of these borrowings may now be written with Latin or anglicized plurals.

cactus—cacti *or* cactuses
medium—media *or* mediums

**b.**  Nouns ending in *o* regularly add *s* for the plural, but many add *s* or *es* (*mosquitos, mosquitoes*), and the following list always *es:*

| | |
|---|---|
| echo—echoes | Negro—Negroes |
| embargo—embargoes | potato—potatoes |
| hero—heroes | tomato—tomatoes |
| mulatto—mulattoes | torpedo—torpedoes |

Except for these eight, you may safely form the plurals of *o* words regularly, with *s*.

**c.** Most nouns ending in *f* change the *f* to *v* and add *es* for the plural.

| | |
|---|---|
| calf—calves | scarf—scarves |
| half—halves | sheaf—sheaves |
| knife—knives | thief—thieves |
| leaf—leaves | wharf—wharves |
| loaf—loaves | wife—wives |

(But *chief—chiefs, grief—griefs, handkerchief—handkerchiefs*)

**d.** A few nouns do not change in the plural.

sheep     series

A few others change but rarely.

fish (fishes)     deer (deers)

**e.** Hyphenated nouns add the plural to the most important word.

passers-by     mothers-in-law     courts-martial

Compounded nouns add the plural to the end.

cupfuls     teaspoonfuls     pailfuls

**f.** The plural of letters, numbers, symbols, and words used as words is formed by adding *'s*.

| | | | |
|---|---|---|---|
| a's | 7's | &'s | apple's |
| o's | 2's | *'s | etc.'s |

LEARNING TO SPELL

Dates, however, are now frequently written with only an *s*.

1900's *or* 1900s
1820's *or* 1820s

### 6. Using *ie* or *ei*.

Don't solve this problem by the easy rule of "Make them both look like *e* and put a dot in the middle"! Learn the useful old jingle:

Put *i* before *e*
Except after *c*
Or when sounded like *a*
As in *neighbor* and *weigh*.

| believe | receive | vein |
| niece | ceiling | freight |

**Exceptions:** All of the common ones are contained in the easily memorized sentence, "The weird foreign sheiks and financiers neither forfeit leisure nor seize heights."

Although there aren't many of them, these rules cover large enough numbers of words to make them worth memorizing; in fact, they cover the tricky spots in nearly a fifth of several hundred words in a recently published list of "spelling demons." But for the most part you must memorize individual spellings. Use any tricks you can to keep difficult words in your mind, such as visualizing "sepArate." These associations will help with a few others:

principle—a rule (of conduct, science, etc.)
principal—all other meanings
stationery—paper from a stationer
stationary—all other meanings
capitol—the building with the dome
capital—all other meanings
despair—comes from desperation
attendance—dance

# SP H / SPELLING—HYPHEN

***Spell with a hyphen.***

The history of word combinations is often that they begin as two words (*basket ball*), become hyphenated through frequent use together (*basket-ball*), and ultimately, if used long enough with a single meaning, become one word (*basketball*). *Weekend* has only recently completed this cycle. What stage a given combination of words has reached in common use is best verified through a recent dictionary (compare *flash flood* and *flashback, air rifle* and *airplane*).

**1. Two or more words used as a single adjective are commonly hyphenated (but not an adjective and a noun).**

an air-mail letter (But *air mail*)
a motion-picture theater (But *motion pictures*)
a ten-dollar hat (But *ten dollars*)

Such hyphens are often necessary to a clear meaning.

Compare:    thirty odd presidents    thirty-odd presidents
little worn shoes    little-worn shoes

There are so many possible combinations of words used as compound adjectives that a dictionary cannot begin to list them all. Feel free to make your own, but hyphenate them.

a never-to-be-forgotten day    a once-over-lightly cleaning

The same effect of holding several words together for a single purpose is often gained, particularly in longer combinations, with quotation marks (**P q**).

He is one of those "early to bed and early to rise" boys.

Do not use both hyphens and quotation marks.

## 2. Words combined with adverbs to express a single meaning are commonly hyphenated.

So are all combinations beginning with *self.*

a drive-in    a set-to
a mix-up    self-preservation

## 3. Adverbs combined with adjectives are commonly hyphenated unless they end in *ly.*

a well-known fact (But a *thoroughly known* fact)
the best-loved poems (But *dearly loved* poems)
a fast-moving train (But a *rapidly moving* train)

## 4. Compound numbers from twenty-one through ninety-nine are always hyphenated.

But numbers that precede words like *hundred* and *thousand* are never hyphenated with them, except as compound adjectives.

sixty-seven             five hundred dollars
thirty-two million people    a five-hundred-dollar car

## 5. Fractions are generally hyphenated.

They are not if they are loosely used or if the second term is an already hyphenated number.

exactly one-fourth of a mile    three-sixteenths of an inch
nearly one fourth of them     three thirty-seconds of an inch

## 6. A hyphen is used to indicate that a word has been divided at the end of a line for reasons of space.

Put the hyphen at the end of the line where the division starts, never at the beginning of the next.

There are a number of magazines to which I would subscribe if I had the time to read them.

**a.** Divide words between two syllables: generally between double consonants, after prefixes or before suffixes, or at another clear break in sound.

lit-tle    dis-appear    fight-ing    mel-o-dy

When in doubt about the location of a syllable break, see the dictionary entry.

knowl-edge    cul-ture    dom-i-nant

**b.** Do not divide a word after or before a single letter.

a cross    ba-nan a

**c.** Do not divide a word pronounced as one syllable even though it may be long or have a suffix.

breadth    thought    coughed

In consulting entries in your dictionary, be sure to distinguish between the true hyphen and the usually smaller mark that only separates syllables.

cop-out    cop • per

# SP O  /  SPELLING—ONE WORD

***Spell as one word.***

Check your dictionary as suggested above (**Sp h**) when in doubt as to whether a combination of words is now spelled as one.

### 1. A word to which a prefix or a suffix has been added usually remains a single word.

unnecessary    hypersensitive    easement
supernatural    vengeful    useless

But if the word to which the suffix is added is capitalized, the combination is hyphenated.

un-American     non-Aryan

**2. Combinations with adverbs (*in, out, over, under,* etc., used first or last) are commonly spelled as one word.**
So are all words beginning with *non.*

intake, within     overrated, popover
output, walkout    upgrade, hookup
onrush, underpaid  downcast, shakedown
offspring, takeoff nonalcoholic

But combinations of three or more words are usually hyphenated.

up-to-date     out-of-doors

**3. Compounded connectives are spelled as single words.**

furthermore    nevertheless
inasmuch       notwithstanding

**4. Compounded indefinite pronouns and adverbs are regularly spelled as single words.**
(But see **Sp t 1,** below.)

everything     somehow
somebody       anywhere

**5. The verb *can* is regularly compounded with *not,* but other verbs aren't except in contractions.**

cannot     do not     don't

Do not by careless penmanship write as two words those you intend as one, nor run together those that should be separated. Some confusion was once caused by a large campus sign that appeared to read "THE TAXI." Properly spaced, it was revealed to be "THETA XI."

# SP T / SPELLING—TWO WORDS

*Spell as two words or more.*

Any words that do not form a single combination or a hyphenated compound should be spelled separately. The modern dictionary lists many phrases as well as single words. If the group you wish to use does not appear, write the words singly. But be sure to give the meaning you intend.

**1. The indefinite phrase *no one* is two words unless contracted to *none.***

Do not use the compounded indefinite pronouns when your meaning calls rather for a simple noun or pronoun modified by an adjective.

*Anyone* may ride free on the bus. (Pronoun meaning *all*)
Does *any one* of you wish to ride with me? (Adjective and pronoun meaning *one only*)
*Everybody* should start when I say the word.
*Every body* has been recovered from the ruins.

**2. An adverb and a preposition should not be confused with a compound preposition.**

Turn your paper *in to* your instructor. (*In* is an adverb modifying *turn*.)
The instructor came *into* the room.
He walked *on to* the next corner. (*On* is an adverb modifying *walked*.)
He stepped *onto* the platform.

**3. An adverb should not be confused with an adjective modified by an adverb.**

Notice the difference in spelling and meaning between

He has *already* gone.
He is *all ready* to go.

*Almost* is one word, but *all right* is always two; the form *alright* has not yet been accepted.

Do not by careless penmanship write as one word those you intend as two.

# SP C / SPELLING—CAPITAL

*Spell with a capital letter.*

Certain kinds of words, and other words in certain positions, should be capitalized—spelled with initial capitals.

**1. Capitalize the beginning word of each sentence, even of a sentence quoted within another.**

The mechanic answered, ''That will be a long job.''

But do not capitalize the clause indicating a quotation unless the sentence begins with it.

''That,'' the mechanic answered, ''will be a long job.''
''That will be a long job,'' the mechanic answered.

Do not capitalize a sentence inserted in another within dashes, parentheses, or brackets.

My brother—he's a great hand at sports—has gone out for football.
We think (we wouldn't want this repeated) that he will resign.
Campbell writes, ''The later years of Harper's life [he died in 1939] were spent in poverty.''

Do not capitalize a sentence following a colon unless it is

Quoted: The king then replied: ''Show me a wise man and I'll show you an old one.''

Formal: His final advice to his sons may be summed up in these words: Do your duty to your fellowmen and put your trust in God.

The first of several introduced by the same colon:

> Our speech teacher gave us a number of pointers:
> Avoid the use of notes. Enunciate clearly. Use
> easy, natural gestures.

**2. Capitalize the first word in every line of poetry if the poet did.**
Many modern poets do not.

I think that I shall never see
A poem lovely as a tree.

Ladders of luck, let us
climb your yellow rungs.

**3. Always capitalize**
a.  The first person pronoun *I*
b.  The interjection *O* (But not *oh*)
c.  Nouns and pronouns indicating objects of religious veneration: God, He, Almighty, the Lord, the Bible, the Koran
d.  Days of the week: Monday, Tuesday
e.  Months of the year: January, February, but not the seasons: spring, fall, summer, winter
f.  Names of the planets: Mars, Jupiter, Venus, but not the sun, moon, earth
g.  Names of peoples: English, French, Negro
h.  Names of places (cities, countries, mountains, rivers): London, Germany, Everest, the Danube
i.  Sections of the United States: the East, the South, the Midwest, but not directions: go west, southeast
j.  Subjects originating from names of peoples: French, Latin, English, but not other subjects: chemistry, mathematics, history

## 4. Capitalize all proper nouns and any adjectives formed from them.

Proper nouns are those that name particular persons, groups, and places, historical terms, and courses; common nouns are those that name classes of such.

**a.** People:

A man I admire is George Jackson.
The Dean has mentioned me to a professor.
He told me his father had spoken to Mother about us. (After the possessive pronoun, the noun is common; without it, a proper noun, used as a particular name, is customary.)

**b.** Groups:

As an immigrant curious about army life, he enlisted in the United States Army at the age of twenty-seven.
He has been a boy scout for years, having joined the Boy Scouts as soon as he was old enough.
That is company policy, I think, with the Standard Oil Company.

**c.** Places:

We live on a street called Sycamore Street.
The Ohio River is one of the important rivers of the Midwest.
We headed east on Route 6, the route that led to our destination, the East.
This class will meet in Room 112 until a better room is found.
The building we meet in, the Chemistry Building, is almost new.
In 1973 I was a junior in a large high school—Seymour Technical High School.

**d.** Historical terms:

The costliest war in history was World War II.
Our rights as individuals are defined in the Bill of Rights.
One of history's least productive ages was the Dark Ages.

**e.** Courses:

I am taking a course in mathematics called Mathematics 12.

A few words derived from proper names now regularly or frequently appear uncapitalized from long general use.

China—chinaware        India—india ink
Turkish—turkish towels    Chauvin—chauvinist
French—french fries      Pasteur—pasteurize

**5. Capitalize all the words in a proper name, including initials and titles.**

But titles alone are not capitalized, except for very important ones.

Yesterday John H. E. Balfour and Susan Elizabeth Jones were married.
I think Professor Thomas and Judge Henry are on the committee.
The professor and the judge frequently disagree.
He went with his cousin and Uncle William.
You may ride with Cousin Charles and your uncle.
The president of our club lives in a white house.
The President lives in the White House.

**6. Capitalize the first word and all important words in titles (T t).**

The unimportant ones are prepositions, conjunctions, and articles. This rule applies equally to large and small: books, magazines, newspapers, essays, stories, poems, and your own themes. (The beginning article is not usually considered a part of the titles of newspapers and magazines but is of all others.)

*The Lord of the Flies* (book)
the *New Yorker* (magazine)
the *Chicago Tribune* (newspaper)
"The Lady or the Tiger" (story)
"On a Subway Express" (poem)
"Piloting a Helicopter" (theme)

A preposition or a conjunction used as the final word of a title, or one more than five letters long, is usually capitalized, as is *to* when it is the sign of the infinitive.

"A Father To Be Proud Of"
"A Trip Around the World Because of Curiosity"

### 7. Capitalize proper nouns within compounded words after a hyphen, but not in forms written as one word.

pro-German    Afro-American    unchristian
anti-British     Anglo-French     ungodly

(Such trade names as *VistaVision, CinemaScope,* and *Bank-Americard* are exceptions to general practice.)

In titles, the secondary parts of hyphenated words are capitalized if they would be, standing alone, but not otherwise.

"The Tell-Tale Heart"    "A Head-on Collision"
"Twice-Told Tales"     "An Unheard-of Demand"

# SP A / SPELLING—APOSTROPHE

***Spell with an apostrophe.***

The apostrophe in the English possessive leads to a shocking number of errors, for its size. Master its few rules and observe them.

### 1. Spell the possessive of all nouns and indefinite pronouns with an apostrophe.

*Do not* use it in other pronouns, which undergo form changes in the possessive.

Where is my *wife's* car?    My bark is losing *its* bite.
It is *anybody's* guess.    *Whose* raincoat is this?

**a.** The singular possessive of nouns is regularly formed by adding *'s* to the singular.

boy—a boy's coat    mother—my mother's ring

If the singular noun already ends in *s,* an apostrophe alone may be added, but only if the word can be read without an extra syllable.

Burns—Burns' poems (one syllable) or Burns's poems (two syllables)
lass—the lass's curls (two syllables needed)

**b.** The plural possessive of nouns is regularly formed by adding an apostrophe to the plural.

boys—boys' games    ladies—ladies' ready-to-wear

But if the plural does not end in *s,* *'s* must be added.

man—men's suits    children—children's toys

**2. Use the apostrophe in phrases expressing time and distance, even though no actual possession is indicated.**

a month's pay         a stone's throw
two weeks' vacation   a mile's walk

**3. Use the apostrophe to show the omission of one or more letters in contractions or colloquial pronunciations.**

hasn't—has not    You feelin' sickly?
we'd—we would     I said it an' I meant it.

**4. Use the apostrophe to help form the plural of letters, figures, symbols, and words used as words.**

Dot your *i's* and cross your *t's.*
Don't make your *7's* look like *4's.*
He was born in the early *1900's.* (Now often *1900s*)
Notice how many *merely's* you have in the first paragraph.

# SP AB  /  SPELLING—ABBREVIATION

***Use abbreviations rarely, and when you do, use
them correctly.***

Abbreviations are shortened *spellings* of words indicated by terminal periods. Do not confuse them with contractions (*we'll, can't*) and other shortened word forms that are used in speech as well as in writing and do not require the period; these are a diction rather than a spelling problem. The two are easily distinguished by pronunciation: the abbreviation *Prof.* is pronounced "professor," but the shortened form *prof* is pronounced "prof." *Me.* (read "Maine," not "me") and *Aug.* (read "August," not "aug") are abbreviations. But *he'd* (read "heed," not "he would") is a contraction, and *math* (read "math," not "mathematics") is a shortened form. Most groups of initial letters for agencies and the like, so frequently used these days, are shortened forms rather than abbreviations. Some are pronounced as the letters themselves (AFL-CIO, PTA), others as words formed by the letters, called acronyms (NASA, UNICEF), but all are now customarily written without periods (see **P pd**).

Abbreviations should generally be avoided in any but the most informal and hasty types of writing, such as note-taking. A few, however, are accepted or even required.

**1. The abbreviations *Mr.* and *Mrs.* are always used when the words for which they stand appear as titles before names.**

The newer *Ms.* (drawn from *Miss* and *Mrs.,* and pronounced "Miz") is now used as a title for any woman, regardless of marital status, and is punctuated as an abbreviation even though there is no word for which it stands. (*Miss,* please note, is not an abbreviation.)

> Mr. Jones and Mrs. Smith were elected to the school board.
> I addressed the letter to Ms. Leona Jackson.

Dr., as a title, follows the same pattern.

> I saw Dr. Wharton yesterday. He is our family doctor.

Do not abbreviate other titles, such as *major, professor, superintendent,* in ordinary writing, whether they stand before names or alone. But titles after names are regularly abbreviated.

> Robert Lewis, M.D.    Francis Henry Newton, Jr.

The title *saint* is customarily abbreviated in the names of places but not of persons.

> St. Louis     Saint Patrick
> St. Moritz    Saint Agnes

*Fort, port,* and *mountain* are not usually abbreviated.

> Fort Lauderdale    Port Arthur    Mount Everest

**2. Given names may be abbreviated to initials, and a few men's names to shortened spellings, if the individual so signs himself.**

> Robert W. Hamilton    Wm. Hathaway
> W. G. Nelson    Chas. Richter

The name of a firm should be written as the company writes it.

> B. Altman & Co.    The Aluminum Company
> Sears, Roebuck and Co.     of America
> The Jos. Garneau Co., Inc.    Carillon Importers, Ltd.

**3. A few other abbreviations are in common use.**
**a.** Time: a.m., m., p.m. (or in printing, small capitals: A.M., M., P.M. ), B.C., A.D.

We left at 4:30 P.M.
The battle occurred in 439 B.C.

**b.** *Temperature: C., F.*

Water freezes at 32°F, 0°C.

**c.** Academic degrees: B.S., M.A., Ph.D.

He went to Harvard to work on his M.A.

**d.** Latin terms: e.g., i.e., vs., ca., cf., q.v. (Their English equivalents are more frequently used now, except in scholarly writing.)

Later the Franco-Prussian War (q.v.) began.

# SP N / SPELLING—NUMBER

**Express numbers correctly.**

The problem of "spelling" numbers is the choice between expressing them in words or numerals.

**1. Write out numbers under one hundred and express in figures those over.**
This general practice takes into consideration the number of words involved.

twenty-three games    146 students

In recent editorial practice, however, the change is often made after ten.

nine policemen    11 team members

But if a series is involved, violate either rule rather than change in midstream (using *seventy-nine* with *112,* for example, or *five* with *11*), sometimes done but distractingly illogical.
Always use figures if more than one number is involved for statistical comparison:

a football score of 13–6
an attendance range from 82 to 127

And always write out a "round" (approximate) number, regardless of size:

about fifteen members
nearly a hundred and fifty students

## 2. Use figures for specific purposes such as

**a.** The hours, when A.M. or P.M. , follow.

He works a night shift from 11 P.M. to 7:30 A.M.
He doesn't get home until nine o'clock or even ten.

**b.** Dates: both the days of the month, and years

November 11, 1918

**c.** Addresses

Box 101, Route 66, Cullowhee, N.C. 28723

**d.** Book references

Volume IV, chapter 17, page 119
Act II, scene iv, line 82
Genesis 8:13

**e.** Route numbers, room numbers, telephone numbers

Highway 441      Room 113
Interstate I-40    704-293-9668

## 3. Do not, except in the most formal legal documents, express the same number in both words and figures.

Six months after date I promise to pay the sum of fifty dollars ($50).

## 4. Punctuate figures with a comma before every third digit from the right, except for those in dates and addresses.

(The comma is often omitted when only four digits are present.)

In 1974 the new company grossed $12,564,432.
He paid $35,500 for the duplex at 19732 Chalmers Avenue, making a down payment of $5000.

**5. Do not begin a sentence with a figure, since it cannot be capitalized.**

Write out the number or rearrange the sentence.

Two hundred and sixty-three students graduated last year.
Last year 263 students graduated.

# SP P / SPELLING—PAIR

*Be on guard against spelling the wrong word.*
(Exercise 2, pp. 104–105)

Homonyms (pairs or groups of words that are pronounced alike but have different meanings and often spellings) are a frequent cause of error. Be sure that you have not only spelled a word correctly but that it is the correct word for your purpose.

| | |
|---|---|
| their—there | to—too—two |
| break—brake | sight—cite—site |

# SP PRO / SPELLING—PRONOUNCE

*Pronounce the word carefully as a guide to its spelling.*
(Exercises 3–4, pp. 105–107)

Pronunciation, as we have seen, is by no means a sure guide to English spelling, but pronouncing a word carefully will help you to avoid a good many common spelling errors. Be particularly careful with pairs of words which are pronounced and spelled very similarly although they have different meanings and uses.

| | |
|---|---|
| perspective—prospective | allusion—illusion |
| affect—effect | accept—except |

Inexact pronunciation contributes to the misspelling of numerous other words. Train yourself to enunciate precisely, neither adding nor omitting letters or syllables.

| | |
|---|---|
| invariably | mathematics (Four syllables, not three) |
| arctic | athlete (Two syllables, not three) |

## EXERCISES

SP S  /  SPELLING—STANDARD
(Discussion, pp. 80–81)

**1.** The following "demons" are a hundred commonly used, frequently misspelled words. Get someone to read them to you while you write them. If you miss any, add them to the list of your misspellings suggested on page 79, and review them occasionally until you have mastered them.

| | | | |
|---|---|---|---|
| 1. | academic | 28. | desperate |
| 2. | accommodation | 29. | disease |
| 3. | acknowledge | 30. | divide |
| 4. | acquaintance | 31. | eligible |
| 5. | across | 32. | embarrass |
| 6. | adequate | 33. | exaggerate |
| 7. | amateur | 34. | excellent |
| 8. | anxiety | 35. | exercise |
| 9. | apparatus | 36. | exhaust |
| 10. | around | 37. | existence |
| 11. | audience | 38. | fascinate |
| 12. | awkward | 39. | fiery |
| 13. | bachelor | 40. | forty |
| 14. | calendar | 41. | fundamental |
| 15. | campaign | 42. | gauge |
| 16. | cemetery | 43. | grammar |
| 17. | challenge | 44. | grandeur |
| 18. | coliseum | 45. | grievance |
| 19. | column | 46. | guarantee |
| 20. | committee | 47. | huge |
| 21. | competent | 48. | indispensable |
| 22. | competition | 49. | inquiry |
| 23. | complexion | 50. | instructor |
| 24. | conscientious | 51. | intercede |
| 25. | criticize | 52. | interfere |
| 26. | criticism | 53. | irresistible |
| 27. | dealt | 54. | laboratory |

LEARNING TO SPELL

| | | | |
|---|---|---|---|
| 55. | license | 78. | recommend |
| 56. | medicine | 79. | rehearsal |
| 57. | menstruate | 80. | religious |
| 58. | mountain | 81. | reminiscence |
| 59. | muscle | 82. | repetition |
| 60. | musician | 83. | restaurant |
| 61. | mysterious | 84. | rhythm |
| 62. | occasion | 85. | sacrifice |
| 63. | odor | 86. | sandwich |
| 64. | pamphlet | 87. | Saturday |
| 65. | parallel | 88. | schedule |
| 66. | pastime | 89. | separate |
| 67. | permissible | 90. | skeptical |
| 68. | persuade | 91. | specimen |
| 69. | physician | 92. | stretch |
| 70. | physiology | 93. | suburb |
| 71. | pneumonia | 94. | susceptible |
| 72. | prejudice | 95. | threshold |
| 73. | privilege | 96. | Tuesday |
| 74. | probably | 97. | village |
| 75. | pronunciation | 98. | visible |
| 76. | psychology | 99. | Wednesday |
| 77. | questionnaire | 100. | written |

## SP P / SPELLING—PAIR
(Discussion, p. 102)

**2.** Most of the words in the following two lists of troublesome homonyms are familiar to you, but you may find it helpful to be aware, in using any one, of the fact that the other one or two exist and must be avoided.

a. Show your familiarity with these homonyms by using them in a distinguishing context. If any are unfamiliar, look them up.

| | | | |
|---|---|---|---|
| 1. | air, heir | 5. | altar, alter |
| 2. | ascent, assent | 6. | bare, bear |
| 3. | aisle, isle | 7. | berth, birth |
| 4. | allowed, aloud | 8. | bridal, bridle |

|    |                          |     |                        |
|----|--------------------------|-----|------------------------|
| 9. | buy, by, bye             | 35. | knew, new              |
| 10.| canvas, canvass          | 36. | know, no               |
| 11.| capital, capitol         | 37. | lead, led              |
| 12.| cents, sense             | 38. | lessen, lesson         |
| 13.| cite, sight, site        | 39. | mantel, mantle         |
| 14.| coarse, course           | 40. | passed, past           |
| 15.| complement, compliment   | 41. | peace, piece           |
| 16.| core, corps              | 42. | pedal, peddle          |
| 17.| council, counsel         | 43. | plain, plane           |
| 18.| dear, deer               | 44. | principal, principle   |
| 19.| desert, dessert          | 45. | presence, presents     |
| 20.| dual, duel               | 46. | rack, wrack            |
| 21.| dew, do, due             | 47. | rap, wrap              |
| 22.| dyeing, dying            | 48. | right, rite, write     |
| 23.| fair, fare               | 49. | road, rode             |
| 24.| forth, fourth            | 50. | role, roll             |
| 25.| grate, great             | 51. | rung, wrung            |
| 26.| groan, grown             | 52. | sew, sow               |
| 27.| hair, hare               | 53. | shone, shown           |
| 28.| heal, heel               | 54. | staid, stayed          |
| 29.| hear, here               | 55. | steal, steel           |
| 30.| heard, herd              | 56. | straight, strait       |
| 31.| hole, whole              | 57. | threw, through         |
| 32.| holy, wholly             | 58. | troop, troupe          |
| 33.| incidence, incidents     | 59. | waist, waste           |
| 34.| instance, instants       | 60. | weak, week             |

b.  Do not confuse a word with a contraction of two words
    which has a similar sound.

|    |                |    |                |
|----|----------------|----|----------------|
| 1. | its, it's      | 4. | wont, won't    |
| 2. | there, they're | 5. | your, you're   |
| 3. | whose, who's   | 6. | cant, can't    |

**SP PRO  /  SPELLING—PRONOUNCE**
(Discussion, p. 102)

**3.**  You can avoid difficulty with these near-homonyms by
being careful to pronounce them distinctly. Show your familiarity

LEARNING TO SPELL

with them by using each in a distinguishing context. If any are unfamiliar, look them up.

| | | | |
|---|---|---|---|
| 1. | accept, except | 31. | formally, formerly |
| 2. | access, excess | 32. | genius, genus |
| 3. | advice, advise | 33. | hoarse, horse |
| 4. | affect, effect | 34. | human, humane |
| 5. | allusion, illusion | 35. | hurdle, hurtle |
| 6. | altitude, attitude | 36. | ingenious, ingenuous |
| 7. | an, and | 37. | irrelevant, irreverent |
| 8. | angel, angle | 38. | later, latter |
| 9. | bath, bathe | 39. | lightening, lightning |
| 10. | born, borne | 40. | loath, loathe |
| 11. | breath, breathe | 41. | loose, lose |
| 12. | Calvary, cavalry | 42. | marital, martial |
| 13. | choose, chose | 43. | medal, metal |
| 14. | clothes, cloths | 44. | moral, morale |
| 15. | comical, conical | 45. | personal, personnel |
| 16. | conscious, conscience | 46. | perspective, prospective |
| 17. | corps, corpse | 47. | precede, proceed |
| 18. | counsel, consul | 48. | quite, quiet, quit |
| 19. | dairy, diary | 49. | respectfully, respectively |
| 20. | decry, descry | 50. | sense, since |
| 21. | descent, dissent | 51. | shudder, shutter |
| 22. | detract, distract | 52. | statue, stature, statute |
| 23. | device, devise | 53. | than, then |
| 24. | dominant, dominate | 54. | thorough, through |
| 25. | eminent, imminent | 55. | topography, typography |
| 26. | entymology, etymology | 56. | track, tract |
| 27. | ethical, ethnical | 57. | weather, whether |
| 28. | ever, every | 58. | were, where |
| 29. | finally, finely | 59. | which, witch |
| 30. | forebear, forbear | 60. | woman, women |

**4.** Careful pronunciation will help you to avoid common errors in the spelling of a number of troublesome words.

1. drowned (Only one syllable, not *drownded*)
2. manufactur<u>er</u> (Five syllables—*manufacture* is four)

3.  government, recognize, quantity
4.  auxiliary, miniature, convenience, variety
5.  children, hundred, instrument
6.  perform, prescribe
7.  February, library
8.  forty, fourteen
9.  sophomore, temperament
10. maintenance (Compare *maintain*)
11. pronunciation (Compare *pronounce*)
12. disastrous, hindrance, wondrous
13. optimistic, ridiculous
14. eighth, twelfth
15. length, strength (Compare *height*)

# 6 BUILDING THE SENTENCE

The three preceding chapters have had to do, in one way or another, with words. Now we must turn to the business of assembling them into sentences, for the sentence is the basic unit through which we communicate with others. The sentence, with its systematic arrangements of various kinds of words, makes possible the refinements of meaning that put our living language so far beyond the conjectured "grunt" stage of the primitive. Since these arrangements are a major function of grammar, a number of grammatical terms are used here. If you need to refresh your memory of them, you can locate them quickly in the alphabetized Glossary of Grammatical Terms (pp. 293–313), where they are briefly defined, explained, and illustrated.

## S P / SENTENCE—PARTS

(Exercises 1–2, p. 124)

The English language is traditionally divided into eight kinds of words known as the **parts of speech,** which are the building blocks for all the sentences we construct. We could begin our study of the sentence by examining a long construction like this one:

> The big American flag that flew from the pole in front of the post office quickly lost its new look, when winter came, from the continual whipping of the wind.

That sentence looks complicated, doesn't it? But it won't seem so after we have worked our way up to it from the simplest. This is the two-word sentence consisting of a **noun** (or **pronoun** that means the same thing) and a **verb—statement words** that are the most important of the parts of speech. You may think "Listen" is a one-word sentence, but it isn't; it's just a short way of saying "You listen"—and there is our pronoun and verb.

When a man and a woman marry, he becomes a husband to her, she a wife to him. And when we use a noun with a verb to make a statement, the noun becomes the **subject** of the verb, and the verb becomes the **predicate** of the noun. Together, subject and predicate form a basic sentence which for convenience we shall shorten to **S-P:**

> Mary writes.

Fine. But if she sits there writing for very long, we get to wondering *what* she is writing. Hah! a letter! And that becomes the **object** of her effort and of the sentence, which we'll now call **S-P-O:**

> Mary writes a letter.

Don't worry about the *a* that slipped in; like *an* and *the* it's a little word called an **article,** used only as a handle for nouns. But we should notice that some verbs can't be followed by an object (*run, look,* for instance) and so are known as **intransitive** (usually marked *v.i.* in your dictionary).

> Mary laughed.

But most verbs imply some kind of action on the part of their subjects, and we look for an object to receive it. These are called **transitive** (marked *v.t.* in most dictionaries). We can test verbs by temporarily putting "something" after them;

Mary couldn't *laugh* something, so that is just an **S-P** sentence, but she can *write* something—the letter.

Now we have a complete statement—complete grammatically, but our curiosity isn't satisfied. Looking over Mary's shoulder, we see that she started off with "Dearest George." So,

> Mary writes George a letter.

She isn't "writing George," though—she's still writing the letter, but it is *to* George, which makes him an **indirect object,** and we now have a basic structure of **S-P-IO-O.**

Now let's start over again with George, who is a popular boy at school. In another **S-P-O** sentence, we find

> The class elected him.

But to what office?

> They elected him president.

What *president* does is to *complete* the idea of *him,* the object, giving us an **object complement** in a sentence we'll call **S-P-O-OC.**

All of these three kinds of **S-P-O** sentences are in what is called the **active voice:** the subject does the action expressed by the verb to the object (Mary did the writing to the letter, the class did the electing to George). But sometimes, if we don't know the doer or if we wish to emphasize the receiver, we change the sentence to the **passive voice:** the receiver of the action, formerly the object, becomes the subject, and a **helping verb** is added to the predicate to make the change clear:

> George was elected president.

Although George is the subject, he doesn't do any more acting than he did before; if we wish to include the doer, we can put it into a prepositional phrase (see p. 113):

> George was elected president by the class.

BUILDING THE SENTENCE

We looked at the object complement, above; now we must turn briefly to another kind of complement. Earlier we found "Mary laughed" to be a complete sentence in itself, since *laughed* is intransitive. But there are other intransitive verbs that require something to complete their statements. We can't stop with "George *is*" or "He *seems*"; these are **linking verbs** needing something to connect to their subjects.

George is a leader.
He seems popular.

*Leader* is a noun that rounds out the sentence by meaning the same thing as the subject *George;* being part of the predicate, it is called a predicate nominative, or **predicate noun.** *Popular* is an adjective in the predicate and similarly completes the statement by describing the subject *he;* it is therefore called a **predicate adjective.** Together they are known as **subject complements,** and we have **S-P-SC** sentences. Try fitting some of your own words and ideas to these five basic patterns (**S-P, S-P-O, S-P-IO-O, S-P-O-OC,** and **S-P-SC**) to be sure you understand them before we go on to more elaborate construction work.

These basic sentences have been satisfying as far as they went, but we want to know more. Let's put in two parts of speech that change the meaning of the kinds of words we have been using, or "modify" them, as we say grammatically, by adding ideas. These are **adjectives,** which modify nouns, and **adverbs,** which modify verbs, adjectives, and even other adverbs. For instance, what kind of letters does Mary write George, and when?

Mary writes George a *long* letter *daily*. (*Long* is an adjective modifying the noun *letter, daily* an adverb modifying the verb *writes*.)
Mary writes George a *very* long letter *almost* daily. (*Very* is an adverb modifying the adjective *long; almost* is an adverb modifying the adverb *daily*.)

Words are often used in a sentence not singly but in two kinds of groups called **phrases** and **clauses,** which take us to

**112**

another set of building blocks—mortar, rather—the **connecting words.** One set of these is the **prepositions.** A very common type of phrase is called the **prepositional phrase** because it is made up of a noun that is connected to another word in the sentence by a preposition. These may be used as adjectives modifying nouns or as adverbs modifying verbs.

> They elected George president *of the class.* (*Of* is the preposition, *class* is its object, and the whole phrase is used as an adjective telling which president.)
> They elected George president *at the meeting.* (*At* is the preposition, *meeting* is its object, and the whole phrase is used as an adverb telling where about *elected.*)

All of these model sentences have been **simple,** meaning that they have only one subject and one predicate. They are still simple if one of those parts is compound:

> *Mary and George* are very good friends.
> The class *knows and trusts* George.

Notice the *and* in both, called a **coordinating conjunction** because it connects equals (two nouns, two verbs). It can also be used to connect two sentences, which we then call a **compound sentence.** It contains two **independent clauses**—*independent* because they can stand alone, *clauses* because they are now joined together in one sentence, and because (unlike phrases) they contain subjects and predicates.

> Mary wrote George a letter. She wrote her family only a postcard. (Two simple sentences)
> Mary wrote George a letter, *but* she wrote her family only a postcard. (One compound sentence: two independent clauses connected by the coordinating conjunction *but*)

The coordinating conjunctions are few (*and*—addition, *but*—contrast, *or* and *nor*—alternatives). But the **subordinating conjunctions** are many, allowing **complex sentences** that greatly enrich our language. They are called *subordinating* because they connect **dependent** (subordinate) **clauses** to independent clauses, in which they may serve as nouns, adjectives, or adverbs. The **relative pronouns** *who, which,* and *that* may also serve as connectives for noun and adjective clauses. These clauses may express a wide variety of relationships:

> Mary tells George *that she loves him.* (Noun clause, object of *tells,* connected by the subordinating conjunction *that; George* is, as before, the indirect object.)
> Mary, *who loves George,* writes to him daily. (Adjective clause, modifying *Mary,* connected by relative pronoun *who*)
> Mary writes to George *because she loves him.* (Adverb clause of reason, telling why she writes, connected by subordinating conjunction *because*)

And many others. Try using *if* to introduce a condition clause; *although,* a concession clause; *when,* a time clause; *where,* a place clause; *so that,* a purpose clause; *as . . . as,* a comparison clause; *so . . . that,* a result clause.

We should notice that when two independent clauses are modified by one or more dependent clauses, we have a **compound-complex** sentence:

> Mary loves George, and she writes to him often, *although she should study.* (Adverb clause modifying *writes* in second independent clause)

And an independent clause modified by a dependent clause which in turn is modified by another dependent clause is called a **complex-complex** sentence:

> Mary, *who always writes to George* (Adjective clause modifying *Mary*) *when she has time* (Adverb clause modifying *writes*), is still a good student.

Now we are ready to go back to page 110 to that sentence about the American flag. It's still a long one but not forbidding any more, for we now know all about its parts and their relationships. Its independent clause is easily recognized as the basic **S-P-O** pattern: "flag lost look." Add its modifying adjectives and adverb, and we have an intelligible statement:

> The big American flag quickly lost its new look.

But the whole sentence is richer than that; it has two dependent clauses, both of the simple **S-P** type: "that flew," recognizable as an adjective clause by its connecting relative pronoun *that* and by its modifying the noun *flag;* and "when winter came," seen to be an adverb clause by the subordinating conjunction *when* and by its modifying the verb *lost.* And all those other words? Just two simple strings of prepositional phrases, each a part of one of those two clauses:

> First:     *from the pole*—used as adverb modifying verb *flew*
>
>              *in front*—used as adjective modifying noun *pole*
>
>              *of the post office*—used as adjective modifying noun *front*
>
> Second:   *from the continual whipping*—used as adverb modifying verb *lost*
>
>              *of the wind*—used as an adjective modifying noun *whipping*

And there we are at the end of what proved to be a complex sentence, with a place for everything and everything in its place. One is inclined to agree with the linguist who once remarked that "Grammar is one of the greatest of human inventions." Without it, how could we distinguish between such pairs as *corn ground* and *ground corn,* or, having said that "We water the land," be equally understood when we say "We land on the water"? It's a complicated system, but it works!

Before we go on to the next sections, on sentence variety, we should notice what a very well-behaved sentence the one about the American flag is. If we draw a line between *office* and *quickly,* we shall have neatly divided it into two parts: the subject (*flag*) and all its modifiers, known as the **complete subject,** and the predicate (*lost*) and all its modifiers and words used to complete its meaning, known as the **complete predicate.** This is the normal order in English, but it is varied in many ways and for many purposes, as we shall see shortly (**SV o**). For instance, if we want to emphasize the time element, we might put that dependent adverb clause first:

**115**

When winter came, the big American flag that flew from the pole in front of the post office quickly lost its new look from the continual whipping of the wind.

We'll see other possibilities for variety in the next sections: variety of type (**SV t**), of construction (**SV c**), of order (**SV o**), and of length (**SV l**).

But first we should look at three interesting kinds of hybrids —curious words that start out as verbs but wind up being used as several other parts of speech instead. They are called **verbals,** and they won't cause you any trouble in sentence building, now that you know how to handle the parts of speech they will be used as. But you should be able to recognize them for what they are. A curious thing about them is that they are used in the sentence as adjectives, adverbs, or nouns, but their verb ancestry enables them to have objects or complements and to be modified by adverbs!

The **participle,** usually ending in *ing,* is used as an adjective (*living* things). Accompanied by other words it becomes a **participial phrase,** which works as a unit just as the prepositional phrases we have looked at do.

The driver, *quickly turning the wheel,* avoided the dog. (The participle *turning* has an object, *wheel,* and is modified by an adverb, *quickly;* the whole phrase modifies the noun *driver.*)

The **gerund,** like the participle, usually ends in *ing,* but is always used as a noun (human *beings*). Accompanied by other words it becomes a **gerund phrase.**

*Recklessly operating an automobile* can result in arrest. (The gerund *operating* has an object, *automobile,* and is modified by an adverb, *recklessly;* the whole phrase is subject of the predicate *can result.*)

The **infinitive** consists of its "sign," *to,* plus a verb (*to know*). Accompanied by other words (it can even have a subject!), it becomes an **infinitive phrase,** which can be used as adjective, adverb, or noun.

My desire *to go around the world* is growing stronger. (The infinitive *to go* is modified by the prepositional phrase *around the world* used as an adverb; the whole infinitive phrase modifies the noun *desire* as an adjective.)

I went *to draw my pay.* (*Pay* is the object of the infinitive *to draw;* the whole infinitive phrase modifies *went* as an adverb.)

*To hear him* is *to know him to be honest.* (Three gerund phrases here, all used as nouns: *to hear him* is the subject of *is; to know him to be honest* is a subject complement meaning the same as *to hear him.* But within this second phrase is a third, used as the object of the infinitive *to know: him to be honest,* in which *to be* is the infinitive, *him* its subject (the only kind of subject that is in the objective case), and *honest* an adjective used as a subject complement modifying *him.*)

Now we can look at three additional uses of nouns. These aren't much involved in building the sentence; in fact, we usually set them off by commas to indicate their relative independence. One of them is related to a verbal we have just been looking at; it is a phrase consisting of a noun modified by a participle and called a **nominative absolute.** What could have been a sentence is made into an incomplete construction, but it does not "depend" grammatically by occupying a place in the accompanying sentence, as other phrases do. Compare:

The taxi was late. We missed our connection. (Two sentences)
*The taxi being late,* we missed our connection. (Nominative absolute)

Another kind of noun use is that of one noun immediately following another noun, expressing its meaning in different words. The second noun is thus in apposition to the first, and so is called an **appositive.**

George, a *student,* is president of his class.
Mary is very fond of her boy friend *George.*

A still more independent noun is called a **nominative of address,** which does nothing more than call someone's attention to the fact that we are addressing him:

*Mary,* come here a minute.
I'm coming, *George.*

**117**

BUILDING THE SENTENCE

And last—did anybody notice that we've mentioned only seven of the eight parts of speech? That's because the eighth isn't really a part of the construction job either, it's just an independent word called an **interjection.** That's an exclamation that adds more or less emotion to our sentence—mild, like *oh* and *well,* strong like *ouch* and a lot of profanity and

*Whew!* we almost left it out!

# SV T / SENTENCE VARIETY—TYPE

(Exercise 3, p. 125)

All the sentences we use may be divided into four types according to the intention of the user. Generally we want to make statements, as we did in all the sample sentences used in this chapter so far; these are called **declarative sentences** and are normally punctuated with a period (**P pd**).

> The doctor is here.
> He will know what to do.

If, instead of having information to give, we need some, we will ask a question, putting the predicate or a part of it, a helping verb, in front of the subject. This gives us an **interrogative sentence,** which we punctuate with a question mark (**P qs**).

> Is the doctor here?
> Does he know what to do?

Sometimes we want to tell someone to do something, to give an order. Now we have an **imperative sentence.** Here the word order is normal, except that the subject is seldom stated; it is always understood, however, to be *you.* Like the statement, the imperative sentence, or command, will be closed with a period (**P pd**).

> Call the doctor.
> Find out what to do.

Our fourth purpose is to show strong feeling, which we will do in an **exclamatory sentence.** This kind sometimes involves a change in word order, beginning with *how,* perhaps, or *what,* but not necessarily. We emphasize it by punctuating it with an exclamation point (**P e**).

How late the doctor is!
I wish he would come!

Notice that this last example, minus the emotion, would be just a statement. In fact, an interrogative or an exclamatory sentence may be declarative in form, the purpose of questioning or exclaiming being indicated by punctuation only.

**Compare:**    I must go tomorrow. (Declarative)
I must go tomorrow? (Interrogative)
I must go tomorrow! (Exclamatory)

To these choices in types of sentences, we can add other kinds of variety to our own writing, for our sentences must be not only accurate but effective, and variety is one of the best means of achieving effectiveness. We should consciously work to vary the kinds of sentence construction we use, the order of words within our sentences, and our sentence lengths.

# SV C / SENTENCE VARIETY— CONSTRUCTION

*Use a variety of sentence constructions.*
(Exercises 4–5, pp. 125–126)

Now that you are familiar with the various sentence constructions possible in English, use them. A child's style may consist mainly of simple "I see the cat" sentences or of compound sentences made up of several such simple statements strung together with *and's* and *but's.* But mature writers avail themselves of all types of subordinating constructions; these not only add variety but also express more subtle shades of meaning. Examine the following expressions of the same two basic ideas.

| | |
|---|---|
| **Two simple sentences:** | 1. Mr. Smith was a rich man. He went around the world. |
| **One compound sentence:** | 2. Mr. Smith was a rich man; he went around the world. (The semicolon expresses a closer relationship between the two ideas than separate sentences do.) |
| | 3. Mr. Smith was a rich man, and he went around the world. (The coordinating conjunction expresses a still closer relationship.) |
| **One complex sentence:** | 4. Mr. Smith, who was a rich man, went around the world. (The idea of his wealth, put into a dependent adjective clause, is subordinated to that of his travels.) |
| | 5. Mr. Smith, who went around the world, was a rich man. (This is the same construction as sentence 4, with the emphasis reversed to suit a different purpose.) |
| | 6. Mr. Smith went around the world because he was a rich man. (The idea of his wealth, put into a dependent adverb clause, becomes the reason for his travels.) |

SV C / SENTENCE VARIETY—CONSTRUCTION

7. Mr. Smith must be a rich man, for he went around the world. (This is the same construction as sentence 6, but with his travels made evidence of his wealth.)

**One simple sentence:**

8. Mr. Smith being a rich man, he went around the world. (This is the same relationship as sentence 4, but with the idea of wealth being subordinated in a nominative absolute phrase.)

9. Mr. Smith, being a rich man, went around the world. (The idea of wealth is still further subordinated, in a participial phrase.)

10. Mr. Smith, a rich man, went around the world. (The idea of wealth is reduced to an appositive phrase.)

Study the effects and the effectiveness of these ten versions. When you write, avail yourself of all kinds of sentence types to express the relationships you intend as exactly and effectively as you can. In general:

1. Use a series of simple sentences or a compound sentence only when the ideas expressed are on the same level of importance.

2. Use complex, compound-complex, and complex-complex sentences whenever you need dependent clauses to express some ideas at lower levels of importance.

3. Reduce independent or dependent clauses to phrases when it is possible to do so without loss of meaning; a simple sentence modified by such phrases is usually preferable to a compound or a complex one if it says the same thing.

# SV O  /  SENTENCE VARIETY—ORDER

***Vary the order of words within your sentences.***
(Exercises 6–8, pp. 126–127)

The normal order of the English sentence, as we have seen, is that of "The cat ate the rat": subject, predicate, and object or complement, with their respective modifiers, if any. Such a sentence is called **loose** because it can be cut off at any one of a number of points.

> The old man sighed with relief as he watched the boat come into the harbor bearing his only son and a good catch of fish for the next day's market.

This sentence could end (a statement having been made) after *sighed, relief, watched, boat, come, harbor, son, catch,* or *fish.*

A good occasional variation of the loose construction is the **periodic,** in which the main idea is withheld until the end.

> As he watched the boat come into the harbor, bearing his only son and a good catch of fish for the next day's market, it was with relief that the old man sighed.

Such periodic word order has two advantages: being less common, it is more emphatic; and saving the main idea until the end, it creates suspense.

Between these two extremes of word order lie a great many possible variations. As you revise your first draft, look particularly to your sentence beginnings. If you find you have consistently opened with the subject (or the adjectives that directly modify it), try substituting other constructions for variety.

| | |
|---|---|
| Subject: | The *bells* rang softly as evening approached. |
| Adverb: | *Softly* the bells rang as evening approached. |
| Adverb and verb: | *Softly rang* the bells as evening approached. |
| Prepositional phrase: | *In the evening* the bells began to ring softly. |
| Adverb clause: | *As evening approached,* the bells began to ring softly. |
| Participial phrase: | *Being perfectly in tune,* the bells rang softly as evening approached. |
| Infinitive phrase: | *To mark the approach of evening,* the bells began to ring softly. |
| Nominative absolute: | *Evening approaching,* the bells rang softly. |

# SV L / SENTENCE VARIETY— LENGTH

***Vary the length of your sentences.***
(Exercises 9–10, pp. 127–128)

To the question "How long should a sentence be?" there is no definite answer. A writer can express a thought in a single word if it is an imperative verb; or he can use a hundred or more words in one sentence if he has a firm command of sentence structure. The occasion makes a difference. Informal writing calls for shorter sentences, generally, than formal; a letter or a brief report, for shorter ones than a literary essay.

But in general too many short sentences are likely to sound childish and choppy; too many long ones, pedantic and heavy. A common average in adult prose is about twenty words per sentence, but it is only an average, drawn from individual sentences which may range from one to fifty or more words. (Our flag sentence had thirty.) You may find it revealing to count the numbers of words in each sentence in a page of your own writing and average them; but the average will be less important than the range in sentence lengths and the order in which they occur. A good general rule is to vary the length of your sentences pleasingly, interspersing shorter ones, for emphasis, among longer ones, for fluency.

**EXERCISES**

SP / SENTENCE PARTS
(Discussion, pp. 109–118)

**1.** In the following sentences,
    a. Draw a line between the complete subject and the complete predicate.
    b. Underline the simple subject and the simple predicate.

      1. Troubles come.
      2. My father was engrossed in the sports section.
      3. The real truth of the matter is his dislike of the work.
      4. What kind of information is printed on those cards?
      5. The little old lady with the big brown suitcase is standing up in the aisle.

**2.** In the following sentences,
    a. Rewrite in normal subject-predicate word order.
    b. Then draw a line between the complete subject and the complete predicate.
    c. Underline the simple subject and the simple predicate.

      1. Can you see his signals from here?
      2. Down came the rain.
      3. After a short time the gates were opened.
      4. Bring me the wastebasket.
      5. Every night after the attack the number of troops guarding the palace was doubled.

## SV  T  /  SENTENCE VARIETY—TYPE
(Discussion, pp. 118–119)

**3.** In the following sentences,
    a.   Name the type of sentence used.
    b.   Explain the word order and the punctuation in
        terms of the purpose of the sentence.

    1.   Please go away.
    2.   The clock has stopped.
    3.   The clock has stopped!
    4.   Must you leave so soon?
    5.   What a wonderful day it is!
    6.   The deadline is Monday.
    7.   The deadline is Monday?
    8.   He held his hat in his hand.
    9.   Give me a little time.
  10.   What is the reason for your absence?

## SV  C  /  SENTENCE VARIETY—CONSTRUCTION
(Discussion, pp. 119–122)

**4.** Recast each of the following pairs of simple sentences
into as many types of construction as you can. Name
the types used.

    1.   My brother loves airplanes. He is going to join
        the Air Force.
    2.   Madison is an old town. It is located on the Ohio River.
    3.   Professor Alexander can't be a young man. He was
        born before 1900.
    4.   Her sister went to Vassar. She goes to Wellesley.
    5.   Tom was in an automobile accident. He walks
        with a limp.

**5.** Rewrite the following paragraphs from a student theme,
retaining the essential facts  expressed but recasting them

into sentences with a greater variety of length, order, and type, reducing predications wherever feasible.

> I would like to tell you about my home town. My home town was named Lafayette for the famous French general. It has a population of about eighty thousand people. The Wabash River runs through it. Many industries are located in and near it. It is a busy city. It has the friendliness of a small village.
>
> Many parents may wonder what Lafayette can offer them. We have a very fine school system. The finest city park in the Midwest is located here. It has a zoo, a swimming pool, a lake, and many other fine recreational facilities. Our greatest love is sports. Basketball has an enormous following. We would rather see a basketball game than eat. There is also a softball league here. Married couples with children could not ask for a better sports program. Their children might some day become great athletes.
>
> I would like to tell you how I have benefited from living in Lafayette. I had the opportunity of attending Jefferson High School. Here I had the opportunity of preparing for college. Our school system was adapted to the college system as much as possible. We had to take six college courses in order to graduate. We had psychology, English, and many other fine college-level courses. I have always been glad that I was brought up in Lafayette.

## SV O / SENTENCE VARIETY—ORDER
(Discussion, pp. 122–123)

**6.** Using your revision of the theme in Exercise 5, check your sentences for order.

   a.   How many begin with the subject or its direct modifiers?

   b.   What kinds of beginning constructions are used in

the others? How many kinds? (Any one construction used habitually can become monotonous.)

**7.** Rewrite the following loose sentences, making them periodic.

1. The car plunged over the hill.
2. The answer lay in the bigger yield of corn per acre.
3. The flood waters washed down through the parched canyons.
4. The boy's cry rang high up among the mountain peaks.
5. The children stole down the stairs early on Christmas morning to see what Santa Claus had brought them.

**8.** Recast the following subject-predicate sentences, beginning each with as many different kinds of construction as you can. Name the kinds used.

1. My father often took me to the circus when I was a child.
2. I lay down wearily on the bed when I got back from classes.
3. The escaping convict ran around the corner at full speed.
4. I left my home regretfully in an effort to get a job.
5. The patient showed improvement quickly after he reached the hospital.

**SV L / SENTENCE VARIETY—LENGTH**
(Discussion, pp. 123–124)

**9.** Using one of the themes that you have already written,

a. Count the words in each sentence.
b. Note the shortest; the longest.
c. Find the average. How does it compare with the general average?
d. How many of your sentences are shorter than your average? How many are longer?

**10.** Using a page from a magazine article, repeat the process in Exercise 9; then compare the two sets of results. Does the comparison suggest any desirable changes in your own style?

# 7 CORRECTING THE SENTENCE

A good writer must have a *feeling* for a good sentence—a sense best developed, like many other writing skills, through good reading. In the hands of an inexperienced writer, a sentence may stray from the path of effective expression in many directions. Most serious of these errors are the incomplete sentence, the fused sentence, faulty coordination, and faulty subordination; these are violations of the basic intention of the sentence —of sentence sense.

## S I / SENTENCE—INCOMPLETE

**Avoid the incomplete sentence.**
(Exercise, pp. 174–175)

An incomplete sentence is a group of words that looks like a sentence but isn't. It begins with a capital letter and ends with a period, but its construction fails to satisfy the reader's expectation of a meaningful statement. Experienced writers sometimes use, with good effect especially in descriptive writing, sentence fragments that are grammatically incomplete ("Damascus—city of enchantment!"). But as an amateur you will do well to keep to complete sentences, for your fragments are likely to be careless and confusing rather than intentional and effective. The unintentionally incomplete sentence is a serious breach of sentence sense.

Completeness is not a matter of length but of construction. "He went" is a satisfying statement, having the required subject and predicate; but add a word, writing "After he went," and you leave the reader waiting, with a question in his mind, for you to finish what you have only started to say.

The incomplete sentence is usually the result of carelessly cutting a dependent construction off from the main predication. Combine the two by changing the punctuation, or expand the dependent construction into an independent one.

Incomplete: Stamp-collecting takes a good deal of his time. Having been his favorite hobby since childhood. (The second part is a participial phrase, not a sentence.)

Complete: Stamp-collecting takes a good deal of his time, having been his favorite hobby since childhood. (The phrase is now properly attached to the main predication, modifying— and therefore depending upon—*stamp-collecting.*)

Complete: Stamp-collecting takes a good deal of his time; it has been his favorite hobby since childhood. (The phrase has been expanded into an independent predication in its own right.)

Incomplete: I fished all afternoon. My little brother rowing the boat. (The second part is a nominative absolute, not a sentence.)

Complete: I fished all afternoon, my little brother rowing the boat.

Complete: I fished all afternoon. My little brother rowed the boat.

Incomplete: Because he lacked money for his tuition. He hoped to get a scholarship. (The first part is a dependent adverb clause, not a complete sentence.)

**Complete:** Because he lacked money for his tuition, he hoped to get a scholarship. (Adverb clause modifying *hoped*)

**Incomplete:** I like all my courses this semester. Particularly the one in mathematics. (The second part is an appositive phrase expanding *courses,* not a sentence.)

**Complete:** I like all my courses this semester, particularly the one in mathematics.

Since the semicolon (**P s**) is close to the period in force (too bad it wasn't named a "semiperiod"!), it is equally inappropriate when used to separate dependent constructions from independent predications.

**Separated:** She drove the car East; her husband having preceded her by plane.

**Joined:** She drove the car East, her husband having preceded her by plane.

**Separated:** When all the cleaning-up was finally completed; we started for home.

**Joined:** When all the cleaning-up was finally completed, we started for home.

# S F / SENTENCE—FUSED

***Avoid fusing two or more sentences through inadequate punctuation.***
(Exercise, p. 175)

The fused sentence is the stringing together, with no punctuation or only a comma between them, of two or more complete thoughts not connected by a coordinating conjunction. It is the opposite of the incomplete sentence, in which an incomplete construction is erroneously separated from the main predication by a period or a semicolon; but it springs from the same failure to understand basic sentence structure and shows an equally serious lack of sentence sense. Correct it by placing a semicolon or a period between the clauses or by adding a coordinating conjunction (**P s**).

| | |
|---|---|
| **Fused:** | I listened to the football game all afternoon my wife went to the movies. |
| **Still Fused:** | I listened to the football game all afternoon, my wife went to the movies. |
| **Semicolon:** | I listened to the football game all afternoon; my wife went to the movies. |
| **Period:** | I listened to the football game all afternoon. My wife went to the movies. |
| **Comma and conjunction:** | I listened to the football game all afternoon, but my wife went to the movies. |

Do not mistake an adverbial conjunction for a coordinating conjunction.

| | |
|---|---|
| **Fused:** | I played some tennis afterward I studied. |
| **Fused:** | I played some tennis, afterward I studied. |
| **Semicolon:** | I played some tennis; afterward I studied. |
| **Comma and conjunction:** | I played some tennis, and afterward I studied. |

# S C / SENTENCE—COORDINATION FAULTS

***Do not overcoordinate, or coordinate unequal ideas.***
(Exercise, pp. 175–176)

Coordinate constructions are correctly used to join ideas of equal importance; they become a fault when they are overused or when unequal ideas are expressed as if they were equal.

## 1. Avoid overcoordination by subordinating less important ideas.

A child may express every thought in a separate sentence (**SV c**).

> We bought a car. We drove to Yellowstone. Our car was stolen. We took a plane home.

This style is only slightly improved by connecting these ideas with coordinating conjunctions.

> We bought a car, and we drove to Yellowstone, but our car was stolen, and we had to take a plane home.

The mature writer distinguishes between the important and the less important ideas, and learns to use a variety of subordinate constructions to show differing levels.

> Having bought a car, we drove to Yellowstone. (The less important idea is put into a participial phrase dependent on the main clause.)
> Because our car was stolen, we had to take a plane home. (A new sentence is made of the second pair of ideas, and the first clause of this is shown to be what it is—the cause of the second, therefore a subordinate—adverb—clause.)

## 2. Do not coordinate ideas which are not logically of the same level of importance.

The student who concluded a letter home with "I hope you are all well, and please send me twenty dollars" needed to use separate sentences—or even separate paragraphs—for his two unrelated ideas.

> Faulty:    We studied about DDT, and it is a very dangerous insecticide. (Our study of it is hardly on a level with its danger.)
> Improved:  We studied about DDT, which is a very dangerous insecticide. (Its danger is now shown to

> be subordinate to what, for this writer, is the more important—his study of it.)

**Compare:** We studied about DDT, and we experimented with it in the laboratory. (Proper use of co-ordination for two ideas of the same level)

## 3. Do not put ideas which are not logically similar into a coordinate series of words, phrases, or clauses.

**Illogical:** On Main Street you will see a gas station, a tavern, a hardware store, and a grocer. (Three are places of business; one, a kind of business-man.)

**Logical:** On Main Street you will see a gas station, a tavern, a hardware store, and a grocery. (Four places of business)

**Illogical:** I'm going to try and find a loan. (Not two actions, trying and finding)

**Logical:** I'm going to try to find a loan. (You are going to try "something"—the infinitive *to find* is used as a noun, the object of the infinitive *to try*.)

**Doubtful:** In the next five years she produced two novels and three daughters. (Literary output and biological offspring are hardly coordinate—avoid, except for a deliberately humorous effect.)

**Better:** In the next five years, during which her three daughters were born, she wrote two novels. (The daughters are subordinated.)

**Or:** In the next five years, during which she wrote two novels, her three daughters were born. (The novel-writing is subordinated.)

Which of these last two versions to use depends on the writer's purpose; the idea more important to it must be put into the main clause.

# S S / SENTENCE—SUBORDINATION FAULTS

***Do not oversubordinate, or subordinate incorrectly.***
(Exercise, p. 176)

Most inexperienced writers can improve their styles, as shown above, by subordinating more frequently, but even a good device can be badly used.

**1. Avoid a long chain of dependent clauses, each subordinate to the preceding—the weak "house that Jack built" style.**

Awkward:    We went to a movie that was playing in the theater that is located on Oak Street, which is on the other side of town.

Better:    We went to a movie in the Oak Street theater on the other side of town.

**2. Avoid "upside-down" subordination, in which the more important idea is placed in the dependent clause, the less important in the dependent.**

Upside down:    I left the hospital just as my father died. (Leaving a hospital is a common thing; the fact to be emphasized is your father's death.)

Right side up:    Just as I left the hospital, my father died.

Or:    My father died just as I left the hospital. (Same construction with clauses reversed for emphasis)

**3. The same clause cannot be both coordinated with and subordinated to another.**

Bad:    In 1973 he suffered the loss of all his investments, and which created a crisis in his life. (*And* coordinates; *which* subordinates.)

**Better:**   In 1973 he suffered the loss of all his investments, and it created a crisis in his life. (Coordinate)

**Best:**   In 1973 he suffered the loss of all his investments, which created a crisis in his life. (Subordinate)

**4. Avoid the use of the conjunction *so* in formal writing; it has been weakened by colloquial overuse.**

Use a stronger adverbial conjunction indicating result or, better, recast the sentence, subordinating the preceding clause into one of reason.

**Weak:**   I needed money for college, so I decided to get a job.

**Better**   I needed money for college; therefore I decided to get a job.

**Best:**   Because I needed money for college, I decided to get a job.

### COMMON ERRORS IN SENTENCES

In addition to the four major errors in sentence sense discussed above, there are many other common problems in the writing of correct and clear sentences. Fifteen types of frequent errors are illustrated and explained below. If you need help in understanding those that involve grammatical terms, consult the Glossary of Grammatical Terms in the Appendix.

# A V  /  AGREEMENT—VERB

*Make the verb agree with its subject in number and person.*
(Exercise, pp. 176–177)

A verb must agree with its subject (noun or pronoun) in those properties that statement words share—number (singular or plural) and person (first, second, or third). In problems of verb agreement you have first to find the subject, next, to determine its number and person. Then make the verb agree.

CHAPTER 7

### FINDING THE SUBJECT

**1. The verb must agree with its subject regardless of any other nouns or pronouns between them.**

*One* of the reasons for his many mistakes *is* his deafness.
The *coach,* like his boys, *deserves* a holiday.
*I,* a responsible citizen and taxpayer, *am* waiting to ask a
   question.

**2. The verb agrees not with its subject complement but with its subject, which comes first.**

Our greatest *need is* more hospitals.
More *hospitals are* our greatest need.
My *hope* for both teams *is* more runs.

**3. The verb agrees with its subject even if the subject follows it.**
Change the sentence back to normal subject-predicate order to determine the subject.

On the desk *lie* a *pencil,* a *pen,* and a *notebook.* (A pencil, a pen,
   and a notebook lie on the desk.)
There *are* a good many *reasons* for his collapse. (*There* is only
   an expletive, an introductory word, not a noun used as a subject: A good many reasons for his collapse are [= exist]).

**4. If the subject is a relative pronoun, the verb must agree with its antecedent.**
Such a pronoun doesn't show number or person but shares them with the word it stands for.

It is *I who am* afraid of the dark. (I am)
He is a *man who* always *knows* his own mind. (Man knows)
He is one of those *men who* always *know* their own minds. (Men
   know)

(Watch this last construction; it's a frequent source of error. It
means that there are men who know their own minds, and he

**137**

is one of them. Compare it with the preceding sentence in which only he is discussed.)

### DETERMINING THE NUMBER OF THE SUBJECT
A singular noun normally takes a singular verb; a plural noun, a plural verb. (Notice that while an *s* ending on a noun regularly indicates the plural, an *s* ending on a verb indicates the singular, though only in the third person, present tense.)

A rat bite*s.*
Rat*s* bite.

But appearances may be deceiving.

### 5. Some nouns which, ending in *s,* appear plural, are actually singular.
When in doubt, consult your dictionary.

The *news is* good.
*Mathematics was* my most difficult subject.

### 6. A collective noun looks singular but may take a singular or a plural verb.
It is singular when the group is stressed, plural when its individual members are considered.

The senior *class has* voted Jim its most popular member.
The senior *class* of '74 *have* already become widely scattered.

### 7. The indefinite pronouns take singular verbs even when they express a plural idea.

*Everybody is* going to the picnic; *each* of us *is* taking a lunch.
*Nobody is* willing to stay home, but *somebody has* to.
*Everything* that *either* of them *wants is* all right with me.

*None* takes a singular verb if it clearly means *no one* or is followed by a singular noun.

None *is* needed, thank you.
None of the food *was* spoiled.

But it is now usually followed by a plural verb if it means no persons or things.

None of the apples *have* rotted.
None *are* more concerned than we who voted for him.

### 8. Certain idiomatic expressions with plural meanings take singular verbs.

*Many a child has* been punished for less.
*More than one student has* learned to study after he reached college.

### 9. A plural noun takes a singular verb if it means one thing.

Ten *books are* on the table. (Ten things)
Ten *dollars is* a big price for that sweater. (One sum)
Ten *miles is* a long way to walk. (One distance)
*Three-quarters* of a pie *is* all I have left. (One fraction)
*The Arabian Nights is* excellent reading. (One book)

### 10. A compound subject with parts connected by *and* is usually plural.
But it is singular if it means only one thing.

The *secretary and the treasurer have* made their reports. (Two people)
The *secretary and treasurer has* made his report. (One person)
*Ham and eggs is* a good breakfast dish. (One combination of food)

### 11. A compound subject with parts connected by *or* or *nor* may be singular or plural.
It is singular (since only one is meant) if its parts are singular, plural if they are plural.

CORRECTING THE SENTENCE

*Tom, Dick, or Harry is* to report to the office. (One boy)
*Neither boys nor girls are* to use the gym this period. (Both plural)

If one part of the subject is singular, another plural, the verb agrees (for the sake of sound) with the one closer to it.

*My two brothers or my sister is* to have this bedroom.
*My sister or my two brothers are* to have this bedroom.

**12. The number of a verb may be obscured by a contraction.**
Expand it, to see what is needed.

Grammatical:    I don't care to go. (I do not.)
Ungrammatical:   He don't care to go. (He do not? He *doesn't.*)

# A P  /  AGREEMENT—PRONOUN

**Make the pronoun agree with its antecedent in number, person, and gender.**
(Exercise, pp. 177–178)

A pronoun must agree with its antecedent in the grammatical properties they share—number, person, and gender. Of these, number gives the most trouble.

**1. A pronoun must agree with its antecedent in number.**
Finding the antecedent is simple enough: it is whatever word in the same or the preceding sentence the pronoun stands for.

The *company* has adopted a new policy. Hereafter, *its* dividends will be payable semiannually.
As the *students* swarmed onto the court, *they* cheered wildly.

Occasionally the pronoun appears before the word for which it stands. It must still agree.

As *they* swarmed onto the court, the *students cheered wildly.*

The rules for determining the number of the antecedent are the same as for determining the number of the subject (**A v**); a noun that would as a subject require a singular verb will as an antecedent require a singular pronoun. But mistakes in agreement occur much more frequently with pronouns than with verbs, perhaps because a pronoun is likely to be farther from its antecedent than a verb from its subject, so that sound is less useful as a substitute for grammatical know-how.

One group of pronouns deserves special mention in this connection: the indefinites *everyone, everybody, someone, somebody, anyone, anybody, nobody.* Technically these are all singular, and no one would think of using plural verbs with them, as is now done with *none* (see p. 138, rule 7); the ear would flinch at *everybody were* or *anyone are.* But because they evoke a plural concept and the pronoun is far enough away for the ear not to be offended, the use of a plural pronoun has increased until it is accepted colloquially—a not uncommon case of usage triumphing over rules.

| | |
|---|---|
| Standard: | *Everybody* brings *his* lunch to school these days. |
| Colloquial: | Everybody brings *their* lunch to school these days. |
| Standard: | *Nobody* is going to pay me to help *him.* |
| Colloquial: | *Nobody* is going to pay me to help *them.* |

If a choice of verb prevails, as with *none* and the collective nouns, however, the pronoun must agree with the number chosen:

*None* was willing to sacrifice *his* free time. (Pronoun singular, like verb)
*None* of the students *were* willing to sacrifice *their* free time. (Pronoun plural, like verb)
The baseball *team has* decided on *its* mascot. (As a group)
The baseball *team have* disagreed about *their* training rules. (As individuals—note plural verb *and* pronoun.)

Compound singular subjects connected by *and* require a plural pronoun as well as verb; connected by *or,* a singular.

*John and Harry are* busy with *their* books. (Both of them)
Either *Sue* or *Ellen* is practicing *her* piano lesson. (Only one or
the other of them)

## 2. A pronoun must agree with its antecedent in person.

You may write correctly in the first, the second, or the third person, but you should not aimlessly shift from one to another while writing of the same thing.

| | |
|---|---|
| **Confusing:** | *I* like to take a cold shower because *one* feels good when *you* do. |
| **Clear:** | *I* like to take a cold shower because *I* feel good when *I* do. |

The second person, *you,* may be used informally to stand for people in general, but be consistent:

*You* have to work hard to keep up *your* grades.

The third person, *one,* is preferred for more formal generalities:

*One* has to work hard to keep up *one's* grades.

## 3. A pronoun should agree with its antecedent in gender.

Unlike the European languages you may have studied, with their arbitrary assignment of masculine and feminine gender to inanimate as well as animate objects, English has "natural" gender, masculine pronouns being used only for male creatures, feminine for female. True, some neuter objects, such as ships and countries, are often referred to by feminine pronouns, and others, such as the sun, by masculine, especially if there is an element of personification present.

The Royal Viking Line's *Star* was beautiful as *she* steamed into the harbor.
*Switzerland* is noted for *her* mountain scenery.
All summer the *sun* blistered the sidewalks with *his* fierce heat.

But on the whole, gender offered few problems in English until recently, a man being referred to as *he,* a woman as *she,* and a person (sex unspecified) by masculine pronouns used generically (meaning "for the genus," here the whole human race) to refer to either.

> The *boy* resembles *his* mother; the *girl, her* father.
> The *child* should have full inoculations before *he* is two.

This matter of using masculine pronouns generically, however, has come up for reevaluation in these days, when the rising self-consciousness of women is changing *chairman,* for example, to *chairperson.* What is needed is a dual-purpose pronoun, but arbitrary suggestions such as *himmer* and even *him-her* will probably be slow to find a secure place in so headstrong a system as language. Since only singular pronouns indicate gender, one solution can be found in the increasing turn to the plural, "Everybody should do his share" becoming "Everybody should do their share" (see p. 141). We also have recourse to "his or her," long used when a distinction between the sexes was called for:

> *Everybody* performed *his* or *her* household duties in the pioneer family.

But that is too awkward a construction to appeal for regular use. There is the indefinite pronoun *one,* however, which stands for both sexes.

> *One* ought to do *one's* duty by *one's* country as *one* sees it.

But that repetition is so stilted that *one* has customarily been replaced, after its first appearance, by the masculine pronoun used generically.

> *One* ought to do *his* duty by *his* country as *he* sees it.

And that, of course, brings us back to the masculine again. We may find an increasing turn to the plural throughout.

> *People* ought to do *their* duty by *their* country as *they* see it.
> *Children* should have full inoculations before *they* are two.

# C / CASE

***Use the case required by the use of the word in the sentence.***
(Exercise, p. 178)

A pronoun, as we have just noticed, must agree with its antecedent in number, person, and gender; but it *does not agree in case,* for its case is determined by its own position in the sentence.

The *boy* fell off *his* bicycle because I pushed *him.*

*His* and *him* are both singular number, third person, and masculine gender because their antecedent, *boy,* is. But as for case, *his* is possessive because it is used as an adjective specifying whose bicycle, and *him* is objective because it is the direct object of the verb *pushed.* Both are entirely unaffected by the fact that *boy,* being a subject, is nominative.

Nouns and pronouns alike may be in the nominative, the objective, or the possessive case, depending on whether they are used in the sentence as subject words, object words, or modifying words. But the form of nouns changes only in the possessive, where the apostrophe is used. (Errors of this sort are treated as spelling problems, **Sp a**.) Most pronouns, on the other hand, have different forms in the nominative and the objective cases. Pronouns, therefore, are responsible for most case problems, which you can solve only by determining use.

### 1. Determine case by the use of the word in the sentence.

**a.** Use the **nominative case** of a pronoun that is a subject, a subject complement, a nominative absolute, a nominative of address, or an appositive following a nominative word.

**b.** Use the **objective case** of a pronoun that is a direct object, an indirect object, an object complement, an object of a preposition, a subject of an infinitive, or an appositive following an objective word.

**c.** Use the **possessive case** of a noun or pronoun that is used as an adjective showing possession about the noun it modifies, or as an appositive following such an adjective.

## 2. Guard against case errors that may occur in compound nouns.

If the first part doesn't show case, you may misjudge the last.

| | |
|---|---|
| Ungrammatical: | Father scolded Rob and I because we were late. (Scolded *I?* Object of verb) |
| Grammatical: | Father *scolded* Rob and *me* because we were late. |
| Ungrammatical: | Just between you and I, we'll lose both games. (Between *I?* Object of preposition) |
| Grammatical: | Just *between* you and *me,* we'll lose both games. |
| Ungrammatical: | The culprits, my buddy and me, were soon discovered. (*Me* was discovered? In apposition to subject) |
| Grammatical: | The *culprits,* my buddy and *I,* were soon discovered. |

## 3. Don't be confused by the fixed position of a relative pronoun.

Most troublesome of case uses are those involving relative pronouns, for neither the eye nor the ear but only a knowledge of sentence structure can supply the correct form. The reason is this: in normal sentence order the subject comes before the verb and the object after; in the relative clause the relative pronoun, whether subject or object, must always come first, as it must immediately follow its antecedent, which the clause modifies. Fortunately *that, which,* and *what* have the same forms in the nominative and the objective, leaving only *who* and *whom, whoever* and *whomever* as troublesome choices. And the trouble ends as soon as you see how they are used. Diagrams showing the basic sentence structure are helpful here.

Pattern: <u>subject | predicate | object</u>

CORRECTING THE SENTENCE

I met a man *who* once knew my father. (*Who* is subject of predicate *knew* in adjective clause.)

who | knew | father

I met a man *whom* my father once knew. (*Whom* is object of *knew*.)

father | knew | whom

Give the book to *whoever* comes to the door. (Not *whoever* but whole noun clause is object of preposition *to*. *Whoever* is subject of predicate *comes*.)

whoever | comes

Put the shoe on *whomever* it fits. (Again, whole noun clause is object of preposition *on*. *Whomever* is object of predicate *fits*.)

it | fits | whomever

She is a person *who* I believe *will go* far. (*I believe* is an independent insertion.)

who | will go

**4. Be sure to recognize the subject of an elliptical clause, in which the verb is omitted but understood.**
Do not confuse it with the object of a preposition.

He thinks he is wiser than *I*. (Than I *am*)
I'm glad I don't have as hot a temper as *he*. (As he *has*)
We tried to walk like *him*. (Object of preposition)

**5. Put nouns and pronouns preceding gerunds into the possessive case, to be logical.**

Ungrammatical:    *Us* losing the game was a shame. (*Us* an object?)

**146**

| Grammatical: | *Our* losing the game was a shame. (*Our* is a possessive adjective modifying *losing*.) |
| Questionable: | She dislikes her husband swearing. (Dislikes her husband?) |
| Preferable: | She dislikes her *husband's* swearing. (Dislikes the swearing, which belongs to him.) |
| Compare: | We left *him* lying there. (Correct—we actually left *him; lying* is a modifying parti- |

## 6. Use the possessive form for only certain nouns.

These are the ones meaning people, animals, things personified or regarded as animate, and time and distance.

| | |
|---|---|
| the child's wagon | the ship's course |
| the horse's tail | a mile's run |
| the sun's rays | a year's leave |

For other nouns the alternate prepositional construction is generally preferred to indicate possession.

the bark of the tree    the roof of the building

Or nouns not in the possessive may be used as adjectives with much the same effect:

the street corner    the carpet pad

## 7. Informally, the nominative is often used instead of the objective.

The reason is that we have come to expect a nominative before a verb, an objective after.

| Formal: | It is *I*. (Subject complement—nominative) |
| Informal: | It's *me*. (After verb—expected objective) |
| Formal: | *Whom* do you wish to see? (Object of *to see*—objective) |

**147**

| Informal: | *Who* do you want to see? (Before verb—expected nominative) |
|---|---|
| Formal: | I am not interested in *whom* they elect. (Object of *elect*—objective) |
| Informal: | I don't care *who* they elect. (Before verb—expected nominative) |

(Notice the change of tone from formal to informal in other parts of these sentences also.)

# R  /  REFERENCE

**Make your pronoun refer clearly to the antecedent noun or pronoun.**
(Exercise, p. 179)

A very frequent cause of confusion to the reader is the writer's failure to handle his pronouns properly. Remember that by definition a pronoun takes the place of a noun, and be sure that every personal pronoun you use in the third person has a near, clear, and specific antecedent. Note, however, that no antecedent is expressed for the first and second persons— *I, we, you;* the indefinites—*one, somebody,* etc.; the interrogatives—*who, what,* etc.; and the general *it.* (See Chart of Pronouns in Appendix.)

## 1.  An antecedent should be near its pronoun.

As a general rule, see that it is not only in the same paragraph but in the same or the immediately preceding sentence.

*Gerald* hopes to get a job with a large and well-known firm. It is located in Philadelphia, where it specializes in commercial building. All in all, it offers an excellent opportunity for advancement. *He* sent in his application early this spring.

To avoid this long gap between pronoun and antecedent, repeat *Gerald* for *he;* or replace *he* with a synonym such as *the boy;* or better, recast the entire paragraph to bring the two uses closer together.

### 2. Two possible antecedents cause confusion; stick to one.

| | |
|---|---|
| Confusing: | My mother and my sister went to the dentist to get her teeth fixed. (Whose teeth?) |
| Awkward: | My mother and my sister went to the dentist to get my sister's teeth fixed. |
| Clear: | My mother took my sister to the dentist to get her teeth fixed. |
| Confusing: | Bob told Bill that he was late. (Who was late?) |
| Clear: | Bob said, "Bill, you're late." (Or "Bill, I'm late.") |

### 3. An antecedent should be a noun, not an adjective.

| | |
|---|---|
| Confusing: | After a half hour of the mechanic's time, he had our car repaired. |
| Clear: | After a half hour of the mechanic's time, our car was repaired. |
| Clear: | After the mechanic had worked a half hour, he had our car repaired. |

### 4. An antecedent should be in a form to which the pronoun can clearly refer.

| | |
|---|---|
| Vague: | My mother wants me to be a teacher, since it is the profession she herself chose. |
| Clear: | My mother wants me to go into teaching, since it is the profession she herself chose. |
| Vague: | It has been a long time since I have been on skis, which used to be my favorite sport. |
| Clear: | It has been a long time since I have done any skiing, which used to be my favorite sport. |

**149**

**5. If a whole statement is used as an antecedent, be sure your sentence isn't ambiguous.**

Clear: The first punch I threw at my opponent connected, which made me feel great. (*Which* clearly refers to the whole idea.)

Confusing: My new car arrived with a major defect, which greatly annoys me. (What is the antecedent of *which,* the preceding sentence or the word *defect?*)

Clear: My new car's arrival with a major defect greatly annoys me. (You are annoyed by the whole situation.)

Clear: The major defect in my newly arrived car greatly annoys me. (Only the defect does.)

**6. The indefinite pronouns *it* and *they* should not be used unnecessarily.**

Vague: When you enter college, *they* give you a battery of tests. (Who?)

Clear: When you enter college, you are given a battery of tests. (The pronoun is eliminated by using the passive voice; see **V v**.)

Repetitious: In the newspaper *it* says that Mr. Roberts was elected.

Direct: The newspaper says that Mr. Roberts was elected.

The indefinite *it* is idiomatically necessary in many general expressions.

*It* is very sultry today; I hope *it* rains tonight.

*It* is also commonly used as an introductory word—a grammatical subject that delays the phrase or clause logically the subject.

*It* was advisable for us to rent our house. (For us to rent our house was advisable.)
*It* is certain that he is making a mistake. (That he is making a mistake is certain.)

**7. Use a reflexive pronoun only after an antecedent noun or pronoun.**

With them *I* always enjoy *myself*.
The *Governor himself* will deliver the address.
I think *they* do *themselves* an injustice.

There is an increasing tendency to use the reflexive colloquially when it doesn't "reflect" at all, apparently to escape the case decision involved in using a personal pronoun.

My best friend and *myself* have quarreled. (Standard use—I)
My aunt left all her money to my sister, my brother, and *myself*. (Standard use—me)

**VERBS**

Many errors in the work of inexperienced writers are due to carelessness in the handling of the numerous forms of verbs: helping verbs, principal parts, tense, voice, and mode. Actually, English verb forms are comparatively simple, and the errors reduce themselves to a few points which can be easily cleared up with a little understanding of basic principles.

# V H / VERB—HELPING

### Use the correct helping verb.

Helping (auxiliary) verbs offer little trouble except for those with which the future tense is formed—*shall* and *will*. Many distinctions between them are disappearing, perhaps from the frequent informal use of the contraction *I'll* (which could mean either) or of the idioms *I am going to go* or *I am to go* instead of the regular future tense, *I shall go*.

But many careful writers still distinguish between an expression of simple futurity (what will happen in the natural course of events) and one of determination (what it is determined shall take place). In this distinction the verb forms traditionally shift according to person as well as intention—a complicated pattern that perhaps deserves to be increasingly ignored. Here it is, for the curious.

| | | **CHOICE OF HELPING VERB** | | |
| PERSON | SUBJECT | SIMPLE FUTURITY | DETERMI-NATION | **MAIN VERB** |
| --- | --- | --- | --- | --- |
| 1st | I (we) | shall | will | go. |
| 2nd | You | will | shall | go. |
| 3rd | He (she, it, they) | will | shall | go. |

Here are two sentences helpful in remembering these distinctions:

**Simple futurity:**   1st Person          3rd Person
*I shall* drown, and *nobody will* save me. (Accident)

**Determination:**   *I will* drown, and *nobody shall* save me. (Suicide)

While these academic distinctions are still observed by many, there is an increasing tendency to use *will* for all future forms, *shall* for those expressing determination. Certainly Churchill's famous "We shall fight on the beaches, we shall fight on the landing grounds, we shall fight in the fields and in the streets" and MacArthur's "I shall return" were both intended to express determination—and succeeded.

# V P  /  VERB—PRINCIPAL PART

***Use the correct principal part of the verb.***
(Exercise, pp. 179–180)

Among the most conspicuous deviations from standard English grammar are misuses of the principal parts of verbs. There are four of these from which all verb forms are drawn: the present, the present participle, the past, and the past participle (example: *help, helping, helped, helped*). The present pratciple is always the same (*ing* added to the present), leaving only two parts that concern us. Among regular verbs, like *help,* the past and past participle are always formed by adding *ed* to the present. It is the irregular verbs that cause most of the trouble: *see, saw, seen; eat, ate, eaten;* and many others. When in doubt about what the parts of a verb are, consult your dictionary.

### 1. Distinguish between the past and the past participle of an irregular verb.

The past is *never* used with a helping verb, the past participle *always* is.

Nonstandard: I *seen* my duty and I *done* it. (Past participles used for past tense.)
Standard: I *saw* my duty and I *did* it.
I *have seen* my duty and I *have done* it.
Nonstandard: I had *saw* him before he left. (Past tense used for past participle.)
Standard: I had *seen* him before he left.

### 2. Irregular verbs should not be forced into the pattern of regular verbs.

Nonstandard: He *drawed* a picture of a man he *knowed* well.
Standard: He *drew* a picture of a man he *knew* well.

### 3. The endings of regular verbs should not be lazily omitted, in either speech or writing.

Incomplete: Yesterday the teacher *ask* us if we were *suppose* to be in the study hall.
Complete: Yesterday the teacher *asked* us if we were *supposed* to be in the study hall.

**4. The preposition *of* should not be confused in writing with the contraction of the helping verb *have,* pronounced similarly.**

| | |
|---|---|
| Ungrammatical: | You could *of* asked him about it. |
| Grammatical: | You could'*ve* asked him about it. |
| Grammatical: | You could *have* asked him about it. |

# V TI / VERB—TRANSITIVE, INTRANSITIVE

*Change the transitive verb to an intransitive, or vice versa.*
(Exercise, p. 180)

Some verbs may be either transitive or intransitive, depending on whether or not, in a particular sentence, they have an object.

| | |
|---|---|
| Transitive: | He *ran* a race. (Object is *race.*) |
| Intransitive: | He *ran* out of the house. (No object) |

Your dictionary will tell you in what senses such a verb may be used, each way. It will also label the verbs that are always transitive or always intransitive. Most mistakes in this area are made by confusing similar words of three pairs of verbs—*lie, lay; sit, set; rise, raise*—the transitives most often being wrongly used for the intransitives.

| TRANSITIVE<br>(Must have an object) | INTRANSITIVE<br>(Cannot have an object) |
|---|---|
| lay, laying, laid, laid | lie, lying, lay, lain |
| set, setting, set, set | sit, sitting, sat, sat |
| raise, raising, raised, raised | rise, rising, rose, risen |

Notice that (to the sorrow of every student and teacher) the transitive present of the verb *lay* is identical—except in use—with the intransitive past of *lie*. Watch out for them!

| Nonstandard: | I had *laid* there about an hour before I *set* up. |
| Standard: | I had *lain* there about an hour before I *sat* up. (No objects, intransitive) |
| Nonstandard: | We left him *laying* there, and *set* down to rest. |
| Standard: | We left him *lying* there, and *sat* down to rest. (No objects, intransitive) |

| Nonstandard: | He *raised* from his pillow and then *set* on the edge of the bed. |
| Standard: | He *rose* from his pillow and then *sat* on the edge of the bed. (No objects, intransitive) |
| Standard: | He *raised* himself from his pillow and then *set* his feet on the floor. (Objects, transitive) |

# V T / VERB—TENSE

***Use the correct tense.***
(Exercise, pp. 180–181)

The English tense system allows for numerous variations in the expression of time through verbs. Consult the Chart of Verb Forms in the Appendix.

### 1. Use the correct tense to indicate the time you intend.

| Confusing: | I *have seen* him in school yesterday. (*Saw*—in the past, not continuing to the present) |
| Confusing: | I *lived* here ever since my freshman year. (*Have lived*—continuing into the present) |

### 2. Keep to the same tense while writing of the same general period of time.

| Confusing: | We *lived* on the same street. One day he *comes* over and *suggests* going fishing. So we *went* off. Jack *gets* the first bite, but I *catch* the biggest fish just before we *went* home. |

Either the past or the narrative present (used to make happenings seem more immediately real) is appropriate above, but be consistent, since all of the verbs used indicate events within the same general time area.

| | |
|---|---|
| Inconsistent: | The students *cheered* when the principal *announces* a holiday. |
| Consistent: | The students *cheered* when the principal *announced* a holiday. (Past) |
| Consistent: | The students *cheer* when the principal announces a holiday. (Present) |

## 3. Use the proper sequence of tenses to indicate changes in time.

My grandmother *had lived* in this house before she *bore* my
(past perfect)        (past)

father, she *lived* here while Dad *grew* up, and she *has lived*
(past)      (past)      (present perfect)

here ever since he *left* home. She *lives* here today and I expect
(past)      (present)

she *will have lived* here for a half century, by the time of her
(future perfect)

death, for she *insists* that she *will live* here all the rest of her life.
(present)      (future)

| | |
|---|---|
| Not clear: | Last week I *met* a friend whom I *knew* in high school. (*Had known,* before the meeting) |
| Not clear: | He *worked* in the same factory ever since he came to town. (*Has worked,* from then till now) |
| Not clear: | Since my mother's death I *have realized* how much she *had meant* to me. (*Meant.* Past perfect is too far past for indicating time before the present perfect; use past.) |
| Clear: | After my mother's death I *realized* how much she *had meant* to me. (Past perfect, for time before the past) |

### 4. Use the present tense to indicate general truth, even in a sentence where another verb is past.

Newton demonstrated that all bodies *gravitate.* (Always do)
We visited the Rocky Mountains, which *are* higher than the Appalachians. (Always are)
In high school we studied "The Pit and the Pendulum," which *is* a short story by Poe. (Still is)

### 5. The tenses of participles and infinitives are controlled by those of accompanying verbs.

However, since verbals have fewer tenses (see Chart of Verb Forms in Appendix), they cannot always agree directly, but they should agree logically nonetheless.

Clear:  *Being rich,* he *has* everything he *wants.* (Present participle with present verbs)
Clear:  *Being rich,* he *had* everything he *wanted.* (Present participle with past verbs)

If the action or state of being expressed by the verbal was completed before that of the verb, use its perfect form.

Not clear:  *Being* rich before the Depression, he now *finds* poverty difficult. (The state of being expressed in the participle took place before the time of the main verb.)
Clear:  *Having been* rich before the Depression, he now *finds* poverty difficult. (Perfect participle expresses state of being completed before the time of the verb.)
Not clear:  I *wanted to have seen* him in the senior play. (Not to see him before you wanted to)
Clear:  I *wanted to see* him in the senior play. (Same time)
Not clear:  I *had hoped to have finished* my paper before vacation. (Not to do the finishing before you did the hoping)
Clear:  I *had hoped to finish* my paper before vacation.

(Present infinitive even with a past perfect verb, to indicate the same time)

Clear:      I *ought to pay* him. (Now that you feel an obligation)

Clear:      I *ought to have paid* him. (Before the present, which is the time you feel the obligation)

# V V / VERB—VOICE

***Change the voice from passive to active, or from active to passive.***

(Exercise, p. 181)

**1. The passive voice of a verb exists when the receiver of the action is the subject.**

It is very useful:

**a.**      Whenever the doer of the action is unknown.

That fender *was dented* while I was shopping.

**b.**      When the receiver of the action, rather than the doer, needs to be emphasized.

Cars parked here *will be towed* away by the police.

**c.**      In formal report writing, where it is conventional for the writer to keep out of the picture.

The experiment *was performed* and the following results *were obtained.*

But do not use the passive voice pointlessly.

**2. The passive voice should be avoided if the more direct active can be used instead.**

Roundabout:      He *was given* a clock for his birthday by me.

Direct:      I *gave* him a clock for his birthday.

**3. Shifts from active to passive should not occur during the same flow of thought.**

Inconsistent:    I *put* the skillet on the fire, and then the grease *was added.*

Consistent:    I *put* the skillet on the fire, and then I *added* the grease.

# V M / VERB—MOOD

***Use the subjunctive mood as needed.***
(Exercise, pp. 181–182)

The subjunctive mood has so largely disappeared from common English usage that it gives little trouble; but it still occurs occasionally, chiefly in the expression of conditions *contrary to fact.* This rule of thumb will take care of most mood problems: in formal English, use the subjunctive *were* instead of the indicative *was* after the verb *wish* and in *if* clauses unless they express possible fact.

Colloquial:    I wish I *was* going to be with you.

Formal:    I wish I *were* going to be with you. (Contrary to fact)

Colloquial:    If I *was* in his place, I would do differently.

Formal:    If I *were* in his place, I would do differently. (Contrary to fact)

No problem:    If I *was* in poison ivy yesterday, I didn't know it. (Possible fact)

The subjunctive is also used in *that* clauses containing proposals:

Indicative:    He *will be* left alone.
Subjunctive:    He asks only that he *be* left alone.

Indicative:    She *will see* a doctor.
Subjunctive:    I urge that she *see* a doctor.

**159**

Indicative:     The nominations *will be* closed.
Subjunctive:   I move that the nominations *be* closed.

But just as it is being increasingly disregarded, colloquially, the subjunctive is being increasingly evaded by the use of other constructions ("He asks only to be left alone." "I urge her to see a doctor.") The sentence about the nominations, however, is so traditional that we shall probably continue to move that they "be" closed, for a long time.

# DM / DANGLING MODIFIER

***Correct any dangling modifiers.***
(Exercise, p. 182)

A dangling modifier is a phrase used as an adjective but lacking a noun or pronoun to modify. It is usually a verbal (a verb form—see Glossary). It may easily slip into your writing, causing confusion or unintentional humor. Here is a familiar example:

*Walking down the street,* the post office comes into view.

There are four kinds of dangling verbals, all of which may be corrected in either of two ways: (1) by supplying a noun or pronoun that the verbal can logically modify; or (2) by expanding the verbal into an adverb clause which will modify the verb.

## 1. A dangling participle

Dangling:    *Being a small puppy,* I fed him plenty of milk. (*Who* is the puppy?)
Clear:       *Being a small puppy, he* was fed plenty of milk. (*He* is.)
Clear:       *Because he was a small puppy,* I fed him plenty of milk. (Adverb clause modifying verb *fed*)

## 2. A dangling gerund

Dangling: *After buying some groceries,* a meal was cooked. (*Who* bought the groceries?)

Clear: *After buying some groceries, we* cooked a meal. (*We* did.)

Clear: *After we had bought some groceries,* we cooked a meal. (Adverb clause modifying verb *cooked*)

## 3. A dangling infinitive

Dangling: *To drive a car well,* much practice is needed. (*Who* is driving the car?)

Clear: *To drive a car well,* a *person* needs much practice. (A *person* is.)

Clear: *If a person is to drive a car well,* he must practice a good deal. (Adverb clause modifying verb phrase *must practice*)

## 4. A dangling elliptical clause

That is one with vital words omitted so that it has only the value of an adjective phrase. (Note that the introductory word is not a preposition, as in a gerund phrase (#2 above) but a subordinating conjunction.)

Dangling: *When studying at night,* a good lamp should be available. (*Who* is studying?)

Clear: *When studying at night, one* should have a good lamp available. (*One* is.)

Clear: *When one studies at night,* a good lamp should be available. (Adverb clause modifying verb phrase *should be*)

Dangling modifiers most frequently occur at the beginning of a sentence, as in the examples above. But be on the watch for them in any position, making sure that every sentence into which you write a verbal adjective has as its subject a noun or a pronoun which can be or do the verb idea present in the verbal.

| | |
|---|---|
| Dangling: | Breakfast was served after getting up in the morning. |
| Clear: | We were served breakfast after getting up in the morning. |
| Clear: | Breakfast was served after we got up in the morning. |

| | |
|---|---|
| Dangling: | The crankcase was not refilled, causing serious engine damage. |
| Clear: | Not refilling the crankcase caused serious engine damage. |

Even prepositional phrases used as adjectives can dangle, if there is no noun in the sentence that they can logically modify.

| | |
|---|---|
| Dangling: | Like most students, Jack's work was never finished. |
| Clear: | Like most students, Jack never finished his work. |
| Clear: | Like most students' work, Jack's was never finished. |

# WO / WORD ORDER

***Change the word order.***
(Exercise, pp. 182–183)

Even in a grammatically sound sentence, there may be a faulty ordering of parts—a modifier or other sentence element badly placed. This kind of error, like the dangling modifier, may lead to confusion or to unplanned amusement. Changes in word order are sometimes necessary not only for clearness but also for euphony or even politeness.

**1. Place adjective phrases and clauses as closely as possible to the words they modify.**

Otherwise you may produce more unmeant humor than clarity.

Confusing: This table was made by an old carpenter with carved legs.
Clear: This table with carved legs was made by an old carpenter.

Confusing: A man drove past in an automobile that was completely bald.
Clear: A man that was completely bald drove past in an automobile.

**2. Place adverb phrases and clauses where they clearly modify the word intended.**

Adverbs have a wider range of positions than adjectives do, but will bear watching.

Confusing: He was born while the Boer War was in progress in England.
Clear: He was born in England while the Boer War was in progress.

Confusing: Hawkins developed cancer shortly after he married and died.
Clear: Shortly after he married, Hawkins developed cancer and died.

**3. Avoid placing an adverb between two verb forms where it can be read as modifying either.**

Confusing: He wished *fervently* to express himself.
Clear: He fervently wished to express himself. (Fervent wishing)

Clear:       He wished to express himself fervently. (Fervent expressing)

Confusing:  The student who studies *often* is worthy of help.

Clear:       The student who often studies is worthy of help.

Clear:       The student who studies is often worthy of help.

**4. Put such adverbs as *hardly* and *only* directly before the words they modify.**

They frequently creep in too soon to say what they mean. The fact that this error is found even in professional writing doesn't make the results any more logical.

Illogical:   He *hardly spoke* a word all evening. (Did he write, or whisper?)

Logical:    He spoke *hardly a word* all evening.

Illogical:   I *only drank* one cup of coffee this morning. (What else could you have done with it?)

Logical:    I drank *only one* cup of coffee this morning.

Consider the variety of meanings that *only* expresses in the following positions:

*Only* Jack said that he wanted it. (Nobody else said so.)
Jack *only* said that he wanted it. (He didn't mean it.)
Jack said *only* that he wanted it. (He said nothing else.)
Jack said that *only* he wanted it. (Nobody else wanted it.)
Jack said that he *only* wanted it. (He didn't expect to get it.)
Jack said that he wanted *only* it. (He wanted nothing else.)

**5. Guard against the equally common and still more illogical placing of *not*.**

It frequently appears too late to say what it should.

Illogical:   All people are *not* as clever as you are. (You are more clever than everybody else?)

Logical:    *Not* all people are as clever as you are. (You're just more clever than some.)

**Illogical:** He learned to his sorrow that all newspapers are *not* trustworthy. (But some are, surely.)

**Logical:** He learned to his sorrow that *not* all newspapers are trustworthy. (Yes, some are—but some aren't.)

## 6. Your modifiers may cover more ground than you intend.

**Confusing:** We consulted a lawyer and a banker *who had gone to Yale.* (All right, if they both went to Yale.)

**Clear:** We consulted a banker who had gone to Yale and a lawyer.

**Confusing:** For lunch we had fruit, milk, and hot rolls *served in a basket.* (What a mess!)

**Clear:** For lunch we had hot rolls served in a basket, fruit, and milk.

## 7. Two adjective phrases or clauses cannot follow the same noun, unless coordinate.

**Awkward:** She is one person *with red hair who isn't hot-tempered.* (Phrase and clause)

**Better:** She is one red-haired person who isn't hot-tempered. (Clause)

**Coordinate:** She is a girl with red hair and a sunny disposition. (Coordinate phrases)

**Coordinate:** She is a girl who has red hair and who isn't hot-tempered. (Coordinate clauses)

## 8. Use two introductory adverb clauses only if they are coordinate or one is dependent on the other.

**Awkward:** *When you are late, if you want to get an excuse,* go to the principal.

**Better:** When you are late, go to the principal if you want to get an excuse.

**165**

Coordinate: When you have been absent or when you wish to be excused from a class, go to the principal.

Dependent: When you have been absent because you were ill, go to the principal. (Second clause dependent on the first)

### 9. Insertions may need to be moved to avoid interrupting the flow of your sentence.

Awkward: He, *in the twinkling of an eye,* pinned the snake to the ground with a forked stick.

Smooth: In the twinkling of an eye he pinned the snake to the ground with a forked stick.

Awkward: My little brother will, *by the time Christmas comes,* have twenty dollars in the bank.

Smooth: My little brother will have twenty dollars in the bank by the time Christmas comes.

### 10. An infinitive may be split if a better reading results.

The old rule for keeping adverbs out from between *to* and the following verb form has been successfully broken by many excellent writers. Whether or not a given infinitive should be split is a matter of euphony, not grammar. Place the adverb wherever it makes for the smoothest reading.

Split, awkward: He said that he wanted me *to not go.*

Not split, better: He said that he wanted me *not to go.*

Not split, awkward: Before I die, I want *really to live.* (This not only lacks fluency, but is confusing: does *really* modify *want* or *to live?*)

Split, better: Before I die, I want *to really live.*

Helping verbs and main verbs are regularly separated by adverbs, if the effect is logical and euphonious.

I will *not* go. (But: I will go *quickly.*)
He has *already* finished. (But: He has finished *rapidly.*)
We shall *certainly* do it. (But: We shall do it *thoroughly.*)

### 11. A sentence may end with a preposition if a better reading results.

The old restriction is ridiculed in the comment Churchill is reported to have written to a secretary who had made such a correction on his manuscript: ''This is errant pedantry up with which I will not put.'' As with the split infinitive, sound is the best guide. Don't hesitate to end a sentence with a preposition if it would be stiff and pedantic, *in the context,* not to do so.

| | |
|---|---|
| Informal: | That's the novel I was telling you *about.* |
| Formal: | That is the novel about which I was telling you. |
| | |
| Informal: | It depends a lot upon which circles you move *in.* |
| Awkward: | It depends a lot upon in which circles you move. |
| Formal: | It depends greatly upon the circles in which you move. |

### 12. Put yourself last in a series, for politeness.

| | |
|---|---|
| Impolite: | I and Mr. Simpson are going to take tickets at the game. |
| Polite: | Mr. Simpson and I are going to take tickets at the game. |
| | |
| Impolite: | My uncle got tickets for me and my girl friend. |
| Polite: | My uncle got tickets for my girl friend and me. |

## COM / COMPARISON

***Correct error in comparison.***
(Exercise, p. 183)

A comparison fault arises from an attempt to compare two or more things in a sentence. It may take one of several forms.

## 1. Distinguish between the comparative degree and the superlative.

The comparative is used in comparing one thing with another, the superlative in comparing one with two or more.

Imprecise: The doctor succeeded in saving the *strongest* of the twins.

Precise: The doctor succeeded in saving the *stronger* of the twins.

Precise: The doctor succeeded in saving the *strongest* of the triplets.

## 2. A double comparative or superlative, like the double negative, is to be avoided.

Use *-er* or *more, -est* or *most,* but not both (see p. 68).

Double comparative: My pack is *more heavier* than yours.

Single: My pack is *heavier* than yours.

Double superlative: This weather is the *most delightfulest* we have had.

Single: This weather is the *most delightful* we have had.

## 3. Nothing can be compared logically with itself.

Imprecise: Dale is taller than any student in our class. (But he can't be taller than himself.)

Precise: Dale is taller than any *other* student in our class. (He is just taller than the rest.)

Precise: Our instructor is taller than any student in our class. (He is not one of the students and so can be compared with all of them.)

## 4. An elliptical clause may permit a comparison to be interpreted in two ways.

If so, fill in the missing words.

| Ambiguous: | My brother likes music better than his girl. |
| Clear: | My brother likes music better than his girl *does.* |
| Clear: | My brother likes music better than *he* likes his girl. |

Notice that such ambiguity does not occur when the pronoun is used, because the difference in case form makes the meaning clear.

| Clear: | My brother likes music better than she [does]. |
| Clear: | My brother likes music better than [he likes] her. |

### 5. Comparisons should be made only of things that can logically be compared.

| Illogical: | The salary of an experienced man should be greater than a beginner. (A salary must be compared with another salary, not with a person.) |
| Repetitious: | The salary of an experienced man should be greater than the salary of a beginner. |
| Clear: | The salary of an experienced man should be greater than *that of* a beginner. |
| Clear: | An experienced man's salary should be greater than a *beginner's.* |

### 6. A two-level comparison (*as much as* and *more so*) should be completed in the first phrase.

An ellipsis can be left at the end of the sentence.

| Incomplete: | He is as old if not older than his wife. (This needs a second *as;* "He is as old than his wife" isn't idiomatic.) |
| Awkward: | He is as old as, if not older than, his wife. |
| Better: | He is as old as his wife, if not older. (*Than his wife* can be correctly left understood at the end.) |

**169**

CORRECTING THE SENTENCE

# OM / OMISSION

***Words that are needed for clearness should
not be omitted.***
(Exercise, p. 184)

Many words may be correctly omitted from the English sentence. For example, while strict grammatical completeness requires the words placed in brackets below, it is customary to omit them. Such constructions are called elliptical.

[You] Lend me a pencil, please. (Subject of imperative sentence)
We visited a zoo [and] a museum and an aquarium. (All but final conjunction in series)
Jack is taller than I [am tall]. (Predicate phrase in a clause of comparison)

But do not omit any word which is needed for clearness or completeness.

**1. A verb needed twice in a sentence must be repeated unless both uses require the same form and meaning.**

Incomplete: I never have and never will like olives.
Complete: I never have *liked* and never will like olives. (The first verb must be supplied because it is a different form from the second.)
Better: I never have liked olives, and never will. (Ellipsis is correct at end of sentence; see **Com 6** above.)
Complete: I do not and never will like olives. (The first verb can be correctly omitted because it is the same form as the second.)

Incomplete: I was annoyed about his coming, but my parents happy.
Complete: I was annoyed about his coming, but my parents *were* happy. (Different form of the verb *be*)

| Incomplete: | I was an only child and punished infrequently. |
| Complete: | I was an only child and *was* punished infrequently. (*Was* as a main verb cannot be understood later as a helping verb.) |

## 2. One preposition can serve for another only if they are the same.

| Incomplete: | I am familiar and interested in stamp-collecting. |
| Complete: | I am familiar *with* and interested *in* stamp collecting. (The first preposition must be supplied because it is different from the second.) |
| Better: | I am familiar with stamp-collecting and interested in it. |

| Complete: | I have read and heard about a new miracle drug. (The first preposition may be omitted because it is the same as the second.) |

## 3. The same word cannot be omitted from a second phrase if misreading may result.

| Confusing: | He stopped to shave and wash his feet. |
| Clear: | He stopped to shave and to wash his feet. |

| Confusing: | My attention was attracted by the curl of her hair and her complexion. |
| Clear: | My attention was attracted by the curl of her hair and *by* her complexion. |
| Better: | My attention was attracted by her complexion and the curl of her hair. |

## 4. If two things are meant, do not omit the second article.

She has a black and white dress. (One dress, two colors)
She has a black and *a* white dress. (Two dresses, different colors)
I went with my friend and teacher. (One person)
I went with my friend and *my* teacher. (Two persons)

**5. A subordinating conjunction should not be omitted if it will permit even a momentary misreading.**

Confusing:    I doubt his word is reliable. (*Word* is first read as object of *doubt.*)

Clear:        I doubt *that* his word is reliable.

Clear:        She said he would leave tomorrow. (*He,* being a pronoun, shows by its form that it is nominative, so cannot be even momentarily misread as an object.)

# PL / PARALLELISM

*Correct the error in parallel structure.*
(Exercise, pp. 184–185)

Faulty parallelism is a failure to express in gramatically similar constructions two or more ideas that are logically alike.

**1. Always express a coordinate series in grammatically parallel forms.**
A simple listing of its items will help you.

Unparallel:   Last summer I learned tennis, to swim, and riding a horse. (In this series of three, one is a noun, one an infinitive, one a gerund phrase.)

Parallel:      Last summer I learned tennis,
                             swimming, and
(Nouns)             horseback riding.

Parallel:      Last summer I learned to play tennis,
                             to swim, and
(Infinitives)        to ride a horse.

Unparallel:   A man with a large package and armed with a shotgun ran up the street. (Prepositional phrase and participial phrase)

Parallel:     A man with a large package and
                      a shotgun ran up the street.
              (Compound object of preposition)
Parallel:     A man carrying a large package and
                   armed with a shotgun ran up the street.
              (Two participial phrases)

## 2. If your ideas won't fit into a single parallel series, express them in two series.
These will be parallel to each other in their parts.

Unparallel:   He was tall, dark, and wore a long coat. (Adjective, adjective, verb phrase)
Parallel:     He was tall and
                      dark, and
                   wore a long coat.
              (The first *and* connects two adjectives, the second, two verb phrases.)

Unparallel:   My grandfather was a Baptist, a Democrat, and loved to argue. (Noun, noun, verb phrase)
Parallel:     My grandfather was a Baptist and
                              a Democrat, and
                      loved to argue.
              (Compound predicate, the first having a compound subject complement)

## 3. The same grammatical construction should follow each of a pair of correlative conjunctions.

Unparallel:   Not only did he pay his expenses but also started a savings account. (A clause is not parallel with a verb phrase.)
Parallel:     He not only paid his expenses
                   but also started a savings account.
              (Two verb phrases)

CORRECTING THE SENTENCE

| | |
|---|---|
| Unparallel: | I neither wanted to go to the theater nor to the movies. (A verb phrase is not parallel with a prepositional phrase.) |
| Parallel: | I wanted to go neither to the theater <br>                      nor     to the movies. <br> (Two prepositional phrases) |

| | |
|---|---|
| Unparallel: | We found him both cooperative and that he knew the work. (An adjective is not parallel with a noun clause.) |
| Parallel: | We found both that he was cooperative <br>                    and  that he knew the work. <br> (Two noun clauses) |
| Better: | We found him both cooperative <br>                    and  familiar with the work. <br> (Two adjectives) |

## EXERCISES

### S I  /  SENTENCE—INCOMPLETE
(Discussion, pp. 129–131)

Decide which section of the following groups is incomplete, and why. Then change the punctuation so that the incomplete section becomes a part of the complete construction, or change the wording so that you have two complete sentences.

1.   The best hope for peace lies in education. An education that teaches men how to live together.

2.   The steam engine was a beautiful thing at night; sparks climbing high into the sky and the fire box glowing in the darkness.

3.   Our session with the Dean and the President was like a court trial. With the prosecution glaring at the defendants, sure of a conviction.

4.   Signs prohibiting the throwing of trash from automobiles, and heavy fines for those caught doing so. These

**174**

two things would improve the appearance of our roadsides.

5.    When the drug is abruptly withheld, the patient goes through these stages. First, excessive sweating, yawning, and rubbing of the eyes; next, a breaking out in gooseflesh and a dilation of the pupils.

6.    We made our mud pies at the edge of the sidewalk. Really the best place for a thriving bakery.

7.    A British diver finally got down to the wreckage. Measuring the size of the rivets to determine its identity.

8.    For my eighteenth birthday my grandfather gave me his own watch. One that I shall always treasure.

9.    While the motor is warming up; note any excess oil that might mean leaky gaskets or bad rings.

10.    He was often teased by the other boys at school. Because he spoke with a slight lisp.

## S F  /  SENTENCE—FUSED
(Discussion, pp. 131–132)

Correct the following fused sentences by changing or adding punctuation.

1.    In high school I played too much and studied too little, at least I think so now as I look back on those days.

2.    Enjoy yourself it's later than you think.

3.    When I put the paper in the developer, something happened, all right, it turned black.

4.    We had come this far without being noticed, if we could get past the next guard would we be safe?

5.    It had been snowing all day I could barely see the hubcaps of the parked cars.

## S C  /  SENTENCE—COORDINATION FAULTS
(Discussion, pp. 132–134)

Explain any errors in coordination among the following sentences, eliminating them by rewriting as required.

**175**

CORRECTING THE SENTENCE

    1.   I did not like to sweat in smoke and filth, and that fact caused me to come to college.
    2.   The right front tire suddenly blew out, and the car went into the ditch and we were badly frightened, but none of us were hurt.
    3.   Our new home is located at 1216 Maple Avenue, and I like it very much.
    4.   He lives in an old section of town, and there are many apartment houses in his area, and the children have no room to play except in the streets.
    5.   When I speak of jazz I mean modern jazz and not Dixieland jazz.

## S S  /  SENTENCE—SUBORDINATION FAULTS
(Discussion, pp. 135–136)

Explain any errors in subordination among the following sentences, eliminating them by rewriting as required.

    1.   The tables were all taken by the time I arrived, so I sat down on a stool at the counter.
    2.   This is the dog that won the prize that was given at the dog show that was held last week.
    3.   Last year I was taking a chemistry course when the instructor suddenly dropped dead in the laboratory.
    4.   The settlers were an industrious people and who were utterly honest.
    5.   That was the issue that raised the question that you have just asked.

## A V  /  AGREEMENT—VERB
(Discussion, pp. 136–140)

In the following sentences,
a.   Find the subject.
b.   Decide what number and person it is.
c.   Make the predicate agree.

1.  His temperament and his wide experience makes him more patient than most people.

2.  George is one of those boys who never thinks of anything but sports.

3.  Our greatest problem are mosquitoes, which swarm out of the woods in great numbers as soon as evening comes.

4.  Scattered through what I saw during that strenuous week of sightseeing was some very interesting and educational things.

5.  More news of the disasters are coming in hourly.

6.  The team has gone to the locker room to change their clothes.

7.  Bread and milk were our usual Sunday night supper on the farm.

8.  Mr. Jackson or his lawyers has to appear in court tomorrow.

9.  Bill or Bob have to get up early and call the rest of us.

10.  Greg says that he don't care what happens to him.


A   P   /   AGREEMENT—PRONOUN
(Discussion, pp. 140–143)

In the following sentences,
a.  Find the pronouns and their antecedents.
b.  Decide on the number, person, and gender of the antecedents.
c.  Make the pronouns agree.

1.  Bad luck can be very effective in making a person change their mind.

2.  The jury has been working for days to arrive at their decision.

3.  My room has a bed, a desk, a dresser, and a wardrobe in which you can hang your clothes.

4.  When one saw Luke hanging around the post office, they got the impression that he was a loafer.

5.  My family was poor but always ready to help their neighbors.

CORRECTING THE SENTENCE

6.   We watched the *Queen Elizabeth II* as the tugs pulled her away from the dock, ready for its long voyage across the Atlantic.

7.   The crowd was instantly on its feet, yelling at the tops of their voices.

8.   It is necessary to accept each tale as truth, no matter how fantastic they may seem.

9.   One ought to finish one's studying for the next day before he goes to bed.

10.   When we started football practice in August, you got very warm.

## C  /  CASE
(Discussion, pp. 144–148)

In the following sentences,

a.   Correct any errors in case.

b.   Explain your corrections in terms of use.

1.   My parents sacrificed much in order to have we children get good educations.

2.   My mother was opposed to me taking piano lessons while I was in high school.

3.   Seasickness was the first thing that made shipboard life and I disagree.

4.   His music teacher was a motherly person who he dearly loved.

5.   My bunkmate was, unfortunately, a much lighter sleeper than me.

6.   Us boys were the victims of a silly plot hatched by the girls.

7.   He is a minister who works hard and who his parishioners love.

8.   She set out some coffee and sandwiches for whomever was hungry.

9.   That old jalopy is Robert, my brother's, car.

10.   Whom do you think should be appointed, me or him?

R / REFERENCE
(Discussion, pp. 148–151)

Correct any errors in reference in the following sentences, giving the reasons for your changes.

1.  In some states they make you get your eyes tested before you can get a driver's license.
2.  Jack, Bill, and myself are going on a camping trip next summer.
3.  Sam told Harry that he must begin to take his studies more seriously.
4.  When I saw a couple ahead of me ambling along at ten miles an hour in the inside lane, I blew my horn to warn him to pull over to the outside.
5.  I don't believe that people fish solely for the excitement it offers.
6.  He talked about the college's objectives and how it operates.
7.  We escaped from the beehive without being badly stung, but I can still feel the couple I did get.
8.  Because we were so noisy, it interfered with the class in the next room.
9.  My family went off without me so that I had to go alone, which made me furious.
10.  Meg and Susie wrote a letter to her fiancé about the weekend.

V P / VERB—PRINCIPAL PART
(Discussion, pp. 152–154)

Correct any errors in the use of the principal parts of verbs in the following sentences. Consult your dictionary if necessary.

1.  He felled me with such a blow that I thought he had broke my neck.
2.  I don't believe he would of made a good president.

3.    Since hearing his group perform, I have without question became the most rabid rock fan on the campus.

4.    Before the trial, the murderer was taken out of jail by a mob and hung.

5.    I am definitely prejudice against people who eat popcorn in theaters.

### V TI   /   VERB—TRANSITIVE, INTRANSITIVE
(Discussion, pp. 154–155)

Change the verb forms in the following sentences as required, giving your reasons.

1.    The book is laying on the table, right where you laid it.

2.    Yesterday the patient couldn't raise his head, but tomorrow he will be allowed to set up.

3.    I had been laying on my bunk, but I rose when he sat himself down near me.

4.    The sun was rising when we finally laid down to rest.

5.    The curtain raised on the second act, showing our hero setting on a rock.

### V T   /   VERB—TENSE
(Discussion, pp. 155–158)

Make any needed corrections in tense in the following sentences, giving your reasons.

1.    *Mutiny on the Bounty* was the most interesting book that I have ever read.

2.    When I was in college for two years, my older brother graduated.

3.    If I were a freshman again and know what I know now, I should plan my course very differently.

4.    I would have received a scholarship if my use of English during the examination was better.

5.    The radiator burst because ice had more volume than water.

6.    Since seeing the Yankees play, I became a rabid baseball fan.

7.    If I had more time, I would have finished the book.

8.    I intended to have paid this bill when it was due, but I forgot.

9.    Since I have started college, I have failed three courses.

10.    Predicting the weather for any one square mile of ground is a very difficult task because of the many little variations from the prediction that might occur at that one spot.

## V V  /  VERB—VOICE
(Discussion, pp. 158–159)

In the following sentences,
a.    Give the voice of every verb, commenting on its use.
b.    Change voice wherever you find it advisable, giving your reasons.

1.    He dated the letter July 20, but it wasn't postmarked until July 26.

2.    In 1926 Sinclair Lewis was awarded the Pulitzer Prize, but it was refused by him; in 1930 he was awarded the Nobel Prize, which he accepted.

3.    I released the brake, and then the car was put into reverse.

4.    Cars parked here after 5 p.m. will be towed away at the owner's expense.

5.    When I graduated from high school, my father gave me a wristwatch, and I was given a new suit by my mother.

## V M  /  VERB—MOOD
(Discussion, pp. 159–160)

Make any changes in mood required to make the following sentences standard English, giving your reasons.

1.    When the anesthetist put the mask over my face and turned on the ether, I felt as if I was floating through space.

2.  I sometimes wish that I was a child again, with nothing to do but play.

3.  His father has asked that the boy be transferred to the day shift.

4.  If the letter was mailed, it must have been lost.

5.  The veteran in college seldom wishes that he was in the service again.

## DM / DANGLING MODIFIER
(Discussion, pp. 160–162)

Correct any dangling modifiers in the following sentences by giving them subjects they can properly modify or by expanding them into adverbial clauses.

1.  Belching flames and making a roaring sound, I watched the huge rocket leave the ground.

2.  By reading this letter, I hope that you will be convinced.

3.  Morning tea is always served here while still in bed.

4.  In order to be understood, proper articulation and pronunciation are necessary.

5.  I was afraid I would be late, and I was; while still outside the building, the bell rang.

## WO / WORD ORDER
(Discussion, pp. 162–167)

Make any changes in word order that you find advisable in the following sentences, giving your reasons.

1.  I and my brother used to skip school, on spring days, to go fishing.

2.  A song was written about this river that is still popular.

3.  I read so many interesting books this summer that I shall only tell you about one of them.

4.  Steerforth decided to never leave again, now that he and his father were reconciled.

5. The boy I questioned solemnly shook his head.
6. There are many opportunities for people on the staff who are interested in classical music open.
7. I feel with a teacher's license and secretarial training that I shall be secure.
8. Unfortunately, every teen-ager is not able to go to college.
9. The old almanacs used to give cures for common diseases and the weather.
10. Since my mother has been gone, my sister has had to cook herself.

## COM / COMPARISON
(Discussion, pp. 167–169)

Correct any errors in comparison in the following sentences.

1. My experience in playing tournament basketball was very slight compared to the other boys.
2. Playing in a marching band requires more training in teamwork than football.
3. We can now see a game on television as well or better than in the stadium.
4. Faulkner's ideas for bettering the South differ from other individuals.
5. Many of the topics that have been assigned appear to be more for the boys.
6. Of the two possible courses of action still remaining, he can't decide which is the best.
7. The first problem is more harder than any of the others.
8. My twin brother is always arguing with me over which of us is the strongest.
9. Our feeling about television now is comparable to people about radio thirty years ago.
10. Nowadays some boys can cook as well or better than most girls.

CORRECTING THE SENTENCE

### OM / OMISSION
(Discussion, pp. 170–172)

Insert any omitted words in the following sentences, explaining why they are needed.

1. When we arrived at the dance, I was immediately conscious and embarrassed by my lack of formal dress.
2. My home is, has, and always will be, I hope, in Chicago.
3. I have often heard said that experience is the best teacher.
4. To watch a big locomotive come down the track and wave to the engineer was my biggest childhood thrill.
5. I now own both a light and heavy overcoat.
6. Howard has a ride to camp with the owner and director.
7. Nevertheless, I fear his tendency to kleptomania has not been entirely rooted out.
8. The maid having left, Mrs. Thompson had to bake and bathe her baby.
9. All he can talk about is the price of eggs and politics.
10. He came to my room to borrow some black and red ink.

### PL / PARALLELISM
(Discussion, pp. 172–174)

Explain any errors in parallelism in the following sentences and correct them.

1. The deck was strewn with debris, soaking wet, and in a general state of confusion.
2. New uses are constantly being found for television, such as baby-sitting, rocket research, and as a guard in prisons.
3. The automobile of the future should be of higher quality and lower in price.

**184**

4.   When graduation day comes, there will be both tears and laughing among the seniors.

5.   She told me of her past and that she had recently come to the city because of her need for work.

6.   I was told that I could get both a degree in designing and become a teacher.

7.   When we go to the lake on weekends, I have to either sleep in the car or a broken-down bed.

8.   Students often make the mistake of either letting themselves get swallowed up in their activities or in their studies.

9.   In grammar class I was bored, disgusted, and could see no value in studying.

10.   A baseball player must learn how to get along with his coach, to be a member of a team, and good sportsmanship.

# _8

# UNDERSTANDING PUNCTUATION

The faulty use of grammar may lead to adverse judgments from those who hear you speak or who read your writing. But grammar is seldom so misused as to keep a person from being understood, whereas the faulty use of punctuation may lead to serious confusion or even misunderstanding. You have already noticed that the cure for the two most serious violations of sentence sense, the incomplete sentence and the fused sentence (**S i** and **S f**), is just a change in punctuation; other confusing sentences, too, can be clarified without a change in wording through using the proper marks. An example of faulty omission given on p. 171, for instance, is

He stopped to shave and wash his feet.

The source of misreading can be eliminated by completing the second infinitive through the addition of the word *to:*

He stopped to shave and to wash his feet.

But it could also be avoided by the judicious use of a comma:

He stopped to shave, and wash his feet.

UNDERSTANDING PUNCTUATION

The confusing sentence

> For lunch she served coffee and oysters wrapped in bacon.

isn't improved by a change in word order:

> For lunch she served oysters wrapped in bacon and coffee.

But it can be readily made clear through punctuation:

> For lunch she served coffee, and oysters wrapped in bacon.
> For lunch she served oysters wrapped in bacon, and coffee.

The power of punctuation has but to be seen to be believed. Only a couple of marks are needed to move this bit of male chauvinist propaganda over to the arsenal of the women's liberation movement:

> Woman without her man would be a savage.
> Woman—without her, man would be a savage.

A few quotation marks can accomplish a similar about-face:

> Jack Nicklaus says Arnold Palmer is the world's greatest golfer.
> "Jack Nicklaus," says Arnold Palmer, "is the world's greatest golfer."

It took only a single comma added by a mischievous neighbor to turn the nervous householder's posted sign "BEWARE BAD DOG!" into "BEWARE, BAD DOG!"

Punctuation can clarify, it can interpret, and it can emphasize, for it is a system of marks used to help the reader to read a sentence as the writer wrote it. It supplies, in writing, something of what the voice contributes in speaking. Some marks in the system tell the reader that he has reached the end of a thought (period, question mark, exclamation point); some prepare him for something to come (colon, dash); others show pauses or breaks in thought (comma, semicolon, dash); while still others, used in pairs, set off part of a thought as a unit (commas, dashes, parentheses, brackets).

Since these marks constitute a somewhat flexible system capable of aiding in many shades of interpretation, there is no better way for you to become acquainted with it than by attentively reading well-written material, absorbing the ways experienced writers punctuate. In addition, there are certain rules drawn from generally observed practice that you will find useful as guides.

Never put any kind of punctuation mark indicating a pause or a stop (comma, semicolon, colon; period, question mark, exclamation point) at the beginning of a line, no matter how pressed you may be for space at the end of the preceding one. Similarly, never put the first of a pair of quotation marks, parentheses, or brackets at the end of a line. The proper order of punctuation marks used consecutively is discussed under **P p, P b,** and **P q.**

# P C  /  PUNCTUATION—COMMA

**_Use a comma or commas to separate and set off._**
(Exercises 1–2, pp. 219–220)

The comma indicates to your reader a slight pause. It appears more often than any other mark of punctuation, having a wide variety of uses in separating sentence parts or setting them off. One comma is needed to separate two sentence elements or to set off an introductory or a closing one; two, to set off something within a sentence. Be particularly careful to use both where two are needed; it may be a matter of choice as to whether or not any are required, but to unhook an inserted sentence element at one end and not at the other is always wrong.

## SEPARATING WITH COMMAS

### 1. Use a comma to separate two independent clauses connected by a coordinating conjunction.

My chemistry teacher was very easy-going, and we students often took advantage of him.

> We had to sign out in order to leave the building, but we could go to the library without permission.

You may omit the comma if the clauses are short and closely connected in thought.

> He went to New York and his wife later joined him.
> He went to New York, but his wife stayed in Ohio. (Comma retained to strengthen a contrast.)

### 2. Use commas to separate items in a series of coordinate words, phrases, or clauses.

Do not punctuate, however, if there is a conjunction between each two items.

> She bought some apples and some pears and some bananas on her way home.

But it is customary to use a conjunction between the last two items only, a comma taking the place of any conjunctions omitted.

> She bought some apples, some pears and some bananas on her way home.

This is accepted usage. However, because this punctuation tends to make *pears* and *bananas* look more closely related to each other than to *apples,* most writers prefer the extra clarity of another comma before the conjunction.

> She bought some apples, some pears, and some bananas on her way home.

Take your choice, but be consistent. The use of a comma between the last two items is especially advisable when the series is made up of phrases or clauses rather than single words.

> He sprinkles his lawn in the morning, during his lunch hour, and in the evening.
> He wants to get a job, he is trying to get a job, and he is determined that he shall get a job.

Notice that these commas are used within the series only, not before or after, so that a series always requires one less comma than it has items, unless it ends with *etc.,* which is always set off with commas.

All of our furniture, etc., was lost in the fire.
My papers, books, clothes, etc., were stolen from my locker.

(But if the *etc.* is written out, the punctuation will be (1) "All of our furniture and so forth was  . . ." and (2) "My papers, books, clothes, and so forth were.  . . .")

### 3. Use commas to separate coordinate adjectives when they are not connected by conjunctions.
Do not separate adjectives that are not coordinate.

Then began a wearisome, costly, disastrous conflict.
He is a nervous and impatient teacher.
It was a standard American industrial red brick building.

Coordinate adjectives can be distinguished from uncoordinate ones by the facts that usually:

**a.**  They have the same general value.

He is a brilliant, impatient boy. (Both adjectives denote characteristics—coordinate.)
He is a brilliant young man. (The first denotes a characteristic; the other, age—not coordinate.)

**b.**  They can be logically reversed.

It was a bitter, shameful experience. (Or *a shameful, bitter experience*—coordinate)
We were blinded by a bright electric light. (Not *an electric bright light*—not coordinate)

**c.**  A conjunction can be inserted between them.

The nation entered a peaceful, prosperous era. (Or *a peaceful and prosperous era*—coordinate)

The nation entered a prosperous new era. (Not *a prosperous and new era*—not coordinate)

## SETTING OFF WITH COMMAS

### 4. Use commas to set off nonrestrictive elements.

These are words, phrases, or dependent clauses that add information but are not necessary to the basic meaning of the sentence. Restrictive elements, on the other hand, tell "which particular" something, are always necessary to the meaning, and should never be set off. Since proper names and words like *I, my father, the moon,* etc., already tell us which particular one, they are regularly followed by nonrestrictive elements.

| | |
|---|---|
| Clauses: | Bill, who is my best friend, is coming over tonight. ("Bill is coming over tonight" makes complete sense without the adjective clause, which is therefore nonrestrictive.) |
| | The boy who is my best friend is coming over tonight. ("The boy is coming over tonight" is grammatically complete, but it leaves us asking which particular boy; therefore the adjective clause is restrictive.) |
| | Small imported cars, which use relatively little gas, are popular with students. |
| | Cars that use relatively little gas are popular with students. |
| Phrases: | He was born in 1918, just after the close of the First World War. (Since 1918 tells when he was born, the following phrase is just additional information—nonrestrictive.) |
| | He was born just after the close of the First World War. (*He was born* doesn't make much sense alone; the adverb phrase tells at which particular time—restrictive.) |
| | Mr. Roberts, driving the car, was uninjured. |
| | The man driving the car was uninjured. |

**Words:** Wordsworth, the poet, was born in England. (*Wordsworth* tells us who; *poet* is merely additional information—a nonrestrictive appositive.)

The poet Wordsworth was born in England. (*Wordsworth* is necessary to tell which poet —restrictive.)

*Uncle Tom's Cabin,* a novel, deals with the question of slavery.

The novel *Uncle Tom's Cabin* deals with the question of slavery.

Some elements can be interpreted as either restrictive or nonrestrictive. Be sure to punctuate so that your reader will know which of two possible meanings you intend.

The bicycle, which had been lying out on the lawn, was rusty. (You are writing about a rusty bicycle, and add that it had been lying out on the lawn.)

The bicycle which had been lying out on the lawn was rusty. (You imply that there were other bicycles also, and that only the one that had been lying out on the lawn was rusty.)

We finally solved the problem, which had given us a good deal of trouble. (You imply that your reader already knows what problem.)

We finally solved the problem which had given us a good deal of trouble. (The restrictive clause tells which problem you solved.)

*Restrictive* and *nonrestrictive* are terms applying only to sentence elements used as adjectives and adverbs; those used as nouns are always necessary, not only to the meaning but to the structure of the sentence. A noun clause is never separated from its main clause by a comma (unless it is a direct quotation—see rule 9, p. 211) because it will be a subject, an object, or a complement—some essential part of the sentence.

The relative pronouns *who* and *which* may introduce either restrictive or nonrestrictive clauses. *That* is generally preferred to *which* in restrictive clauses, however, and cannot be used in nonrestrictives. Punctuate accordingly, or change the pronoun.

> He is a man *who* can be depended on. (*That* could replace *who* —restrictive.)
> This is America, *which* is a free country. (Not *that*—nonrestrictive.)
> It is a question *that* I cannot answer. (Preferred, but may be *which*—restrictive.)

Do not confuse the relative pronoun *that* with the subordinating conjunction *that,* as in "I wish that the plane would arrive." The latter is solely a connective, having no place within either clause (see pp. 113–114).

### 5. Use commas to set off elements not in their normal positions in the sentence, even if they are restrictive.

**a.** Introductory phrases and clauses.

> After a long night of waiting for an answer, we received a telegram. (We received a telegram after a long night of waiting for an answer.)
> Because my brother had driven the car that day, we ran out of gasoline. (We ran out of gasoline because my brother had driven the car that day.)

Short introductory elements need not be punctuated unless you wish to give them special emphasis.

> *Heretofore* I have paid for my own books.
> *By morning* the storm was over.
> *After he left* we began to have a good time.

But set off even short introductory elements if there is a possibility of misreading.

> Before, I liked him. (Without the comma it reads like a dependent clause, *before* appearing to be a subordinating conjunction instead of an adverb.)
> When the blow struck, the country stood united. (Without the comma *country* reads momentarily as the object of *struck*.)

**b.** Phrases and clauses inserted between closely related parts of a sentence.

They, like everyone else, want a share in the profits. (They want a share in the profits like everyone else.)
He is, I think, the best man for the job. (I think he is the best man for the job.)

**c.** Adjectives that follow the noun they modify.

The Norwegian skier, lean and handsome, took his place for the jump. (The lean and handsome Norwegian skier took his place for the jump.)

## 6. Use commas to set off every item after the first in an address or date.

He was born in Chicago while his father was a student.
He was born in Chicago, Illinois, while his father was a student. ("He was born in Chicago, Illinois while his father was a student," sometimes used, splits the sentence rather illogically in two.)
The meeting was held on May 25 in the Armory.
The meeting was held on May 25, 1975, in the Armory.

## 7. Use a comma to set off any element grammatically independent of the sentence structure.

Yes, we'll be over this evening. (The adverbs *yes* and *no*)
Well, I think I should be going now. (Weak interjections)
We walked down the street with his mother, his father bringing up the rear. (Nominative absolutes)
Boys, hand me the binoculars. (Nominatives of address; in "Boys hand me the binoculars," *boys* is the subject.)

## 8. Use commas to set off sharply contrasting expressions, even if they are independent clauses.
Compare **P s.**

I meant to write tense, not tents.
The longer I stay here, the more I want to leave.

He wanted to go, didn't he?
She didn't yell, she bellowed.

**9. Use a comma or commas to set off in dialogue the words that indicate a quoted remark from the quotation itself.**

Do not otherwise put a comma between a verb and its object.

My father said, "It is for you to decide."
"The reason I came," he went on, "is a secret."
"That is a very good argument," he replied.

In quoting from sources the comma is usually omitted if the quotation is made to read smoothly into the structure of the words indicating it.

It is Thoreau's opinion that "The mass of men lead lives of quiet desperation." (Compare: Thoreau said, "The mass of men lead lives of quiet desperation.")
"Never read any book that is not a year old" is Emerson's advice.

**10. Use a comma wherever it may be needed for emphasis or clarity, whether or not one of the above rules applies.**

Our team may, or may not, be included in the tournament. (Emphasis)
After breakfast she swept, and washed the dishes. (Clarity)
Start out on the right, or leading, foot. (To distinguish an appositive rephrasing of the same idea from two alternative ideas, as in "Start out on the right or left foot")
We went downtown, as our neighborhood drugstore was closed; we had to get the medicine, since the doctor had ordered it. (To distinguish *as* and *since* in cause clauses from those in time clauses, substitute *because* for *as* and *since*. In "because," or cause, clauses, the commas are unnecessary.)
Our team has slowed up seriously since the season began. (Time clause—the comma is superfluous.)
I must leave tomorrow; however, I know they will urge me to stay. (A comma is not usually required after an adverbial conjunction, but *however* without a comma might be read in its

purely adverbial sense: "I must leave tomorrow; however much they may urge me to stay, my duty is clear.")

We spent the night with my brother and his wife, and left at daybreak the next morning. (A comma is not usually required between the parts of a compound verb, but here it helps to distinguish between the values of the two *and's*.)

The comma is now used more sparingly than in the past. Every comma in the following sentence, written by a critic in the early part of this century, can be justified:

Complaints, undoubtedly, are, sometimes, made that his atmosphere is becoming difficult to breathe.

But a modern reader finds the atmosphere of such a sentence rather difficult breathing, and a modern writer would probably eliminate all the commas with no loss of understanding and with some gain in fluency.

Complaints undoubtedly are sometimes made that his atmosphere is becoming difficult to breathe.

## NEEDLESSLY USING COMMAS

### 11. Do not allow a sentence to become cluttered with commas.

Some justifiable commas may well be omitted (unless misreading might result) if several have been used in a short space.

Cluttered: I felt that I must have a car, that spring, and, lacking the money, I appealed to my father.

Improved: I felt that I must have a car that spring and, lacking the money, I appealed to my father.

### 12. Do not allow a comma to make any unnatural division in a sentence.

A subject should not be separated from its predicate, a predicate from its complement, a preposition from its object, nor an adjective from its noun.

Faulty:   The boy with the bright red bicycle, came coast-
ing down the hill.

Faulty:   My father thought, argued, and finally decided,
to let us go.

Faulty:   I think it is only a question of, whether we can
afford it.

Faulty:   The cornered, desperate, gunman finally sur-
rendered.

# P S / PUNCTUATION—SEMICOLON

***Use a semicolon to separate equals.***
(Exercises 3–4, pp. 220–221)

The semicolon stands between the comma (a pause) and
the period (a stop) in force, but is closer to the period. (If its
present use were considered instead of its form, it would
preferably, as we have noted earlier, be called a "semiperiod.")
It is a very useful mark for the discriminating writer, but must
be used with care.

### 1. Use a semicolon between two independent clauses not connected by a coordinating conjunction (S f).

Our mathematics teacher insists on accuracy; he penalizes us
severely for carelessness. (No conjunction)
I entered the university as a junior; therefore I hope to graduate
in two years. (Adverbial conjunction)

Compare the various effects of the following versions of two
ideas.

The Indians put a fish in each hill of corn. Modern farmers use
commercial fertilizers. (Two separate sentences—relationship
indicated only by their proximity and their content.)
The Indians put a fish in each hill of corn; modern farmers use
commercial fertilizers. (Compound sentence indicates closer
relationship between the clauses.)

The Indians put a fish in each hill of corn; however, modern farmers use commercial fertilizers. (Adverbial conjunction *however* is transitional rather than connective, so that the semicolon is still needed.)

The Indians put a fish in each hill of corn, but modern farmers use commercial fertilizers. (Coordinating conjunction *but* expresses still closer relationship, so that weaker punctuation is used.)

Do not be confused by an elliptical second clause—one in which words already expressed in the first are omitted and represented by a comma. Such a sentence still contains two independent clauses in thought, and requires the semicolon.

One comma is required to separate; two, to enclose. (The comma indicates the omitted words *are required*.)

**2. Use a semicolon between two independent clauses, even though they are connected by a coordinating conjunction:**

**a.** If they are already much broken up by commas.

It was a small room, but light, airy, and attractive; and I decided to move in at once.

Since the waiters, being students, were eager to get away, they began removing the plates before all the diners had finished; but their supervisor, annoyed, made them slow down.

**b.** If they are exceptionally long.

My father had indicated that he would stop my allowance if I did not make a "B" average during my first semester in college; but my mother got him to stretch a point when my grades finally came in with an average of "C+."

**c.** If you wish to strengthen the pause, for emphasis.

I thought I knew everything; but I didn't.

**199**

### 3. Use a semicolon between the items of a series if they are already punctuated internally by commas.

The party consisted of Jack, my oldest brother; Harry, our cousin from Wisconsin; Bob, a neighbor boy; and me.

He has had the experience of living in Shiraz, Iran; Kirkuk, Iraq; and Aleppo, Syria.

### 4. Do not use semicolons needlessly.

You can avoid serious misuse of the semicolon if you will remember that *it should appear only between equals*—clauses of the same rank or items in a coordinate series.

## P CO / PUNCTUATION—COLON

***Use a colon to introduce, and, between some numbers, to separate.***
(Exercise 5, pp. 221–222)

Despite its name and appearance, the colon has no relation to the semicolon in function. It is usually a mark of introduction, preparing the reader for something that follows.

### 1. Use a colon before a series of appositives.

We caught three kinds of fish: perch, bass, and pike.

A predicate is often followed by a subject complement: a predicate nominative or a predicate adjective. (Without the colon, this might be misread as a series of three.)

### 2. Use a colon between two independent clauses when the second develops the idea of the first.

In this situation, there is a kind of appositional relationship, as in rule 1 above.

He has one thing left to do: he must find a place to live. (The second clause develops *thing*.)

Compare:   He has one thing left to do; then he is ready to leave. (The second clause is an additional, different idea.)

You have only two choices: you must begin to study, or you must leave school. (The second and third clauses develop *choices*.)

### 3. Use a colon before a formal quotation or a long explanation.

He began with these words: "My fellow countrymen, I entreat you to hear me."
His directions to us were as follows: Go out of town south on Highway 43. When you reach the point where Highway 25 intersects, turn right and go a mile and a half. The house is on the left.

### 4. Use the colon between two numbers signifying different things.

**a.** Between the hour and the minutes when time is expressed in figures.

9:30 A.M.      2:39 P.M.

**b.** Between volume and page in a magazine reference.

*New Republic,* 37:11-12

**c.** Between chapter and verse in a Biblical reference.

Genesis 10:16

### 5. Do not use a colon to separate closely related sentence parts.

A verb or a preposition, for instance, should not be cut off from its object. Use a colon before a series only after a complete sentence unit, when the items are in apposition to a general word already expressed. Compare the following sentences with those under rule 1 above.

**Faulty:** Last summer she visited: France, England, Holland, and Belgium. (Omit the colon, or write "Last summer she visited four countries: France, England, Holland, and Belgium.'')

**Faulty:** My favorite subjects are: physics, chemistry, and mathematics.

**Faulty:** The menu offered a choice of: steak, ham, or chicken.

**Faulty:** He likes active sports such as: swimming, skiing, and mountain-climbing.

# P D / PUNCTUATION—DASH

### *Use a dash or dashes.*
(Exercise 6, p. 222)

A dash gives an impression of abruptness. It may be used singly or in pairs. In some situations dashes are the only possible punctuation; in others they are a forceful substitute for other marks of punctuation: commas, parentheses, colons, or semicolons. In handwriting and printing, the symbol for a dash is one long bar; in typewriting, the dash is composed of two hyphens with no space between them.

## REQUIRED DASHES

### 1. Use a dash to indicate hesitation or a break in thought.

You—you don't really mean it?
I believe that I'll—no, I guess I won't.

### 2. Use a dash after an appositive series that precedes a summarizing sentence.

Fishing, swimming, sunbathing—these activities make up my favorite vacation. (Compare the normal order, which requires the colon: "My favorite vacation is made up of these activities: fishing, swimming, and sunbathing.")
The shouting, the cheering, the groaning—all of these are part of the "spectator's sport."

**3. Use dashes instead of commas for clearness, in setting off an insertion that has internal commas.**

Everything that a man could want—love, fame, and fortune—lay before him.

## OPTIONAL DASHES

**4. Use a dash or dashes to indicate informality or emphasis.**

These are alternatives to more conventional punctuation.

| | |
|---|---|
| **Commas or dashes:** | My sister, who is valedictorian of her class, is going to college. |
| | My sister—who is valedictorian of her class—is going to college. |
| **Parentheses or dashes:** | That woman (she's my wife) will be the death of me yet. |
| | That woman—she's my wife—will be the death of me yet. |
| **Colon or dash:** | He asks just three things of life: wine, women, and song. |
| | He asks just three things of life —wine, women, and song. |
| **Semicolon or dash:** | She paused for a moment; then she turned around. |
| | She paused for a moment—then she turned around. |

**5. Do not use the dash as a substitute for thinking through to a smoother construction.**

We went to the movie—you know the one I mean. It was—well, I hesitate to say this, but—really, it was abominable. The actors— they seemed to be interested in anything—anything but the story, that is.

**203**

**6. Do not overdo the dash for emphasis; it gives your writing a chopped-up appearance and soon loses its force.**

Overused: My brother—he is a senior this year—wants to get married in June—but his fiancée—a senior in another school—thinks they should wait a while—at least until they can furnish an apartment.

Improved: My brother (he is a senior this year) wants to get married in June; but his fiancée, a senior in another school, thinks they should wait a while, at least until they can furnish an apartment.

# P P / PUNCTUATION—PARENTHESES

*Use parentheses to enclose.*
(Exercise 7, pp. 222–223)

Parentheses de-emphasize, as dashes emphasize; they "play down" an inserted element in the manner of a stage aside. Unlike the comma and the dash, which may be used singly or in pairs, they are used only in pairs.

**1. Use parentheses to enclose any inserted word, phrase, or clause that is relatively unimportant, to be read quietly.**

Louis Pasteur (1822–1895) was a French chemist and bacteriologist.
The best value (in the long run) will be found in a more expensive brand.
He did say (though he never really meant it) that he intended to be an actor.
The book (I can't remember the title) was about Mt. Everest.

Compare the effects of these three kinds of punctuation on the same material:

His father (a general in the Air Force) retired at an early age. (Subdued)
His father, a general in the Air Force, retired at an early age. (Customary)
His father—a general in the Air Force—retired at an early age. (Emphatic)

## 2. Place parentheses correctly in relation to other marks of punctuation.

No comma is required after parentheses unless it would be needed by the sentence even if the insertion were omitted.

Faulty:  My father (he never went to college), wants me to get a good education. (Comma wrongly separates subject from predicate.)

Correct:  Although my father is self-educated (he never had a chance to go to college), he wants me to get a degree. (Comma needed after introductory clause even if parenthetical clause is omitted.)

A comma (colon, semicolon) is never used before parentheses; if required after, it always goes outside.

My father is an engineer (he never went to college), and he wants me to be trained for his profession. (Comma between independent clauses regardless of parenthetical clause.)

A period (question mark, exclamation point) goes outside if it terminates the larger sentence, inside if it belongs to the insertion alone.

She is always making excuses for Larry (he is her brother).
She is always making excuses for Larry. (He is her brother.)

## 3. Don't overuse parentheses.

Putting in too many "asides" can have a halting effect on your style.

Overused:  David (he plays football) has never taken part in a losing game (or very few). He is (the coach says) our most valuable player.

**Improved:** David, who plays football, has taken part in very few losing games. The coach says he is our most valuable player.

# P B / PUNCTUATION—BRACKETS

**Use brackets to enclose insertions in quoted material.**
(Exercise 8, p. 223)

Brackets are akin to parentheses, and like them are used only in pairs. But they have a single use: to enclose anything which has been added, by way of explanation, to something quoted from elsewhere. Use them whenever you insert something of your own within a quotation from someone else.

Noyes writes, "The papaya [a kind of tropical fruit] is the finest experience in taste known to mortal man." (The person quoting Noyes has added the explanation *a kind of tropical fruit.* Parentheses instead of brackets would have indicated that Noyes himself included the phrase as an aside.)
A prominent critic has stated that "He [Mark Twain] is America's best-loved nineteenth-century author."

The position of brackets in relation to other marks of punctuation follows the same rules as those for parentheses above.

# P Q / PUNCTUATION—QUOTATION MARKS

**Use quotation marks to enclose quoted material and words used in special senses.**
(Exercises 9–10, pp. 223–224)

Quotation marks indicate that the words they enclose are quoted directly from elsewhere or are being used in an unusual sense. They may be single (') or double ("), double being more common in American practice. They are always used in pairs.

**1. Use quotation marks to enclose any words that you quote from someone else.**

Intellectual honesty requires that you never use another's words without such credit, and that you always quote exactly.

> "To be or not to be" is the beginning of a famous Shakespearian soliloquy.
> We began to argue over Bertrand Russell's statement that "International government, whether pleasant or unpleasant, has become a condition of human survival."

Long quotations (usually those which would occupy more than three lines on your page) should be blocked—that is, clearly indented from the left margin, and single-spaced. Since this arrangement alone indicates their status, quotation marks are unnecessary. (Indent as a paragraph only if you are quoting from the opening of a paragraph.)

> In an article on liberal education, the president of Yale University states:
> The conflict which rages around our schools is not a conflict between public and private institutions. It is a conflict between two different types of learning. Until we understand it as such, we are not likely to solve its many problems—the deepening financial crisis, and the curriculum confusion that fill the headlines.

In quoting more than one line of poetry, arrange it and punctuate it as it appears in the original poem.

> I like the sonnet by Wordsworth which begins: "The world is too much with us." His words are even truer today than when he wrote them.

> I agree with Wordsworth when he says,

> The world is too much with us; late and soon,
> Getting and spending, we lay waste our powers:

> His words are even truer today than when he wrote them.

## 2. Use quotation marks to indicate dialogue.

Each speech is paragraphed separately.

> "I'm going to visit the Thomases in the morning," he said.
> "But if they aren't expecting you," I exclaimed, "you can't just barge in on them like this!"

Notice that two complete sets of quotation marks are necessary in a quotation which, like the second above, is split by the words that indicate it.

## 3. Use quotation marks to open every paragraph of an extended quotation.

This procedure keeps your reader reminded that he is still reading quoted material, not yours. Do not close the quotation marks, however, until the end of the entire quotation.

## 4. Use quotation marks to indicate titles of minor works.

These include short stories, articles, and poems, which are usually contained in larger collections such as books, magazines, and newspapers, the titles of which are preferably italicized (**P i**).

> A department consisting of miscellaneous quotations is now appearing in *Harper's* under the heading "Wraparound."
> I enjoyed reading Brendan Gill's short story "The Sunflower Kid" in his collected volume entitled *Ways of Loving.*
> John Hersey's still famous account of the first atomic bombing, "Hiroshima," first appeared as an entire issue of the *New Yorker.*

Titles of motion pictures, plays, works of art, musical compositions, radio and television programs, etc., are usually enclosed in quotation marks, but sometimes italicized. Where usage is divided, either course is acceptable. But notice that newspaper usage is not a safe guide, as newspapers do not customarily use italic type. Follow rather the editorial practices found in serious magazines and books. And in your own writing, be consistent.

**5. Use quotation marks to indicate words used in an unusual sense or at a level other than their context.**

These may be technical words in general writing or slang words in serious writing.

I am the "baby" in my family. (No longer a real baby, just the youngest)
Sometimes a pronoun may be followed by its "antecedent." (Not literally an *ante*cedent, then)
He did one of those "now you see it and now you don't" tricks. (An unusual adjective combination)
"Red" Lewis grew up to become the author of numerous best-sellers. (If a nickname is used repeatedly, drop the quotation marks after its first appearance, to avoid clutter.)
As the light plane approached for a landing, the pilot "feathered his prop."
Gregory listened soberly to the accusations for a time; then he suddenly "blew his cool."

But it is well to ask yourself, particularly of the slang expressions, whether they really serve a useful purpose; it might be better to change your diction (**D o**).

**6. Quotation marks within quotation marks should alternate as to kind.**

Single should be used within double, double again within single.

"As a girl I memorized the poem 'Trees,' " Mother told us.
Frank said, "When I saw Charlie, he asked, 'Are you in earnest, you "landlubber"?' "

**7. Place quotation marks properly among other marks of punctuation.**

The position of quotation marks in relation to other punctuation marks offers some problems. American editors have, for the sake of appearance, adopted a somewhat illogical system. But it is a system, and a simple one—familiarize yourself with it and practice it.

**a.** The comma and the period are *always* placed before the quotation marks, logically or illogically.

"When you come in," she said, "please close the door." (Logical)

I hoped for a grade of "satisfactory," but I got an "unsatisfactory." (Illogical, but accepted practice)

**b.** The colon and the semicolon are *always* placed *after* the quotation marks, logically.

Both sides enjoyed "Yankee Doodle": the British who started it and the Americans who picked it up.

Late at night we read "The Monkey's Paw"; afterwards we were too frightened to sleep.

**c.** The question mark and the exclamation point are used *before* or *after* the quotation marks, logically—before, if they belong only to the quotation; after, if they belong to the larger sentence.

Can you say rapidly, "Peter Piper picked a peck of pickled peppers"?

"Let me go or I'll tell mother!" she screamed.

**d.** Observe these same practices (rules 7a–c) when more than one set of marks is involved.

The leader answered, "Maybe it's what you call 'fair play'; as for me, I don't like it."

He sighed, "I'm getting tired of mediocre pictures advertised as 'super-colossal.' "

I asked, "Why does everybody want to sing 'Three Blind Mice'?"

Quotation marks should never be placed *above* other marks of punctuation, through carelessness or indecision. Make up your mind.

**8. Quotation marks should be used only if a sentence is clearly indicated as the words of a speaker.**

Unacceptable: My brother and I used to run away frequently. "Why did we do this?" It is hard to say.

**9. Quotation marks should not enclose an indirect quotation.**

Unacceptable: He said "that he would give me a holiday."
(Indirect form)

Conventional: He said, "I will give you a holiday." (Direct form)

**10. Quotation marks should not be used around the title at the top of your own theme, unless it is quoted.**
The position of the title alone is enough to set it off.

I Was a Disc Jockey
The Meaning of Hawthorne's "The Birthmark"

But referred to elsewhere, it should be treated like any other title.

Last semester I wrote a paper entitled "A Day at the Olympics."

A subject should not be punctuated as if it were a title.

Unacceptable: I am writing a paper on "airport development."

# P I / PUNCTUATION—ITALICS

***Use italics for titles and certain words, and for emphasis.***
(Exercise 11, p. 224)

Words are italicized to indicate that they are used in certain special senses or with emphasis. In print, italics are indicated by a special sloping type (*in an italicized passage,* by roman type). In handwritten or typewritten papers, italics are indicated by underlining. Usage is somewhat divided between italics and quotation marks for some purposes (see **P q 4,** preceding), but these rules may be safely followed.

UNDERSTANDING PUNCTUATION

### 1. Italicize titles of newspaper, magazines, books, and other separate publications.

The name of the city in a newspaper title was long left un-italicized, and still is, by some editors; but usage is now swinging to what seems the more logical practice of treating it as it appears on the first page—part of the title. Titles of smaller works within the types of publications listed above, such as stories, articles, and poems, are preferably put into quotation marks (**P q**).

His favorite newspapers are the *Christian Science Monitor,* the *St. Louis Post-Dispatch,* and the *Washington Post.*
My father-in-law subscribes to the *Reader's Digest* and *Sports Illustrated.*
I read *The Grapes of Wrath* and *An American Melodrama,* both in hardcover editions.

(Notice that the articles (*a, an,* and *the*) are not usually regarded as part of a newspaper or magazine title but are, of a book.)

Failure to italicize may lead to confusion.

I am very fond of Jane Eyre (The heroine?)
I am very fond of *Jane Eyre.* (The book)

### 2. Italicize the names of trains, ships, and airplanes.

My grandfather once went from Chicago to the West Coast on the Burlington *Zephyr.* Then he flew to Japan on Pan American's *Morning Star,* and sailed back on the President Line's *President Cleveland.*

### 3. Italicize foreign words in an English passage.

But consult your dictionary for their standing, first reading the preface to see how its editors indicate whether a word of foreign origin is still regarded as foreign (*Weltanschauung, faute de mieux*) or has become thoroughly anglicized (rendez-vous, et cetera).

*Au contraire* I shouldn't even consider such a course of action. (French phrase not yet anglicized.)
My young nephews hit our house like a blitzkrieg. (German word already anglicized.)

Foreign words at both levels are useful and acceptable, but their overuse, where simple English ones will say the same thing, hints of affectation.

After the pilot had done a couple of rolls, I told him to get me back to good old terra firma *tout de suite.*

## 4. Italicize words, letters, or numbers used as such rather than as the things they stand for.

Learn to distinguish between *imply* and *infer.*
I misread this *7* for a *4.*
You didn't cross that *t,* and it looks like an *I.*

## 5. Italicize a word that should be read with special emphasis.

He thinks he is *the* man about town.
Our nation must prepare for defense *and* attack.

## 6. Don't overuse italics for emphasis.

Like too many exclamation points or dashes, overused italics soon lose their force and give a kind of cheaply hysterical quality to your writing.

Overdone: I was *so* glad that George dropped by. I hadn't seen him for *ages.* And you should *see* his new sports car—it's a *dream.*

Particularly in formal writing, take time to achieve emphasis by the more subtle means of vivid diction and forceful sentence structure.

# P PD / PUNCTUATION—PERIOD

***Use periods to terminate most sentences and for certain other purposes.***
(Exercise 12, pp. 224–225)

The period terminates a declarative or an imperative sentence, and indicates abbreviations, decimals, or omitted words.

### 1. Use a period after a declarative sentence.

He came home after his last examination.

An indirect question is declarative.

He asked me why I was studying so late.

The clause that indicates a direct quotation, even a question, is declarative.

"Why are you working so late?" he asked.

### 2. Use a period after an imperative sentence.

Send me your address as soon as you are located.

A question that is meant not as a question but as a politely worded command is regarded as imperative.

Will you please send me your latest catalog.

### 3. Use a period after an abbreviation.

Mr. Jones     Mrs. Smith     Ms. Evans

These titles are regarded as abbreviations even though never written out for serious purposes; compare *Miss,* which is a complete word. (English publishers commonly omit these periods, but American practice still includes them.)

| Dr. Johnson | etc. | St. Louis |
| C. L. Bogard | M.D. | Mich. |

### 4. Use a period to indicate decimals.

| 3.1416 | $9.28 (But 28 cents) |
| a .22 rifle | a .45 revolver |

### 5. Use a series of three spaced periods to indicate words omitted from a quotation.

These are also called ellipsis periods or suspension points.

Walker states that "In northern latitudes on the coldest days . . . the air-source pump is at its least efficient." (The words *which is when it is most needed* were omitted as unnecessary to the quoter's purpose.)

If the omission occurs at the end of a sentence, use four periods, the last being the period for the end of the sentence.

### 6. Do not use two periods together, even if two are indicated; one will do the work of both.

**Faulty:** He likes all outdoor sports: golf, tennis, swimming, etc..

### 7. Do not use a period after a declarative or imperative statement inserted in another sentence, nor after such a statement when it is followed by the words indicating a quotation.

**Faulty:** I can jump—you watch me.—as far as that stone.
**Correct:** I can jump—you watch me—as far as that stone.

**Faulty:** "There is no chance of success." he conceded.
**Correct:** "There is no chance of success," he conceded.

### 8. Do not use a period after a title (T t) even if it is a complete sentence.

**Faulty:** I Changed My Mind.

UNDERSTANDING PUNCTUATION

(Compare the question mark (**P qs**) and the exclamation point (**P e**), which *would* be used in the examples in rules 7 and 8, above.)

**9. Do not use periods after combinations of letters standing for the names of organizations, nor after shortened word forms.**
See **Sp ab** for distinction from abbreviations.

| | | |
|---|---|---|
| lab | NATO | FBI |
| exam | CORE | NBC |

# P QS / PUNCTUATION—QUESTION MARK

*Use a question mark to indicate interrogation.*
(Exercise 13, p. 225)

The question mark terminates an interrogative sentence or any sentence with an interrogative meaning.

### 1. Use a question mark after an interrogative sentence.

Can you go with me to the movies tonight?

Writers, like speakers, make frequent use of the "rhetorical question," which is intended to start the reader or listener to thinking rather than to get an answer (which the user will probably provide). But it is a question and should be punctuated accordingly.

We face a crisis. What shall we do about it? Probably nothing.

### 2. Use a question mark after any statement that has an interrogative meaning.

You think you will be able to get away? (Meaning "Do you think that you will be able to get away?")

The small size has gone up ten cents? (Actually an inquiry, not a statement.)

**3. Use a question mark after an interrogative sentence inserted in another sentence, and after a quoted one.**

I mean—do you follow me?—that *x* must equal *a*.
"What is the reason for this commotion?" he asked.
He asked, "What is the reason for this commotion?"

**4. Use a question mark after a title that is an interrogative phrase or sentence.**

After Graduation—What?
Who Should Be Educated?

**5. Do not use a question mark after a statement that merely implies a question or after a question indirectly quoted.**

Faulty:     I wonder what he is doing right now?
Faulty:     He asked me whether I would study with him tonight?
Correct:    He asked, "Will you study with me tonight?"

**6. Do not use a question mark after a polite question which is really a command.**
See **P pd 2.**

Will you please send me two tickets for the opera.

# P E / PUNCTUATION— EXCLAMATION POINT

***Use an exclamation point to give force.***
(Exercise 14, pp. 225–226)

The exclamation point indicates an exclamatory sentence or word.

**1. Use an exclamation point after any statement, command, or question to which you wish to add emotional force.**

My wallet is gone!
Help me!
What do you know about that!

**2. Use an exclamation point after most introductory *what* and *how* constructions, which are exclamatory by nature.**

Oh, what a beautiful morning it is!
Compare: It is a beautiful morning.
How thoughtful it was of you to stop!
Compare: It was thoughtful of you to stop.

**3. Use an exclamation point to set off exclamatory interjections.**

Ouch! that nail came clear through. (Exclamatory interjection, not sentence)
Well, I just don't think I'll go at all! (Exclamatory sentence, not interjection)
Oh! that truck is going over the bank! (Exclamatory interjection and sentence)

**4. Use an exclamation point after an exclamatory sentence inserted in another sentence and after a quoted one.**

The subject of the sentence—pay attention, please!—is a pronoun.
"I won't have anything to do with it!" he shouted.
He shouted, "I won't have anything to do with it!"

**5. Use an exclamation point after a title that is an exclamatory phrase or sentence.**

Hurray for Our Side!
It Can Happen Here!

**6. Do not overuse the exclamation point.**
Like the little boy in the old story who cried "Wolf, Wolf!" when there was no wolf, you will soon wear out its effect.

Rather, strengthen your effect by forceful words and word arrangements.

**Overdone:** The road was slippery! We were going around a curve! There was another car, coming toward us on our side of the road!

**7. Do not pile up exclamation points—one will do the work.**

Overdone: I think I'll be seeing her at Christmas!!!

## EXERCISES

P C / PUNCTUATION—COMMA
(Discussion, pp. 189–198)

**1.** Supply all needed commas in the following sentences, giving your reason for each comma or pair of commas used.

1. Caesar was fighting on the island of Pharos which was besieged by the Egyptians.
2. Our laughter really caused him a great deal of annoyance but he tried hard not to show it.
3. The teacher came up to me and said "Do you have nothing to do but make trouble?"
4. The most amazing character I have ever known was Miss Williams our high school music teacher.
5. On June 20 1975 we reached our destination Miami Florida.
6. Since I didn't have twenty-five dollars with which to pay my fine I had to remain in jail overnight.
7. The dean we had feared proved to be a friendly reasonable just old man.
8. Twelve million years however seems a long time to wait.
9. Oh what is the matter with him now?
10. A foreign car long and sleek stood at the curb.
11. In the third-year course we read a few plays memorized some poetry and wrote several critical papers.

UNDERSTANDING PUNCTUATION

12.   The new quarterback is I believe the best player
on the team.

13.   It is starting to rain isn't it?

14.   The night before we had arrived at St. Augustine
Florida the oldest city in the United States.

15.   The new theory about criminals is that they should
be helped not punished.

**2.**   The following sentences do not read as their writers
intended. Insert in each the comma that clarifies its meaning.

1.   Every night from nine to ten programs of classical
music are broadcast.

2.   For many a college is just a place to play football.

3.   True liars must have good memories.

4.   The night we attended the show was a waste of time.

5.   Well people should know enough to go to a doctor.

P S   /   PUNCTUATION—SEMICOLON
(Discussion, pp. 198–200)

**3.**   Punctuate the following sentences with commas and
semicolons as required, giving your reasons.

1.   That night our team won a smashing victory a holiday
was declared the next day to celebrate it.

2.   Our virgin forests have largely disappeared but new
reforestation programs will slowly replace them.

3.   "You needn't feel so bad about it" she comforted me
"I have often made the same mistake."

4.   Jack smiling and bowing picked up his watch his
notes and his briefcase and although he walked calmly to the
door he hurried from the room faint with excitement.

5.   The house stood alone in a clump of trees before
it ran a small stream.

6.   It snowed heavily all night consequently we spent
the morning shoveling the walks.

7.   The cast consisted of Robert Freel a veteran of

World War II Mary Freel his wife Virginia their only child and
Rufus Jackson a neighbor.

8.   I was wakened by the rumble of thunder before I
could close the windows the rain began to drive in.

9.   He stood for as much as a minute just looking at the
audience then he began to speak in a quiet voice.

10.   I dislike the location of my new job on the other hand
I enjoy the pay envelope.


**4.**   Punctuate these five sentences if and as necessary,
explaining your decisions in grammatical terms.


1.   My father is a strong party man he has always voted
a straight ticket.

2.   My father is a strong party man therefore he has always
voted a straight ticket.

3.   My father is a strong party man and he has always
voted a straight ticket.

4.   My father is a strong party man who has always voted
a straight ticket.

5.   My father a strong party man has always voted a
straight ticket.


P  CO  /  PUNCTUATION—COLON
(Discussion, pp. 200–202)


**5.**   Use colons, semicolons, or commas in the following
sentences as required, giving your reasons.


1.   As we were starting to get supper over the campfire,
a shocking thought struck me we had forgotten to bring
any salt.

2.   He has taken a number of mathematics courses here
at college algebra geometry trigonometry and calculus.

3.   The plane is scheduled to leave at 9 15 a.m. and
arrive at 1 30 p.m.

4.   The good-luck letter directed us to read Matthew 6 11.

5.    The Protestant sects that have churches in my home town are Presbyterian Methodist Baptist and Lutheran.

6.    My brother said "I'd like to help you Jack but I just don't have time."

7.    In high school Arthur starred as a basketball player in college he has made his name in football instead.

8.    We learned to say "I love you" in three languages French German and Spanish.

9.    He ended his remarks with this quotation from Emerson Nothing can bring you peace but yourself.

10.    I have two possible courses to quit school or to get a part-time job.


### P D  /  PUNCTUATION—DASH
(Discussion, pp. 202–204)


**6.**    Use dashes in the following sentences as required, giving your reasons. If a choice of punctuation is possible, mention and explain.


1.    All of my favorite hobbies model building, stamp collecting, and coin collecting cost money.

2.    A home, a family, a job what more could a man ask of life?

3.    I want oh, I don't know what I want.

4.    You are trying to say can you explain it more clearly?

5.    The boy has drive stamina great promise.


### P P  /  PUNCTUATION—PARENTHESES
(Discussion, pp. 204–206)


**7.**    Indicate any places in the following sentences that parentheses might be used. If there is a choice of punctuation marks, explain the effect of each.


1.    He said I don't remember his exact words that he expected us to stand by him.

2.    We read *Moby Dick* by Herman Melville 1819-1891 an American novelist.

3.    I told him and I'm glad I did it that he was a rotter.

4.    Sodium chloride common salt has many uses.

5.    In New York I had my choice of night clubs the legal age for drinking there is eighteen and Broadway shows.

## P B  /  PUNCTUATION—BRACKETS
(Discussion, p. 206)

**8.**    Explain the use of brackets in the following sentences.

1.    "In the course of time the king [Victor Emmanuel II] accomplished his purpose."

2.    He wrote, "I have developed for the Senegalese [q.v.] a warm affection."

3.    "The twentieth century's greatest genius [Einstein] is gone."

4.    "The new model appeared with a bonnet [the British term for automobile hood] that was much easier to open."

5.    His note read, "I shall see you tonite [*sic*] if at all possible."

## P Q  /  PUNCTUATION—QUOTATION MARKS
(Discussion, pp. 206–211)

**9.**    Use quotation marks in the following sentences as required, explaining your reasons. Be careful to place them properly in relation to other marks of punctuation.

1.    Bud complained, But my weekly schedule must include at least forty-nine hours of sack time.

2.    He assigned three stories: Hemingway's The Killers, Mansfield's Bliss, and Forster's The Other Side of the Hedge.

3.    Are you familiar with the old Army expression goofing off? he asked.

4.    Everyone calls him Knobby: that's because his last name is Knoblock.

5.   Here is the weather report from tonight's paper: Mostly fair and cooler tonight and Thursday; possible thundershowers early Friday.

**10.**   Remove or change the order of quotation marks in the following sentences as required, giving your reasons.

1.   He asked "whether we wanted to work on the night or the day shift."
2.   "No"! she exclaimed. "I wouldn't think of such a thing"!
3.   At first he resented the nickname "Shorty;" later he came to like it.
4.   My instructor asked, "What do you mean here by the slang term 'dig it?' "
5.   I decided to write my term paper on "the control of the drug traffic."

### P I / PUNCTUATION—ITALICS
(Discussion, pp. 211–213)

**11.**   Use italics or quotation marks in the following sentences as required, giving your reasons.

1.   There is an article on the home garden in today's Asheville Citizen.
2.   Be sure that you do not confuse the words principal and principle in your writing.
3.   Through that course I became acquainted with Tom Sawyer and Huckleberry Finn, which I had never read as a child.
4.   I've always read the last line of the Gettysburg Address stressing the prepositions: of the people, by the people, and for the people; the actor stressed people instead.
5.   Nicholson has a poem entitled On My Thirty-fifth Birthday in the April Harper's.

### P PD / PUNCTUATION—PERIOD
(Discussion, pp. 214–216)

**12.** Supply all needed periods in the following sentences, giving your reasons.

1. The signature was F R Hankinson, Jr, M D
2. In his trunk they found a 25 automatic and a 38 revolver
3. The price was marked $9 98, but I got it on sale for $7 50
4. Mr Roberts and Miss Snoberger will be married on Sept 18 and will reside at 718 N Chauncey St after a brief honeymoon.
5. The AFL-CIO meeting began at 10 a m and was not dismissed until 1:15 p m

### P QS / PUNCTUATION—QUESTION MARK
(Discussion, pp. 216–217)

**13.** Use any question marks required in the following sentences, giving your reasons. Remove any other marks of punctuation that the question mark replaces.

1. I understood (didn't you say so) that you were leaving tonight.
2. "Where are the people who on New Year's Day made such good resolutions," he inquired.
3. Do you feel that your years of effort have been sufficiently rewarded.
4. "To be or not to be: that is the question" is a quotation from *Hamlet,* isn't it.
5. The theme I wrote entitled "What Can a Student Believe" was read in class.

### P E / PUNCTUATION—EXCLAMATION POINT
(Discussion, pp. 217–219)

**14.** Use any exclamation marks indicated by the following sentences, giving your reasons. Remove any other marks of punctuation that the exclamation point replaces.

UNDERSTANDING PUNCTUATION

1.  The roller coaster climbed leisurely to the top of the incline, then—down we dropped.
2.  Help, help, I'm slipping.
3.  How beautiful the sunlight is across the water.
4.  Oh, what's the use of even trying to please him.
5.  I wish—quit tickling me—that the rain would stop.

# 9
# DOING LIBRARY RESEARCH

The foregoing chapters have been concerned with the correct and effective expression of ideas in written form. Once you have learned the underlying techniques of organization, diction, sentence structure, and punctuation, you are equipped to do well in any kind of writing that may be required of you, in college or out, in the years to come. But for certain specialized kinds of writing there are additional techniques that must be mastered. Two of these types, the library research paper and the business letter, are treated in this chapter and the one that follows.

The library research paper differs from most of the writing that you are asked to do in composition courses in that you will find your material not in your memories of the past nor in your personal impressions of the world about you but in the works of others—primarily in published articles and books. Your object is to survey the available literature on a given subject and to synthesize the materials you find useful into a purposeful and creative whole.

Such is the type of paper prepared by research workers in many fields. New discoveries in science, for instance, do not often just happen, nor are they likely any longer to be the result solely of one worker's genius. Rather, they are the culmination of a long tradition to which many have contributed. The scientist, in preparing his report of new discoveries, must survey and evaluate the work of his predecessors and show where he has torn it down or built upon it.

This type of paper is required in college not only as theses for advanced degrees but as part of the work in numerous undergraduate courses—as term papers and reports on related subjects in both the sciences and the humanities. More important, there will be research projects required of you after college—by your business or your industry or your profession —research to be carried out and properly written up for presentation to your employers or your colleagues. Further, there will arise all kinds of subjects on which you may wish to inform yourself, less formally, or your family or your friends or perhaps fellow club members. A thorough grounding in the location of sources of information and the methods of handling it, now, will stand you in good stead throughout your career. So far you have learned little of man's vast supply of knowledge, here in college; you will learn relatively little more before you leave; and much of what you will need to know in the future hasn't even been discovered yet. Your own knowledge of, and opinions on, many issues, now and later, will be of value to yourself and others only as they are firmly based on the numerous data and conclusions already published.

The library research paper is, however, an original work, differing from other creative writing only in the sources from which it is drawn and the techniques that have been developed by scholars for the convenient handling of such materials. It is an arduous and exacting piece of work that cannot, like some assignments, be dashed off in a moment of inspiration. Its preparation involves long hours of searching for, selecting, and using source materials, and its completion requires great care in the conventions which surround the handling of such materials. Like many another difficult accomplishment, however, it carries its own rewards.

The simple compositions illustrated in Chapter 1 involved only three procedures: choosing a subject, organizing, and writing. The library research project requires five major consecutive steps: choosing a subject, building a bibliography, reading and note-taking, organizing, and writing and documenting.

## CHOOSING A SUBJECT

### Enjoyment

Since the problem of the library research paper is, compared to any other assignment in this course, a long-drawn-out affair that may take you several weeks, it is particularly important that you choose (if you are allowed a choice) a subject that will give you both pleasure and profit. It will probably be one with which you are already somewhat familiar and about which you find yourself sufficiently curious to want additional information. As a city dweller, you may have become interested in social problems such as drug addiction or the increasing crime rate; as a suburbanite, you may be concerned about mass transit or the saving of areas for public recreation. As an amateur in dramatics, you may wish to know more of the little theater movement; in aviation, of the early history of man's long desire to fly. Your travels may have taken you to Boulder Dam or to the Panama Canal, and you feel you would enjoy a study of the problems which had to be met in their construction. Or some college course, by a casual reference to Esperanto or surrealism, may have given you just a glimpse down an avenue that you would like to explore more thoroughly.

Your choice will depend, however, upon a number of factors in addition to your own preference; one is the reading public for which your paper is intended. In years to come you may, as a serious research worker in your field, be surveying the results of others' work for the benefit of fellow specialists. For the time being, however, it would be presumptuous of you to write on penicillin for the bacteriologist or on the Children's Crusade for the historian. Your logical present purpose is to stand as interpreter between the specialist, of whose field you will make as thorough a study as you can, and the relatively uninformed general public, for whom you can thus perform a real service. Assuming, for instance, that you were capable of a complete understanding of Einstein's theory of relativity, there remains the problem of whether or not you could write on that subject simply enough for the information and enjoyment of the average adult. Choose a subject that can become intelligible not only to you but also to the general reader—if for no other reason than that only on such a paper, probably, will your instructor be qualified to judge you fairly.

## Limitation

The choice of a subject for library research involves limitation. At no time is it more necessary to remember the advisability of writing fully on a small subject in preference to sketching briefly the mere outlines of a large one. All the laws of vividness and emphasis require that you narrow your choice to a single phase of the omnibus topic you may conceivably have chosen. Aviation has become an encyclopedic subject; but fascinating research papers of 1000 to 2000 words (a common length requirement) might well be produced on Lindbergh's 1927 flight to Paris, the use of planes in firefighting, the development of the helicopter, and so forth.

## Availability of material

Before settling upon a choice, make sure that there is available for your use an adequate amount of printed or other material on your subject. A full-fledged research worker will overcome any such handicap by negotiating interlibrary loans or by studying at various centers of learning; but you will be wise, for this practice paper, to limit yourself to a subject on which your own college library is well supplied with material available to the undergraduate. The subject of American attitudes toward some international issue as revealed in the cartoons of the daily press of a given period might prove a fascinating choice but futile unless your library has the necessary newspapers available, either in bound volumes or on microfilm.

### BUILDING A BIBLIOGRAPHY

In checking on the availability of material on your chosen subject, you have already begun to take the second step of the research task, the collection of a list of available materials on your subject that is known as a bibliography. Accompanying your completed paper, in acknowledgment of the sources from which you have gathered its basic content, will be a *final* bibliography—a list of materials on which you have actually drawn in preparing the completed paper. In beginning your work, however, you will draw up a much longer list—a *working* bibliography, from which you will later select the items that prove of actual use in your paper.

### Reference guides

A bibliography is literally a list of books, but the materials available for your use may very likely include (depending on your choice of subject) newspapers, popular magazines, specialized journals, bulletins, pamphlets. Your first task will be to become familiar with the many devices available in the modern library to aid you in locating all kinds of materials on any subject. You will therefore begin by looking not for the materials themselves but at the various guides through which you may discover what materials exist and how to find them.

Winchell's *Guide to Reference Books* is a primary aid in this enterprise. Kept up-to-date by occasional new editions and more frequent supplements, it classifies by type and subject matter and describes all kinds of reference works (bibliographies, encyclopedias, etc.) to which you may go in turn for further references as well as for material. There is also Walford's *Guide to Reference Material,* divided into volumes devoted to science, the social sciences, and the humanities. But these days there are many media other than the printed word to consider, and for them there is Hall and Northern's annual *Multi Media Reviews Index* (MMRI), with sections covering reviews of film, filmstrips, records and tapes, and miscellaneous media to be found in a great variety of periodicals and services. Limbacher's *Reference Guide to Audiovisual Information* is another recent guide to nonbook media. How useful these great guides may be to you will depend, of course, on both your choice of subject and the resources of the library you are working in.

Your library's guide to what books are available in it may be, these days, in book form, periodically updated by computer. But it is likelier, still, to be the traditional **card catalog.** In its tiers of drawers are filed, alphabetically, identifying cards, usually several cards for a single book, so that you may locate it not only by title and by author but through any one of a number of subjects with which it deals. Under "Wilson, Woodrow,'' for instance, you will find cards referring you not only to books by Wilson but to books about him. (Be sure to notice whether the catalog you are using has a single alphabetical listing or is divided into author, title, and subject sections.)

Books, however, may constitute only a small part of your source material. Your subject may be one that never attained book stature, or some recent scientific discovery on which books have not yet been published; or, even though you have found books on it, you may wish to supplement them with other material from the periodical press. In locating such material, you have at your disposal a number of invaluable guides.

The *Reader's Guide to Periodical Literature* is the foremost index of its sort. Issued monthly in magazine form, it is ultimately cumulated into volumes covering several years. In it, under author and subject headings, you will find indexed the contents of the better-known American (and a few English) periodicals on general subjects since 1900.

*Poole's Index* is an index of English and American periodical literature of an earlier period, 1802–1906.

*The International Index,* which began as a supplement to the *Reader's Guide* in 1916, indexes a selected list of American and European periodicals in the fields of the humanities, social sciences, and science until 1965. Then the *Social Science and Humanities Index* took over, indexing some 175 American and English periodicals until 1974, when it became separate publications, the *Social Sciences Index* and the *Humanities Index.*

Besides these general indexes, there are numerous others specializing in particular fields—agriculture, engineering, education, psychology, art, industrial art, dentistry, medicine, law—some of them listing books and bulletins as well as articles in periodicals.

The *New York Times Index* is published annually, and through it you can discover the exact location of material in the files of one of the nation's great metropolitan dailies, the *New York Times.* Since most significant news is handled on the same day by all the principal papers of the country, this index is also helpful in using other newspaper files.

Whatever index you consult, familiarize yourself with its scope and its system of symbols, for each has its own plan and method. Intelligently used, these indexes combine to put quickly at your disposal materials that would otherwise lie undiscoverable on the miles of shelves in the stacks of a large library.

Mention should be made here of the most useful reference tool of all—reference librarians. Especially trained in the location of sources, they can help you find all manner of materials. But don't impose on their good nature; in this practice work particularly, proceed as independently as you can. The ability to find your way around a library (and you will find libraries conveniently similar all over the country) will be an asset to you for the rest of your life.

It is well to remember that a college library is often dispersed about the campus—that in addition to a large general library, there may be departmental collections such as chemistry or agriculture located conveniently in the buildings that house those departments. Such materials are usually indexed in the card catalog at the main library building with special notations as to their location.

### Bibliography cards

Before starting to build a working bibliography of your subject, equip yourself with a package of ruled cards of a convenient size. Satisfactory to most is a card 3 x 5 inches, although some who write a large hand prefer a 4 x 6-inch card. As you discover likely items, do not yield to the temptation merely to jot down a list of possible sources in your notebook, but *record each item on a separate card.* Later on, when you are sorting, eliminating, and alphabetizing these items, the time-saving convenience of the card system will be only too apparent.

If the subject you have chosen is one on which books are available, the card catalog is the logical place to begin. You may find yourself overwhelmed with a drawerful of references to books on your subject, obviously more books than you can afford even to look at. In that event the process of selection so important in the research procedure must begin at once. Titles may indicate whether the book is likely to deal with your particular phase of the subject; if you already know something of the field, you may be able to choose the significant authors from the many who have written on the subject; the publication date may indicate whether or not the book will serve your purpose; the brief mention of contents occasionally appearing in the card catalog may help you. When in doubt, fill out a bibliography card; it is much easier to discard items later than to have to return in search of neglected material. A large working bibliography is good assurance that such items as survive to form the final bibliography will be well chosen.

Whenever you discover a promising item, fill out a bibliography card for it, being sure to include all the information that you may later need, for the secret of economical research technique is the avoidance of all unnecessary backtracking. You will need three lines: first, the full name of the author (last name first, always, for convenience in alphabetizing); second, the title (underscored, always, to indicate that it is of a book), including any special information as to volume or edition; third, facts of publication: place, name of publisher, date. All of this will be required in your final bibliography, which must include complete information as to the exact sources used. The library call number from the upper left corner of the catalog card should also be included (probably in the upper right, on your card, where there is more space); this will be a part of the Library of Congress or the Dewey Decimal system, whichever is used in your library, and will make it possible to locate the book on the shelves. Your completed card will look like this (note and follow the punctuation pattern):

PR
6070
.I 45
D3

*Tindall, Gillian*

Dances of Death

New York: Walker, 1973

Moving on to the guides to periodicals, you will again find the need to exercise discrimination in choosing the apparently important out of the many. Since these references appear in volumes collected by date, you need look only at those that concern you. As with books, you may be helped in your selection of promising items by author and title, and additionally by the type of magazine in which the article occurs. Again, be generous; do not encumber yourself with items obviously worthless, but take down any and all that look promising. And again, *use a separate card for each item.*

The information needed for articles will differ somewhat from that required for books. List the author as before. (If the article is anonymous, leave blank the line where the author's name would regularly go, for you will now alphabetize by title instead.) Second comes the title of the article (in quotation marks to indicate that it is only part of a larger whole); and third, the title of the magazine (this should be underscored), the volume number and the date of the copy that contains this article, and the pages that it occupies. Your completed card will look like this:

> Hogg, Tony
> "That Old-time Ignition"
> <u>Esquire</u>, 82 (July 1974), 110–111,
> 159, 162

Again note and follow the punctuation pattern. The conventional position of the volume number *before* the date in parentheses, and the page numbers *after,* makes unnecessary the use of the abbreviations *vol.* and *pp.* here.

The presence of a card in the card catalog is proof that the volume to which it refers is contained in the library in which you are working. Your library may not have some of the periodicals indexed by the guides you have consulted, however, and it may have only certain issues of others. Your next step, therefore, is to consult the periodicals file to discover whether the issues of the magazines you want are available, and if so, whether in bound volumes or microfilm. Jot down any information as to location. Then discard all cards for material that your library doesn't have, unless there is a chance of finding it somewhere else.

### Primary and secondary materials

You cannot be expected to read every word on your chosen subject, either in books or in magazines. One important principle of selection is whether the material in question is firsthand or second. If you perform a laboratory experiment and write up the results, your material is of course strictly firsthand, or primary. If you merely read what others have written about such experiments, it is secondary. Most of the materials you will deal with in this practice piece of library research will probably be secondary, but primary material is always to be preferred when available. A book is primary material for a book review; what the critics have already said about it is, for the purpose, secondary. If you are preparing an account of Thomas Jefferson's views on democracy, the conventional history of his life and times will be secondary, as you will be dealing with someone else's conclusions. On the other hand, an edition of his letters, his speeches, his state papers, will be primary— and just so much more valuable because your access to the material is direct, uncolored by another's opinion of Jefferson's opinions. Similarly, the original version of a magazine article is to be preferred to any condensation appearing later in a magazine digest, where editorial excision has operated upon the author's original material.

### READING AND NOTE-TAKING

You are now equipped with a sizable pack of cards containing references to the most promising materials available on your subject and are ready to proceed to the actual reading and note-taking, two processes so closely allied as to form a single step in the research procedure.

Someone has described the gathering of material for the library research paper as a process of judicious fishing. There is certainly much trial and error involved, and one must reconcile himself to taking wrong steps as well as right ones, to looking over useless material as well as useful, and to generally "wasting time." This is only the kind of waste that is inevitably present in looking for something, however, be it a mislaid object or a rare wildflower, and it combines with the annoyance of false moves something of the exhilaration of the treasure hunt. It is far removed, however, from looking for a needle in a haystack, for you have numerous sources of clues. A knowledge of research techniques plus an intelligent maintenance of perspective will help to eliminate waste motion and speed you to a successful conclusion. But the finished paper, it must be remembered, is a monument to much discarded material as well as to what proved worthy of inclusion.

### Where to begin

It is always best to start with the most general sources in order to see your phase of the subject in its proper relationship to the whole from the beginning. Chief among the general reference works to which you may well turn before settling down to reading books or articles on specific and limited phases of the subject are the encyclopedias (not only the familiar *Britannica, Americana,* and *New International*, but others specializing in a single field such as religion, education, or sociology), collections of brief biographies (*Who's Who* and the *Dictionary of National Biography* for Englishmen, living and dead, and the comparable *Who's Who in America* and the *Dictionary of American Biography* for Americans), collections of facts and statistics such as the *World Almanac* and other yearbooks, and atlases. Spend some time browsing in the reference room of the library, acquainting yourself with the many reference works at your disposal.

### How to read

So much of your reading in school and college has been the word-by-word digestion of the content of textbooks that you may need to be reminded of other ways of approaching printed matter that will take you more rapidly through the masses of material with which you are now faced. First, learn to use that most neglected part of every book, the preface. From it you can often determine whether or not the book is likely to include anything suitable for your purpose. The table of contents is even more useful: a glance at chapter headings may save you the necessity of going farther, or direct you quickly to the one small section which may be all that you will find useful. An index, if the book has one, can serve the same purpose. Next, learn to "skim"—to glance rapidly through masses of material in search of the little that may be significant. By these means, eliminate from consideration as rapidly as you can those items that once looked promising enough to get into your bibliography but that now prove unsuitable. Then you can settle down to a thorough reading of what you have found to be really worthwhile.

### How to take notes

As you read, you must of course take notes; do not depend on your ability to keep in your head the materials needed for such a project. Research technique requires that you keep not only careful notes of the material you will later incorporate into your own paper but also an accurate account of its sources.

Good note-taking will put you far along on the next step in the process, organization. By the time you have acquainted yourself with the general background of your subject and before you have gone far in the detailed reading, you will begin to get a notion of the general pattern into which your handling of the subject will likely fall—of the topics which will constitute the phases of your approach. These topics should become the titles for your notes, and recording under such headings the more important facts and opinions that you run across is the surest way to keep this step of the research process from resulting in a hopeless mass of unclassified data. Use subtitles freely, too, as the need arises, in order to classify your notes further. Notes on "Uses" may become "Uses—industrial" and "Uses—industrial—England" or "Uses—industrial—early."

Your reading notes, like your bibliographical items, should be taken on cards. Convenient sizes are 4 x 6 inches and 5 x 8 inches; choose the size you prefer and stick to it. The important thing is that your notes be uniform in size for convenience in handling and filing.

As with the bibliographical items, *take only one reading note on a card.* You will be tempted to go ahead and fill up a page with successive notes taken from a given work. If you do, you will find, when you come to write your paper, that you have a hodgepodge of information that must be read through time after time in search of pertinent items. Your paper is to be not a series of digests but a composite of information taken from many sources and handled according to a purpose and a pattern of your own. The practice of *limiting each note card to a single titled topic taken from a single reference* will provide you, when your reading is completed, with a mass of notes in which all like material, however varied the sources, appears under a common heading, easy to assemble; it will also make it possible to discard some notes without interfering with the rest. The flexibility of such notes makes the next step, the task of organizing, relatively simple.

You will need to take two kinds of notes, the **summary** and the **direct quotation.** The former you will take most often, jotting down in your own words (as briefly as possible without loss of meaning) the gist of the material you are reading. But there will be times, when you come to write your paper, that you will wish to present a writer's idea just as he expressed it. For this purpose you will need to record his exact words (in quotation marks, always, to indicate that you have done so). While you will perhaps need relatively few such quotations, it is well to remember as you take your notes that the direct quotation can be easily summarized when you write your paper; but a summary cannot be expanded into a direct quotation, should the need arise, without a time-wasting trip back to the original source.

In addition to the classifying title and the note itself, your note card must show clearly the *exact source* of the borrowed material. In your finished paper you will be required to show not only the book or article that the idea came from but the exact page. After every note you take, jot down the page number or numbers on which the information originally appeared. In the upper right corner of your note card, indicate the source of the material by entering the author's last name or a shortened form of the title or both—as brief an identification as possible but full enough to run no risk of confusion with other sources later. A completed note will look like this:

Organization - Camp Monroe                    Pierce
    Entire camp divided into four ident-
ical units, each with own staff, living
quarters, dining hall, and recreational
facilities. Little communication among
the four. "The social and psychological
advantages of the smaller group
have been proven time and time
again."

                                69

Just how to combine the tasks of reading and taking notes can best be determined by actual experience. The practice of taking notes as you read is likely to result in overfull or repetitious notations. On the other hand, reading an entire book without taking any notes is certain to result in a good deal of uneconomical rereading. How much material you can profitably read without taking notes will depend somewhat on its nature and difficulty, somewhat on the retentiveness of your mind. You will soon get a feeling for the most economical procedure.

Do not hesitate to add to your bibliography as you read.

You may get on the track of some of your best material through references to other sources found in your reading and through the useful bibliographies that are often appended. Your working bibliography should remain a fluid collection, subject to constant addition and subtraction as the work goes on.

## ORGANIZING

A summary is only a digest of a given piece of writing—an entirely objective condensation of the material. The writer, having read an opinionated article, can do nothing but condense that opinion. The library research paper is similarly dependent upon others for material, but its author, having run into numerous opinions, will find himself obligated to weigh them and to determine their relative importance. Thus your paper becomes, as mentioned earlier, an essentially creative work (as a house may be made of old lumber yet be a new structure), and its organization involves not only considering the material you have collected but also determining what you wish to accomplish with it.

If your project is concerned with a highly factual subject such as the invention of the phonograph, the need for creative judgment is reduced to a minimum, although even here you must determine what is, for your purpose, the relative importance of the facts. If it is a much-debated subject like amnesty, you are quite likely, in weighing diverse opinions, to arrive at and express some of your own. Whatever the subject of your research paper, you will be faced with the task of making the material yours, of reshaping it to form a well-balanced picture of your subject as you have come to see it, yet to contribute most to the pleasure and profit of your reader. Thus the organization of your material will depend partly upon its nature, with the usual logical patterns of thought operating upon it (origins will reasonably come first, causes precede effects, and so on), but partly upon the handling which you, as author, determine to be most effective for your purpose.

As you read and made notes, your plan no doubt began to take form, and your final organization may involve little more than settling the details of that tentative scheme. Grouping and arranging your material is only a matter of following the principles laid down in Chapter 1 (pp. 7–9), which you have already put into practice many times on a smaller scale. Now, instead of a few ideas in your head, you have a wealth of them on paper; but if your notes have been carefully taken on separate cards and thoughtfully titled and subtitled, organization is a fairly simple matter of shuffling them into the order of your predetermined pattern.

The greater length of the research paper demands that particular attention be paid, as you plan, to the introduction, which may be justifiably a matter of several paragraphs. It may well lie outside the scope of your notes themselves, being concerned with your reason for choosing the subject, with its background, with a discussion of its significance, with a view of the whole of which it is a part—anything calculated to introduce the material appropriately with a maximum of reader interest. The conclusion similarly deserves special thought and may transcend mere summarizing by evaluating the subject or suggesting its future.

Your entire plan should be worked out in a complete sentence outline (pp. 16–17) before you begin the final step, the writing. Not only will the effort of making such a detailed plan help to clarify your pattern in your own mind and to iron out any illogicalities or misplaced emphases, but also the result will be something that will be intelligible to your instructor, who may wish to check your work and make suggestions at this point.

## WRITING AND DOCUMENTING

The problems of writing the library research paper are first those of all writing—accuracy, clarity, and interest. But in addition there are special problems arising from the use of borrowed materials, which require special techniques. Large research centers used to issue their own manuals of style to which their writers adhered, but now there is more general agreement in scholarly circles on these details. They are embodied in the *MLA Style Sheet* (2nd ed., 1970) issued by the

Modern Language Association and now in use in the humanities by most scholarly journals and university presses. The practices illustrated below follow MLA style and should be observed unless your instructor requests certain differences in handling. Whatever patterns you use, consistency in matters of arrangement and punctuation in footnotes and bibliography is important as an indication of care in the preparation of the finished paper.

### Footnotes

Footnotes are a device by which information that should accompany the text but is too cumbersome (or trivial, perhaps) to be given a place in it can appear inconspicuously elsewhere. They get their name from the fact that they traditionally appear at the foot of the page. Footnotes are numbered consecutively in Arabic numerals throughout your paper. These numbers correspond to similar numbers at appropriate points in the body of the paper: after a word, phrase, sentence, or paragraph, whether quoted or of your own composition—always as close as possible to the material to which the footnote applies but always after it. The numbers should follow any punctuation but should not themselves be punctuated, just raised a half space above the line in which they appear, to keep them from being read as part of the text.

The corresponding number preceding the footnote itself is also raised a half line and not punctuated. The first footnote on a page begins three spaces below the last line of text so that it will be promptly recognized for what it is. The first line of each footnote is indented paragraph style, and successive lines, if any, are single spaced, with a period at the end. The notes should be double spaced from each other, however, to allow for the raising of their numbers. The last note may be continued at the foot of the following page, if necessary, following a single continuous line one space below the last line of text; but every note must at least begin on the page where the reference to it appears.

One of the problems in preparing the final draft of the research paper, as you can see, is that of leaving enough space at the bottom of each page for its footnotes. This problem, together with the fact that footnotes tend to make a page look cluttered, has led to an accepted alternative arrangement in which the notes are all grouped together at the end of the paper, as you may have seen them at the end of chapters in some printed books. (They are still called footnotes.) In this practice they are easier for the student to type and may be double spaced, therefore being easier for the instructor to read. Do not bind your finished paper, however, as the reader may wish to lay text and footnotes side by side, for checking. Your instructor will probably express a preference about how you set up your own paper. In the model research paper at the end of this chapter (pp. 252–259), where you can see all these matters of documentation in operation, the footnotes have been placed at the bottoms of the pages for easier reading with the text.

### The source footnote

One of your principal problems in writing the research paper is that of giving credit for the materials you use. The student beginning work on a research project sometimes fears that his paper must necessarily involve a footnote for every sentence; actually, much of the material—your own handling of it and any ideas on the subject that you have found to be generally held—is your own. Credit must be given, however, not only for all words directly quoted but for all facts or opinions which you have found to be the peculiar property of one author, even though you present them in your own words.

All such credit could be included in the body of the paper, but it is generally removed to a footnote to make the text more readable. A comparison of the two possibilities in the following shows why:

A
Once the war had begun, it became generally popular, and, as Bernard DeVoto remarks on page 203 of his book

**244**

*The Year of Decision: 1846,* published in Boston in 1943 by Little, Brown, "The Whigs had the bitter knowledge that most wars increase the power of the party that fights them."

**B**

Once the war had begun, it became generally popular, and "the Whigs had the bitter knowledge that most wars increase the power of the party that fights them."[8]

[8] Bernard DeVoto, *The Year of Decision: 1846* (Boston: Little, Brown, 1943), p. 203.

No item of source information that is included in the text need be repeated in the footnote. If the writer of the passage above includes "as Bernard DeVoto says," as he is likely to do in quoting a well-known authority, the author's name need not be included in the footnote. If he includes the title of the book as well, as he is likely to do in quoting from a well-known book, the title too can be eliminated from the footnote. The footnote is the place for any information about a source that seems awkward or unnecessary to include in the text.

Let's examine some samples. This is a typical book reference in its simplest form:

[1] C. W. Nicol, *From the Roof of Africa* (New York: Knopf, 1972), pp. 143–147.

Notice the items, their order, and the punctuation:

1. The author's name in normal order (there is no alphabetizing to be done here), followed by a comma.
2. The title in italics (underscoring, in typing or handwriting), since it is a whole (as are bulletins and pamphlets), not a part.
3. The facts of publication in parentheses (no comma preceding): the city of publication followed by a colon; the name of the publisher (short form) followed by a comma, and the date of publication.
4. The page numbers, following a comma, with *pages* abbreviated to *pp.* (*page* to *p.*). Note that the full page

number is repeated in a reference to more than one page (avoid the tempting "143–7").

If a work is in more than one volume, the volume number (in Roman numerals) precedes the page number, with no identifying abbreviations needed:

[2] Frank Dalby Davison, *The White Thorntree* (Sydney: Ure Smith, 1970), II, 567.

Information about edition (*rev.* for revised, *2nd,* etc.) precedes the publication data:

[3] Sir James Frazer, *The Golden Bough,* abridged ed. (Chicago: Macmillan, 1905), pp. 371–372.

The name of an editor or translator is followed by the abbreviation *ed.* or *trans.:*

[4] Edward Fitzgerald, trans., *The Rubaiyat,* by Omar Khayyam (New York: Crowell, 1923), p. 17.

The following footnote refers to an anthology of articles by numerous authors, but the particular reference here (note the lower case Roman numerals) is to the foreword, written jointly by the three editors of the anthology. The state (or country, if foreign) is included in the publication data for other than major cities.

[5] Morton Fried, Marvin Harris, and Robert Murphy, eds., *War* (Garden City, N.Y.: Natural History Press, 1968), p. xiv.

Articles collected in books are listed by their own authors, their titles being put into italics to show they are part of a whole. One such article from the anthology cited in sample footnote 5, above, would read:

[6] Margaret Mead, "Alternatives to War," *War,* ed. Morton Fried, Marvin Harris, and Robert Murphy (Garden City, N.Y.: Natural History Press, 1968), p. 225.

Articles in encyclopedias are usually signed with initials, which are identified elsewhere in the set. (If not, your note to an encyclopedia article begins with the title.) Since such articles are arranged alphabetically throughout the set, the volume number is unnecessary, but the number of the edition used (of older sets) or the date (more common now) must be given, and the page, if the article covers more than one.

[7] [Rev.] A[rthur] MacD[onald] A[llchin], "Women's Religious Orders," *Encyclopaedia Britannica,* 1970, p. 631.

(The article cited in sample footnote 7 was signed "A.MacD.A." Reference to the list of contributors provided the full name; hence the brackets.)

References to articles in periodicals also begin with the author's name, followed by the title (a part) in quotation marks, and the name of the periodical (the whole) in italics. No place of publication is needed, however, and there are some differences to note in the handling of dates. The simplest is a footnote to a magazine that numbers its pages consecutively throughout a year's issues, as some quarterlies and monthlies do; as date, only the year is needed, between the numbers indicating volume and page.

[8] Marshall Smelser, "The Babe on Balance," *American Scholar,* 44 (1975), 303.

For a monthly that starts numbering anew with each issue, the month must be included (abbreviate those having over four letters):

[9] Fred Hapgood, "Computers Aren't So Smart, After All," *Atlantic,* Aug. 1974, pp. 40–41.

A reference to an article in a biweekly or weekly magazine must give the full date; military style—day preceding month—saves a comma. (No comma is needed after a title that ends with an exclamation point or a question mark.)

[10] Jean Stafford, "Woodman, Spare that Tree!" *Saturday Review/World,* 13 July 1974, p. 15.

Reference to newspapers may require, in addition to the above, the name of the edition, for big city papers, and the section number; even column numbers are a convenience. The *MLA*

*Style Sheet* italicizes the name of the city, in a newspaper title, as has not always been done in ordinary use.

> [11] John Beaufort, "Hope for American Arts?" *Christian Science Monitor,* Eastern ed., 19 Aug. 1974, 2nd sec., p. 14, cols. 5–6.
> [12] "Pugwash Urges World Arms Parley," *New York Times,* City ed., 5 Sept. 1974, p. 37, cols. 5–6.

The *MLA Style Sheet* may be referred to for guidance in more complicated matters of documenting, but an application of common sense to the models above should enable you to figure out clear, consistent, and conventional footnotes for most of the material you are likely to use.

Now we turn to the use of footnotes in a series. Only in the first reference to a source, fortunately, need the note be as complete as those above. Later footnotes need contain only the surname of the author and the page number of the new reference. If no author, a short form of the title is sufficient, and if an article appears on only one page, this need not be repeated. Thus additional references to the book in footnote 3 and the articles in footnotes 11 and 12, above, may appear as

> [13] Frazer, p. 287.
> [14] Beaufort.
> [15] "Pugwash."

Should you be using two authors by the same surname, or two works by the same author, you would need in later references to make an entry full enough to avoid confusion, such as these for footnote 1:

> [16] C. W. Nicol, p. 192.
> [17] Nicol, *From the Roof,* p. 190.

Later references to a work by three or more authors can be shortened by the use of "et al.," an abbreviation for the Latin *et alii,* meaning "and others." It is not italicized. Footnote 5 thus becomes only

> [18] Fried et al., p. iv.

You can see some of these kinds of references in use in the research paper reproduced at the end of this unit.

## The information footnote

Footnotes are also used to add information that the writer wishes to accompany the text but that is not quite important enough to appear in it. Such information may be an explanation of a term that might not be clear to all readers; an additional example or quotation that is of interest but not essential to the text; a reference to a related work; the author's own opinion of a passage; or a humorous anecdote or flippant reflection suggested by the text but not appropriate to the mood of the paper itself. This information may appear alone in a footnote, or it may follow a source footnote as part of it, or it may be followed, in parentheses, by a source note of its own. The following are typical uses:

**A**

Bach was master of the fugue,[5] and his overture follows the French pattern.

[5] A fugue is a musical form in which the main theme is repeated by the different voices of the orchestra, one after another. [Definition]

**B**

In 1066 the invasion of the British Isles by William the Conqueror was preceded by an appearance of Halley's comet.[2]

[2] Patrick Moore, *The Story of Man and the Stars* (New York, 1954), p. 45. This return of the comet is recorded on the famous Bayeux tapestry. [Additional detail]

**C**

Halley's prediction for the return of the comet was correct to within about half a year.[13]

[13] Thomas Chamberlin, *The Two Solar Families* (Chicago, 1928), p. 289. The error was caused by the influences of planets that had not yet been discovered (Moore, p. 49). [Additional information from a source previously listed in full]

## Bibliography

Appended to the text of your research paper will be your final bibliography—an itemized list of all the sources from which you have used material, quoted or summarized, or to which you feel particularly indebted for general information. The material in the bibliographical item is similar to that in the source footnote, with certain changes of arrangement and punctuation. Since the bibliography is alphabetized, the author's name is reversed, last name first. If several works by the same author appear, they are alphabetized among themselves, by title (always omitting *a, an,* and *the* from consideration), and a bar (followed by a period) replaces the author's name.

The source footnotes we have been looking at each read as a single unit terminating in a period. The bibliographical entry, on the contrary, is divided by periods into three main parts: author, title, and publishing data. For an article, the page numbers given will now be all of those occupied by it in the periodical or volume in which it appears.

The standard bibliographical entry for a book has no mention of pages; consequently no parentheses appear around the publishing data. Besides the three normal items, there may be information as to edition or number of volumes; these will appear between the title and the publishing data, and each will be set off by a period.

If an entry occupies more than one line on the page, carry-over lines should be indented several spaces to keep the alphabetized lead words clearly visible. The bibliography that follows includes some of the works referred to in the preceding source footnotes and a few others for illustrative purposes.

Davison, Frank Dalby. *The White Thorntree.* 2 vols. Sydney: Ure Smith, 1970. [No pages in book entry]

Fried, Morton, Marvin Harris, and Robert Murphy, eds. *War.* Garden City, N.Y.: Natural History Press, 1968. [Only the first-named author is reversed, for alphabetizing.]

Greene, Graham. *The Honorary Consul.* New York: Simon and Schuster, 1973.

————. *The Power and the Glory.* Uniform ed. London: Heinemann, 1949. [Also by Greene, above]

Hapgood, Fred. "Computers Aren't So Smart, After All." *Atlantic,* Aug. 1974, pp. 37–45. [Pages of entire article]

"Problems of Atomic Energy." *New York Times,* 4 Mar. 1951, sec. 6, p. 10. [Article occupies this one page only]

A long bibliography is sometimes divided into classes (books and articles, or primary and secondary sources). Follow your instructor's preference here.

## Quotations

In the section on note-taking earlier in this chapter, the matter of taking direct quotations from the works of others was discussed. Now we must look at certain problems in their use in the research paper. First of all, they must of course be scrupulously acknowledged, not just by a footnote but by quotation marks, to show that they are not only the ideas of the original author but his exact words. Ordinarily such quotations can be run into the body of your text with appropriate transitions; but in a long quotation, as you can readily see, the reader may tend to forget the initial quotation marks and feel that he is reading your own work. To avoid this, custom dictates special handling of quotations that occupy more than a few lines in your manuscript: these are set in a block, single spaced, and indented conspicuously from the left side or both sides. Since this position sets them off sharply from your text, no quotation marks are used.

Another problem is that of omitting from a quotation or adding to it. If within a quotation there is a section that is not applicable to the use you are making of the whole, you can leave it out, indicating such an ellipsis, as it is called, with three spaced periods (. . .) known as suspension points (see p. 215). If the omission occurs at the end of a sentence, use four points, to include the final period. If you have a comment of your own that you wish to make within a quotation, this must be enclosed in brackets, never parentheses. Anything enclosed in parentheses is read as part of the original quotation (see **P b, P q**): "At the same season, during the following year (albeit a month later), the King [Henry VIII] was again married."

Apart from these practices, no changes at all may be made in a quotation, even if it contains what appears to be an error in fact or expression. You can, however, absolve yourself from responsibility by placing, after the questionable spot (and within brackets, of course) the word *sic*. Being Latin (meaning "thus"), it should always be italicized: "Columbos [*sic*] discovered America in 1493 [*sic*]."

# SAMPLE LIBRARY RESEARCH PAPER

The Federal Theatre:  Its Aims.

Problems, and Success

Dianne Johnson

Gino Manelli was an actor.  He had never been a great actor, and
he probably never would be.  But he enjoyed his small parts; acting
was the only life he had ever known.  He had been on stage when candles
were still being used for footlights.  With the beginning of the
twentieth century came the moving pictures.  This did not bother Gino
Manelli; he could still manage to find parts.  Then came the Depression.
People no longer had money to come to the theatre.  The businesses of
the financial backers fell with the Depression; there no longer was
money to put into productions.  Gino Manelli was without a job.  He
had gone through periods of unemployment before, but this time was
different.  There were no interviews, no auditions, no parts to hope for.
The government had initiated a Works Progress Administration, but he
had never done manual labor.  Given a shovel, he could only pretend to
know how to use it.  Then there was his pride; not only was he unable
to do manual labor, but he refused to do it.  Gino Manelli was a lost soul.

It was for people like Gino Manelli that the national government
set up the Federal Theatre Project on August 27, 1935.  It was to be
under the jurisdiction of the Works Progress Administration with
national scope and regional and state operation.[1]

The government had two purposes in mind when it organized the
Federal Theatre.  The first, of course, was to give employment to
out-of-work actors and actresses.  Entertainment was a dispensable

[1]"Federal Theatre Project," <u>Encyclopaedia Britannica</u>, 1963, p. 139.

luxury.  When money dwindled, theatregoing dwindled.  Unemployed actors
found that they had no skills for anything other than acting.  They
were not used to or skilled in manual labor, nor would their self-respect
as members of the arts permit them to stoop so low.[2]  The unemployed
actor had only three choices: to go hungry, to beg, borrow, or steal
from friends and relatives; or to turn to "something useful."[3]  The
Federal Theatre would, it was hoped, employ many actors in the work
they desired, rehabilitate them, and develop their skills.[4]

The second purpose was to bring theatrical entertainment and culture
to the thousands of troubled people who before this time had been unable
to afford theatregoing.  Millions of American citizens in the city slums
and in small towns had never been able to enjoy theatrical entertainment.
In fact, the theatre had become an extravagance for most American citizens.[5]
The Federal Theatre, then, was formed, "not because of an art theory,
but because of an economic necessity."[6]

In the early beginnings of the Federal Theatre, its directors set
additional goals for the project.  A theatre requires more components
than actors alone.  Playwrights, technicians, stagehands, directors,
and all the other people so necessary to a theatrical production found
jobs in the Federal Theatre.  The playwrights were given their own
goal to fulfill.  The country needed a change, and the playwrights were

[2] Willson Whitman, _Bread and Circuses_ (New York: Oxford University Press, 1937), p. 10.

[3] Pierre de Rohan, _First Federal Summer Theatre, a Report_ (New York: WPA, 1937), p. 8.

[4] "Federal Theatre Project."

[5] de Rohan, p. 8.

[6] de Rohan, quoting Hallie Flanagan, p. 8.

called upon to write powerful plays with significance for the people.
Through plays, people could be encouraged to think about the various
government programs and shown how their situations could be helped by
these programs.  Hallie Flanagan, director of the Federal Theatre
Project, said,

> Our Federal Theatre, born of an economic need, built by and for
> people who have found terrific privation, cannot content itself
> with easy, pretty or insignificant plays.  We are not being given
> millions of dollars to repeat, however expertly, the type of
> plays which landed 10,000 theatre people on relief rolls.  By
> a stroke of fortune unprecedented in dramatic history, we have
> been given a chance to help change America at a time when twenty
> million unemployed Americans proved it needed changing.  And the
> theatre, when it is any good, can change things.[7]

The theatre could criticize the times, but in doing so it could also
help the government immensely by illustrating the possible values of
its programs.  The Federal Theatre's goal was not to propagandize, but
to encourage the public to think.[8]

The Federal Theatre also had goals for itself.  Its directors
foresaw a permanent national theatre similar to those in Europe.  They
envisioned the Federal Theatre as a theatre in which there could be
experimentation, a place where new ideas could be aired freely.  They
wanted a permanent theatre in which there could be quality plays for
reasonable prices.[9]  The directors hoped for a renaissance of the
theatre industry through the efforts of the Federal Theatre.

[7] de Rohan, p. 36.

[8] Whitman, p. 137.

[9] de Rohan, p. 10.

The aims of the Federal Theatre, then, were to employ out-of-work members of the theatrical profession, to provide culture and entertainment for the depressed people of America, to promote the government programs for the good of the people, and to improve the theatre industry. In realizing these goals, however, the Federal Theatre faced many problems and a great amount of opposition.

The biggest problem of the Federal Theatre was the necessity to care for people who had little dramatic talent but who could show proof that they had been members of the commercial theatrical industry.[10] Being a government relief program, the Federal Theatre was compelled to accept these people, train them the best it could, and find some position for them.

In addition to the training of the untalented, the rehabilitation of the more adept and experienced actors proved to be a problem.[11] Hallie Flanagan describes this situation:

> Here our problem was to build a theatre out of people who were tired and discouraged, people whose morale was broken, people who were, in many cases, angry and bitter, or, what was more difficult, frightened or ashamed. Our immediate necessity was to put these people to work; for the rehabilitation of an artist, like the rehabilitation of anyone else, starts with a job.[12]

Another great problem was finances. Ninety cents out of every government dollar had to go to labor costs, leaving production financing so small that it was almost impossible to put on the lavish productions

---

[10] Whitman, p. 138.

[11] de Rohan, p. 8.

[12] de Rohan, p. 12.

which the professional people were used to.[13]   Royalties, traveling
costs, legal finances, playbills, and other common expenses of a theatre
had to be paid for from the remaining ten percent.  The directors
solved this problem, in part, by seeking support from various foundations,
such as the Rockefeller Foundation, and from corporations.[14]

The continuous turnover of the many talented people presented a
need for constant revamping of the theatre organization.  As soon as
adept but unemployed actors were given a chance in Federal Theatre
plays, the commercial theatre grabbed them up again.[15]   Actually, this
was fulfilling one of the goals of the Federal Theatre - that of stimulating
employment.  However, the government had to pay for these gains of the
commercial theatre.[16]   This drawing away of the best people became a
great concern to the Federal Theatre.  Indeed, it was difficult to
continue developing a company "if its best members were continually
going off to other jobs, were even expected to do so, and were not
encouraged to remain by any assurance that the work would be continued
past the next appropriation date."[17]   This was a problem that could
not be solved; it could only be tolerated.

The great number of less talented actors far exceeded the number
of jobs available.  To cope with this problem, Hallie Flanagan
introduced the idea of "The Living Newspaper."[18]   This, in essence,

---

[13]de Rohan, p. 8.

[14]de Rohan, Federal Theatre Plays, Triple-A Plowed Under (New York: Random House, 1950), p. vii.

[15]Whitman, p. 137.

[16]Whitman, p. 139.

[17]Whitman, p. 148.

[18]de Rohan, Federal Theatre Plays, p. vii.

was a dramatization of the news and events occurring in the world.

The national government reserved the right to censor the plays, since the Federal Theatre was under its jurisdiction.  It exercised this right for the first time on a "Living Newspaper" production on Ethiopia.[19]  It objected to the stage representation of heads of foreign powers, fearing especially that the dictators would take offense.[20]  The federal government kept a close watch on these productions.

Along with national censorship, there was the problem of local censorship.  Many local authorities shut down plays given by Negro companies.  In Illinois, Paul Green's Hymn to the Rising Sun, performed by a Negro company, was called off by the state WPA director for what he felt to be his "country's good."[21]  The play had previously been given in New York and had been well received.[22]

Obscenity was another complaint heard from the local authorities, especially in the New England states.[23]  Maxwell Anderson's play Valley Forge was banned in Boston as "offensive, profane, and ribald."[24]  Although it was defended by several Boston ministers, the director of the Veterans' Bureau, and the American Legion commander, the play remained closed.[25]

[19] Whitman, p. 94.

[20] Whitman, p. 96.

[21] Whitman, p. 97.

[22] Whitman, p. 95.

[23] Whitman, pp. 97-98.

[24] Whitman, p. 98.

[25] Whitman, p. 96.

One of the greatest criticisms of the Federal Theatre arose from its
presentation of new ideas in social and economic fields (especially in
"The Living Newspaper").[26]    There were many cries of "Red" and "Communist"
in the later years of the Theatre.  The Hearst papers referred to the
play It Can't Happen Here as a "venomed libel upon the D.A.R., the
American Legion, Rotary International and all the non-radical movements
which are on the blacklist of American Communism."[27]    This constant
criticism eventually led to the termination of the Federal Theatre
Project.  On June 30, 1939, in spite of support from leading theatre
people in New York and Hollywood, the Federal Theatre was ended by
the House of Representatives subcommittee on appropriations, mainly
because of the many charges of Communistic tendencies.[28]

The Federal Theatre Project, however, had well fulfilled its goals.
By October, 1938, 2,600 members were again engaged in private employment.[29]
About 25,000,000 people had seen Federal Theatre productions, an
estimated 65 percent of whom had never seen a play before.[30]    The Federal
Theatre had produced many excellent plays and new talent.  It had greatly
aided the government in communicating its ideas to the American people.
Although the Federal Theatre had not lived forever, it had died proudly,
having accomplished its chief purpose - helping the Gino Manellis through
the lean years of the Great Depression.

[26] Whitman, p. 100.

[27] Whitman, p. 97.

[28]"Federal Theatre Project."

[29]"Federal Theatre Project."

[30]"Federal Theatre Project."

BIBLIOGRAPHY

Books and Plays

Clugston, Katherine.  Barnum Returns.  Mimeographed.

New York: Federal Theatre Project, 1936.

de Rohan, Pierre, ed. Federal Theatre Plays, Triple-A

Ploughed Under.  New York: Random House, 1950.

"Federal Theatre Project."  Encyclopaedia Britannica, 1963,

p. 139.

Gagey, Edmond M.  The San Francisco Stage, a History.

New York: Columbia University Press, 1937.

Whitman, Willson.  Bread and Circuses.  New York: Oxford

University Press, 1937.

Whittler, Clarence J.  Some Social Trends in WPA Drama.

Washington, D.C.: Catholic University of America, 1939.

Bulletins and Reports

Bulletin of the Federal Theatre.  New York: WPA, 1935-1937.

de Rohan, Pierre.  First Federal Summer Theatre, a Report.

Multilithed.  New York: WPA, 1937.

## QUESTIONS ON SAMPLE LIBRARY RESEARCH PAPER

**1.** Do you think Gino Manelli (described in paragraph 1) is a real person or a made-up example? What purpose does his presence serve? What is the point of returning to him in the final line of the paper?

**2.** Footnote 4 needs only title, since the full information has already appeared in footnote 1, and the article is complete on one page. Footnotes 5–13 require only surnames of authors and page numbers, having appeared fully in footnotes 2 and 3. But footnote 14, being a second work by an author, has to appear in full, and from then on (see footnote 18), a reference to either must include a short form of its title.

**3.** Study the rest of these footnotes, explaining what each means.

### EXERCISES

**1.** The whole field of human knowledge is open to you when you choose a subject for a library research paper, but you need to remember that you can manage only a very small phase of a tiny section of it. Your instructor may help you in choosing a topic that can be handled adequately in the time he allots and the length of paper he suggests, and that will give you maximum experience in the use of your library's resources. The following are but a hint of the kinds of suitable topics that you can find in various fields: history—the Gulf of Tonkin incident; religion—Zen; exploration—the ocean depths; art—Andy Warhol; literature—James Baldwin; language— an American dialect; music—Rod McKuen; natural history— the ivory-billed woodpecker; comics—"Peanuts"; economics —solar heating; aviation—the SST; space—flying saucers; anthropology—the African Bushman. In fact, about the only types of subject to be avoided are the overly technical, which cannot well be made intelligible to the general reader, and the purely biographical, which too often become little more than digests of existing studies. (But a person may be studied in terms of his accomplishments as an author, artist, scientist, diplomat.)

**2.**   Having chosen your subject, proceed step by step with your bibliography building, reading and note-taking, organizing and outlining, and writing and documenting, following carefully the directions given in this chapter and by your instructor. Remember that your purpose in this project is not only to complete your paper with a minimum of waste motion and a maximum of success, but also to develop research habits which will stand you in good stead when you later do other and longer pieces of research to satisfy course or degree requirements or to submit to an employer or a publisher.

# 10
# HANDLING THE BUSINESS LETTER

Any firm doing business with the public by mail can testify to the confusion and delay caused by the carelessness or ignorance of its customers. Since you will be a rare person indeed if in the course of your life you find no occasion to write a business letter, you owe it to yourself to become familiar with the accepted forms and practices of business correspondence and to make their use a fixed habit.

Should you decide to make business a career, you will find books and courses devoted entirely to the subject of business English, which treats of all manner of commercial problems. Here we shall disregard all types of communication between businesses and from firm to customer, taking up only those kinds of business letters which you as a layman are most likely to be called on to write, along with such matters of letter form and business practice as you will need in the writing.

Such forms and practices have become very highly conventionalized. Liberties, of course, may be taken to obtain special effects; you may find a sales letter beginning, for instance, with an attention-getting "Good Morning!" instead of the customary "Dear Mr. Evans." But the following procedures have come to constitute standard business practice, and within their limits you can work with confidence in your correctness.

## BUSINESS LETTER PRACTICE
(Exercise 4, p. 288)

### What to write with
Type your letter, if possible, making a carbon copy for your own records. If not, write neatly and legibly by hand; a ball-point will also make a good carbon. Never use a pencil.

### What to write on
The preferred stationery for general business use is a good grade of white typing paper (8½ x 11 inches). It should always be unruled (use a ruled guide beneath it, if necessary, to keep your handwritten lines reasonably straight).

### How to arrange the business letter
Try to arrange your letter on the page so that it will look like a well-framed picture. The width of your margins may vary in order to make different letter lengths appear to best advantage, but keep all four approximately equal (from one to two inches); the left side and bottom may, if anything, be rather wider than the right and top. Hyphenate long words at the ends of lines to keep the right margin reasonably straight (check with the dictionary, if necessary, to be sure you have divided them at the accepted places). Single spacing, with double spacing between paragraphs, is the usual practice, but double spacing will help to plump out a brief message. Only an experienced stenographer can judge accurately in advance the space a letter will occupy, but with a little care you can avoid an unnecessarily clumsy arrangement.

Even for long letters likely to occupy more than a page, do not reduce your margins to less than an inch on all sides. Arrange to have at least three lines of letter text on your last page; and at the top of each page after the first, put a page number and repeat the addressee's name and the date:

Sears, Roebuck and Co.        2        September 20, 1975

Never write on the back of a sheet.

### How to send it

Your envelope should match your paper in quality and finish as well as color. For the usual one-page letter, the small commercial size (3⅝ x 6½ inches) is adequate. Fold the letter into six sections as follows:

1.   Bring the bottom up to within a half inch of the top, creasing the fold neatly.
2.   Then fold the right side slightly less than a third of the way across, and crease.
3.   Now fold the left side to within a half inch of the folded right edge, and again make a crease, an edge that will go first into the envelope.

This procedure will not only make the letter fit the envelope but will permit it to be slipped in without catching on the sealed flaps. Further, the recipient who slits the top flap of the envelope will be able to withdraw the letter and flip it open easily.

For letters of more than one sheet or with bulky enclosures, the large legal size of envelope (4⅛ x 9½ inches) will better serve. Lay the sheets in order, then fold into three sections as follows:

1.   Bring the bottom up to about a third of the way from the top, and crease.
2.   Then fold the top down to within a half inch of the creased edge, and crease again.

With the top flap toward you, opening to your right, the letter will again slip into the envelope easily and pull out conveniently.

### BUSINESS LETTER FORM

(Exercises 1–3, 5, pp. 287–288)

The form required by custom in writing a business letter is composed of five essential parts besides the message itself: the heading, the inside address, and the salutation, which precede the message, and the complimentary close and the signature, which end it. As you study the requirements for each part, refer to the model letters on pages 272–274 for illustrations of their use.

The **heading** includes your address and the date on which you are writing; these customarily occupy three lines. Business firms, of course, use stationery on which their letterhead, including their name and address, is already printed. You yourself may have stationery on which your name and address appear; if so, you will need to supply only the date.

The **inside address** contains the name and address of the person or firm to whom you are writing, just as it will appear on the envelope. The address must include the zip code number (if this is unknown, look it up in a directory, if you have one, or inquire at any post office); this number should follow the state name, after a blank space, with no punctuation. The inside address, we might note, is the only part of the business letter form that isn't shared with the social letter; its use is essentially a matter of office procedure for convenience in addressing and filing, but it has become a convention required of all business correspondence.

The **salutation** consists of the words with which you greet the firm or person to whom you are writing. These have been conventionalized into a few set phrases.

Gentlemen: (the standard salutation for a firm)
Ladies: (only if it is known to be run by women)
Dear Sir:
Dear Madam: }(for unknown individuals)
Dear Mr. Doe:
Dear Ms. (Mrs., Miss) Doe: }    (if addressee's name is known)

"My dear Mr. Doe," regarded as more formal, is rarely used, as are "Dear Sirs" and "Mesdames." Note that the first word and all nouns in the salutation are capitalized and that a colon follows. (The comma, which is used after the salutation of a social letter, is the only difference in punctuation between the two types of correspondence.)

The **complimentary close** is the "goodby" of the business letter, the words by which you take your leave. Like the salutation, the close has become conventionalized into a few accepted phrases, of which the following are most frequently used:

Very truly yours, Yours very truly, Yours truly,
Sincerely yours, Yours sincerely, Yours very sincerely, Sincerely,
Cordially yours, Yours cordially, Cordially,

The first group is very impersonal, the second more friendly, the third the warmest. Words like *faithfully* and *respectfully* have gone out of general business use, along with the somewhat subservient attitude they suggest. Choose a close that is appropriate to your salutation and the spirit of your letter, capitalize the first word only, and put a comma after it.

The **signature** should immediately follow the complimentary close. Sign your name as you are in the habit of writing it, and be sure that it can be read. Don't pride yourself on one of those highly distinctive signatures that look more like a meaningless drawing than a succession of letters (experts say they are more easily forged than a decipherable one). If you type your letter, type your name also, below your signature, to make certain of its legibility. If you are writing in any official capacity, your title should appear below your name.

As to social titles, a man never signs himself "Mr.," since that title is taken for granted. Similarly, a woman will not include "Ms." as part of her signature. She may, however, include "Miss" or "Mrs." if she wishes to indicate her marital status. Those titles are not part of a legal signature, however, and should not be written as such, but in parentheses.

**An unmarried woman:**  (Miss) Jane Brown
**A married woman:**  Jane Brown
  (Mrs. Charles R. Brown)

Several minor items sometimes needed in a business letter should be mentioned. One is an attention note ("Attention Mr. Robert Cole"), which may be placed between the inside address and the salutation (following and followed by a blank line) if a letter written to a company should come to one person in the firm. (Note that the salutation should always agree with the inside address, however.) Another is the initials usually present at the left margin and just below the typed signature ("JRM/af"); since these indicate dictator and typist, you won't need them in writing your own letters, and if you have a secretary, all of this will be taken care of for you. Under these, the abbreviation "Encl." will indicate any enclosure, and a number after it will indicate how many, if more than one. In the same position or beneath it, the note "cc: Professor John Nesbitt" will indicate the person to whom a carbon copy of the letter is being sent.

## BUSINESS LETTER STYLE

### Arrangement
In the discussion of the parts of business letter form, above, no mention was made of their positions on the page, for the reason that several different styles are in use. We shall now look in detail at the placing of parts in the three most common.

### Full Block
When at the beginning of this century the typewriter came into common use in business offices, it revolutionized the style of the business letter through the ease with which common margins could be maintained by the typist. Carried to the extreme, this fact has led to the use of the full block style, in which every line of every part of the letter form (and the letter) begins at the left margin. Arranging a letter according to this style, then, is a simple matter of placing the parts of the letter form one after another, in the order in which we have just discussed them, with appropriate spacing between. (See Model Letter A on p. 272.) Nothing could be simpler; yet this style has

not yet become very popular, presumably because, being so "side-heavy" to the left, it lacks the balanced appearance that we are accustomed to.

### Modified Block

This style you will find, if you examine the business letters you receive, is currently the most popular. You may wish to adopt it as your own and familiarize yourself with it thoroughly. In it (as you can see in Model Letter B on p. 273):

1. The heading is placed as far up in the right corner as is required for a good arrangement of your letter length, and just far enough to the left to insure that its longest line will end at whatever right margin you intend to maintain. The date always follows the address. (Should you be using stationery on which your address is already printed, the date may, if you prefer, be centered on the page.)
2. The inside address is placed several blank lines below the date but across at the left margin, as in full block style.
3. The salutation is also placed at the left margin, following a blank line after the inside address. (After another blank line, the letter itself begins.)
4. The complimentary close is begun at the middle of the page, following a blank space after the end of the letter.
5. The name of the writer, if typed, begins under the complimentary close, but with several blank lines between to accommodate the written signature.

In this style you may choose to indent the opening lines of your paragraphs the usual five spaces, but they too are more frequently run to the left margin now. A blank line is left between paragraphs, in either practice. If you double space a short typed letter to make it take up more room, always indent your paragraphs for clarity. (But always single space the heading and the inside address, regardless.) You can also improve the appearance of a short letter by leaving more than the usual space between the heading and the inside address, and between the letter and the complimentary close (*not* between the inside address and the salutation, nor the salutation and the letter).

### Indented

The indented style is an old one, having preceded the typewriter, but it is still used occasionally. Some feel its age lends dignity; others find it preferable when writing by hand, as handwriting does not maintain the neatly blocked margins that typewriting does. In this style the parts are placed on the page as in the modified block style, but successive lines are arranged diagonally by indenting them several letter spaces beyond the preceding (see model letter on p. 274). Your return on the envelope should always be blocked.

### Punctuation

Two types of punctuation, **open** and **closed,** may be used in the business letter; the open is now overwhelmingly more popular. In this (as you can see in the model letters showing the full block and the modified block styles), no punctuation is used after the lines in the parts of the business letter form except, as noted earlier, a colon after the salutation and a comma after the complimentary close. Internal punctuation is of course used as needed: a comma between the city and the state, for instance, and between the day and the year (unless the date is written military style: "12 December 1974").

Closed punctuation is seldom used now, and when it is, it is likely to appear with the indented letter style, since both carry an aura of old times. (Either can be used independently, however.) It is illustrated here in the model of the indented style, less that you are likely to use it than that you will understand what it is when you see it. Closed punctuation requires punctuation after every line in every part of the letter form: periods after final lines in the heading and the inside address and sometimes even the signature, and commas after those that precede them. It is easy to see why, in an age that for efficiency has turned to the block forms, these superfluous marks have generally disappeared.

### Abbreviations

Use the abbreviations *Mr., Mrs.,* and *Ms.;* these are never written out. Also abbreviate before a name the title *Dr.,* and after a name, following a comma, *Jr., Sr.,* and degrees such as *M.D., Ph.D.* Abbreviate given names to initials only if the persons so sign themselves (J. Robert Dent, George R. LaRue, H. P. Kelsey), and words in the names of firms only if they do so (Harper & Row, Klipsch and Associates, Inc., New England Realty Co.). In addresses, follow custom: St. Louis (but Fort Wayne), 1070 Massachusetts Avenue, N.W. (designating a section of a city), Washington, D.C., U.S.A. But do not, preferably, abbreviate the names of states nor, in the date line, of months. Such shortenings are generally frowned on, the slight saving of time being insufficient to offset the appearance of haste or laziness and the sacrifice of custom and dignity accompanying their use.

### Envelope

If your envelope is not printed, block your name and address in the upper left corner, single spaced. Then copy the inside address (complete with name), in the lower right quarter of the envelope face, also single spaced. (The use of the two-letter official zip code abbreviations for states may now be used in this mailing address. See Appendix, p. 317.) Any special directions such as an attention note, "Personal," or "Please Forward" should be placed in the lower left corner. Attach the stamp well within the upper right corner; it will look better and be less likely to be torn off than if allowed to hang over the edges.

### Model letters

On the following pages are three typical business letters, two typed, the third hand-written. Study carefully the form and style—parts, arrangement, and punctuation—of each. The contents of the letters we shall look at in the next section.

March 17, 1975

3240 Lincoln Avenue
Syracuse, New York    13202

Icelandic Airlines
630 Fifth Avenue
New York, New York    10020

Gentlemen:

I have just read with great interest your advertisement about Iceland in the April issue of
Southern Living.  As a result I am writing to
you rather than filling out the coupon you provided, in the hope of getting more than routine
information.

First, I shall shortly be studying about Iceland
in a college geography course, and would therefore
like to have any literature that you can send me
about the country, including if possible a list
of books that you can particularly recommend.

Next, a friend of mine and I are considering a
hiking trip through Iceland at the earliest opportunity.  Can you advise me as to what months in
the year it would be feasible to camp, on such a
trip, and what kind of accommodations we could
expect to find in the back country, at roughly
what price?  If not, perhaps you can refer me to
some other source.  Thank you for your trouble.

Very sincerely,

*Herbert I. Roudebush*

Herbert I. Roudebush

**Model Letter A:** Inquiry. *Full block style, open punctuation*

Greenbrier Apartments #20
1563 S. Congress Street
Ypsilanti, Michigan    48197
23 October, 1974

Mr. Kenneth Ward, Manager
The Ken 'n' John Printing Company
520 Delsey Boulevard
Fort Wayne, Indiana    46801

Dear Mr. Ward:

I have just received the 500 sheets of printed personal stationery that I ordered from you on October
10, and am sorry to have to report that they are not
satisfactory.

If you will check my original order, you will find
that my name and address are clearly and correctly
typed there.  Your printer, however, as you will note
from the enclosed sheet, made an error in spelling my
last name, from Schumacher to Schumacker.

I hope that you can get a corrected order to me promptly.
If you wish the whole misspelled order returned to you,
in addition to the sheet I am sending as evidence, please
let me know.

Sincerely yours,

*Mary Jane Schumacher*
Mary Jane Schumacher

Encl.

**Model Letter B:** Complaint. *Modified block style, open punctuation*

Route 66, Box 74,
Huron, South Dakota 57350,
November 17, 1974.

Shoe Importers, Inc.,
10 Confederate Avenue,
Savannah, Georgia.

Gentlemen:

Please send me one pair of Belgian loafers, #2952, color wine, as advertised in your recent flyer for $18.00. My usual size is 7½ AAA, but at your suggestion I am sending a pencilled outline of my feet to insure a correct fit.

I enclose my personal check for $18.75 to cover price plus postage.

Yours truly,
Harriet McCloud

Encl. (2)

**Model Letter C:** Order. *Indented style, closed punctuation*

## BUSINESS ENGLISH

"Business English" is not a new and different kind of expression; it is concerned no more and no less with clearness and correctness than is all your other writing. But, being of a very practical nature with the aim of getting something done rather than of merely informing or entertaining, the English of business tends to be simpler and more direct. The most easily discernible difference between it and "literary" English is its use of shorter paragraphs, even shorter words—a conciseness designed less to charm than to be readily understood. There is little room in most business correspondence for plays upon words or other delightful but time-taking rhetorical devices; your business letter should say what it has to say as clearly and as briefly as is consistent with expressing all the necessary facts graciously and effectively.

Two tendencies distinguish modern business correspondence from that of an earlier day. One is its adoption of a more personal and friendly manner. Once, the businessman was regarded—and regarded himself—as a kind of vassal, a necessary but inferior creature who humbly begged, and was grateful for, small favors. This attitude led to such salutations as "Respected Sir" and to such closes as "Your humble and obedient servant." The modern businessman is an equal in enterprise who offers rather than begs, and his improved status is reflected in the natural, even conversational, style of his letter writing.

The other modern trend is a sharp turn away from the great formality of the past, a formality which once reduced the business letter to little more than a series of elaborate set expressions. As a publisher devoted to better business letters put it:

Most correspondents simply mimic the style of the person who preceded them. And their predecessors mimicked the style of the fellow before them.

If we're not careful, the standard terminology of business letters can be pretty silly. Used thoughtlessly, it can be downright insulting. Here are some common expressions— with the possible reactions of a modern reader:

*I have before me your letter* . . . . . . Okay, answer it!
*In due course of time* . . . . . . After the usual boondoggling.
*I wish to state* . . . . . . Why wish? Just say it!
*We are this day in receipt of* . . . . . . By George, they got it!
*Kindly advise the undersigned* . . . . . . Who's writing
   this letter, anyhow?
*Please accept our order* . . . . . . Any time!
*Thank you for your patronage* . . . . . . Patrons went out
   of style a century ago.

Such time-wasting patterns have now been ruled out in favor of a direct and sincere reply, simply and freshly worded to suit the particular circumstances that call for it. Participial beginnings such as "Replying to your letter of March 6," and endings that glide into the complimentary close ("Hoping to hear from you soon, we remain") are now taboo, largely because they recall unpleasantly the day of stereotyped business phrases.

The modern demand for simplicity sometimes goes to an undesirable extreme known as the telegraphic style, however, in which the writer lops off words as though they were costing him so much each.

Received your letter. Adjustment suggested is satisfactory. Will return goods at once and await immediate refund.

Make your business English the language of natural speech; but remember that the complete sentence is usually desirable, even in speaking.

## TYPES OF BUSINESS LETTERS
(Exercise 6, pp. 288–289)

### The inquiry
See Model Letter A, p. 272.
You will frequently need to write to a business firm to ask for information, prices, catalogs, types of accommodations. Beyond following the matters of form already discussed, your letter should observe three requirements.

### 1. Be explicit.

Be sure that your request is clear, and that you have included enough details to make a definite reply possible. A letter to a hotel asking if it has rooms available is aimless unless you include the date; one inquiring about rates is equally time-wasting unless you mention the size of your party and the type of accommodations desired. Make your inquiry so clear that the reply can be an answer instead of a request for more specific information, with consequent additional correspondence and delay.

### 2. Be brief.

Include all necessary details, but none that are beside the point. A request for information about a company's procedures will appropriately include the use to which you plan to put it, but an inquiry about tickets for the theater need not include your reasons for wishing to see the play.

### 3. Be courteous.

Even though your inquiry will likely lead to business which the firm will be only too glad to get, you should remember that, at the moment, you are asking a favor. "Send me your catalog" will doubtless get results, but a more gracious wording is to be preferred; although servility in business correspondence is a thing of the past, *please* and *thank you* are still welcome grease in the gears. Avoid, however, the hackneyed "Thanking you in advance." Should your inquiry ask for information or material that will benefit you alone (except for the good will the company may win by supplying it), the need for courtesy is of course sharply increased.

### The order

See Model Letter C, p. 274.

The habit of buying goods by mail has been firmly established during the last couple of generations through the rise of the great mail-order houses, whose care in building up public confidence has led to a tremendous increase in all sorts of sight-unseen buying. Many firms provide their customers with order blanks on which spaces are carefully provided for all the information required in this type of business communication. Lacking such, you will need to write a letter in which you are careful to include three kinds of information:

1. The exact description of the article desired: quantity, catalog number (if known), size, color, and price.
2. The method of shipment: parcel post, express, freight, air; the "fastest" or the "cheapest" way; special delivery; prepaid or collect.
3. The arrangement for payment: C.O.D.; cash, stamps, check, draft, or money order enclosed; charged to account or credit card.

The words *immediately, promptly,* and *at once* appended to the shipping directions in order letters are so generally used as to be almost useless. However, if you must have the goods by a certain date, or if for any reason you want shipment postponed until a specified time, an explanation of the circumstances, accompanied by the exact date, will usually secure for your order the special attention it requires.

### The complaint
See Model Letter B, p. 273.

Business transactions frequently produce difficulties that require correction. Goods fail to arrive, they are damaged in transit, the wrong thing has been sent or the right one proves unsatisfactory—such situations call for the letter of complaint. In this type of correspondence not only is courtesy a pleasing grace but it pays, for, as the old saying goes, more flies are caught with honey than with vinegar. To the business firm the "customer is always right"—particularly if he is reasonable as well.

### 1. Be sure that your cause for complaint really exists.
Better to wait a day or two, for instance, than to send a complaint of nonarrival which is likely to cross the shipment. You may find yourself too close for comfort to the situation of the

old farmer in the anecdote who sent a thundering letter complaining of a delay, to which he had to add: "P.S. The mailman just now brought the stuff."

### 2. Be equally sure that your complaint is just.

Check your order to make sure that you wrote the size correctly, before you assign the blame for the failure of the shoe to fit.

### 3. When you are certain that something for which you are not responsible is amiss, write your complaint, being both courteous and reasonable.

Be exact and clear in recounting the cause for your dissatisfaction, and suggest what you regard as a suitable adjustment.

Someone has observed that the wise man will handle every unpleasant situation in terms of the results he wishes rather than of the immediate emotion that he is tempted to express. This observation certainly has a particular truth for the writer of the letter of complaint.

### The application

See Sample Letters A–C, pp. 283–286.

Unless you are one of those fortunate individuals who have jobs waiting for them the minute they get out of college, you will probably start writing application letters very seriously in the last term of your final year or sooner. Perhaps you have already written them for summer work; you may have occasion to write them again, later in your career.

Since such a letter is likely to mean your very bread and butter, it is probably the most important business type that you will ever be called on to write. Courtesy and clearness are sufficient graces for the letter of inquiry, the order, the complaint; but to these virtues the application must add appeal. It is well to think of the letter of application for what it is—a sales letter—and to remember that individuals, like businesses, do not get very far in the face of modern competition without some knowledge of the psychology of salesmanship.

HANDLING THE BUSINESS LETTER

### 1. Do not be diffident.

The door-to-door salesman who used to go up to house-wives saying, "You don't want to buy some magazines, do you?" may have got a few orders out of pity, but he didn't get rich. Never begin with such expressions as "I don't know whether I would succeed in this position or not," or "I have never had any experience in your type of work." In applying for a job, it is not enough to put your best foot foremost; keep the other one safely out of sight.

### 2. Do not be boastful.

A statement like "I have always been a supersalesman ever since I was a child," or "I have always outranked every other student in my class" may be perfectly true, but it is likely to antagonize. Leave such information for others to supply in the letters of recommendation they write for you.

### 3. Never sound superior to the work for which you are applying.

No employer was ever won by such remarks as "I am willing to work for you until I can find a place that suits me better," "My previous experience has been with bigger firms than yours," or "I should not be looking for a job except for recent financial reverses in my family."

### 4. State honestly but modestly the actual achievements that may fit you for the job, but do not include irrelevant items from your past.

Remarks that may be entirely justified in one application may be mere boasting in another. "All through high school I spent my spare time caring for the neighbors' children" might be relevant information in an application for work in a nursery school, but hardly for a stenographic position. "In college I was elected the most popular man in my class" might be fit and useful information if you are asking for work in a sales organization, but inappropriate boasting if you are applying for work as a laboratory technician.

**280**

**5. Remember that a prospective employer is more interested in what you can do for him than in what he can do for you.**

This is so even in this age of social conscience. "Because of my lifelong interest in and study of aviation, I believe that I can make myself useful to the X Airline" is a more ingratiating remark than "I want to work for you because my girlfriend lives in X-ville," or "because I like your retirement plan."

**6. Use every legitimate means at your disposal to make your letter stand out favorably from others.**

It may reasonably be one among dozens or even hundreds received from qualified persons. But do not mistake mere freakishness for individuality. The application letter is an essentially serious and dignified performance, not lending itself readily to the extreme devices often employed in other types of sales letters.

The material included in your letter of application will normally fall into five main sections: introduction, personal data, qualifications, list of references, and conclusion.

### Introduction

How you begin your letter will depend on the kind of circumstance that called it forth.

1. If you are answering an advertisement, you will of course begin with a reference to that fact.
2. If you have learned indirectly of an opening, you will probably mention the name of the agency or the friend who informed you.
3. If you have no knowledge of a particular opening but are sending out a number of letters to employers for whom you think you would like to work, you may begin with some mention of the reasons which have induced you to apply to this one in particular.

### Personal Data
You will include a list of objective facts about yourself as an individual, apart from any qualifications you may have for the job. This may include your age, height, weight, health, sex, marital status, and if pertinent, your religion, nationality, race.

### Qualifications
Most important is a statement of the qualifications that fit you for the job applied for: your education, experience, inclination, aptitude.

### References
List the names, official positions, and addresses of the people whom you have chosen as best qualified to speak for you as to both character and ability for the kind of position for which you are applying. (And don't forget to ask their permission in advance, and to thank them later for writing in your behalf.)

### Conclusion
Like every good sales letter, the application should end with some effort to induce action: a request for an interview; mention of an enclosed stamped, addressed envelope; an expressed hope for an early and favorable reply.

Which of these many items to stress and which to omit will depend, of course, on the nature of the work for which you are applying. Religion would be a more important issue in getting a teaching position in a church-supported school, for instance, than a business job. Experience will play the major role in the application of a person already well-established in his profession; education (with specific reference to relevant courses) and recommendations will be the chief stock-in-trade of most college students.

### Data sheet
If the material that you find necessary or wise to include in a letter of application will involve a long letter—more than a page—it is a good practice to shift the *objective,* or factual, in-

formation (personal data, qualifications, references) to a separate unit called the résumé or data sheet. Here it can be arranged neatly and clearly, under suitable headings and subheadings easy for the prospective employer to consult and file if he is interested, or to avoid the trouble of reading if he is not.

The greatest advantage of the use of the data sheet is that the application letter itself is thus not only shortened and made more readable but freed to concentrate on the more important task of making your personal appeal. In it you will present your *subjective* material: an account of your interest in the job, your general aptitude and inclination for it, and the hopes you have for accomplishment in the field. Remembering that the letter of application is first of all a sales letter, you will recognize the importance of these remaining items and of the impression they will make on the reader, who will read not only the lines but between the lines, and who may be more impressed—favorably or not—by what he thus discovers of you as an individual than by all the facts ascertainable through the data sheet.

In the sample data sheet on pp. 286–287, the most important items are placed first, to catch the reader's eye: the present address, the most significant activity, the major reference. For the same reason the items under "Education" and "Experience" read chronologically but from bottom to top.

Sample Letter A: Answering an Advertisement

### THE ADVERTISEMENT

Wanted: capable, experienced young men to work as counsellors at large boys' camp, July–Aug. Write Box 192, *Wolverine Recorder.*

### THE LETTER

I have just noticed in the May 21 issue of our college paper, the *Wolverine Recorder,* your advertisement for camp counsellors for the upcoming summer sessions, and I would like very much to be considered for one of these positions.

My age is 18, my height 5'10", and my weight 145 pounds. I have had no previous counselling experience, but I have been a camper myself, for a couple of sessions, so that I understand something of the problems involved. I am good with boys, having been a boy scout for several years and having helped my uncle, a scoutmaster in my home town of Harwood, at odd times since.

I have always been fond of the outdoors, and am experienced in several activities and sports, notably swimming, canoeing, and tennis. I also sing (mostly country music) and play the guitar passably, for simple accompaniments.

My first year at Wolverine College, where I am majoring in Physical Education, will end this week. Mr. James Reuther, head of that department (phone Wolverine 293-9668) has offered to speak for me, if you find that you can consider me for a position.

I shall of course greatly appreciate a personal interview, at your convenience.

Sample Letter B: About a Known Opening (to a Doctor)

I have learned through a friend of mine, Miss Amy Beutell, a registered nurse who once worked with you, that there may be an opening in your office about the first of the year for a licensed practical nurse. As I expect to be available at that time, I am writing to ask you to consider me for the position.

I am twenty years old, and have just completed at Murdock Community College (which, as you perhaps know, has recently been accredited by the Southern Association of Colleges and Schools) the four quarters of work prescribed for those wishing to become licensed practical nurses. My record in both its study courses and its clinics has been very good throughout, and I have every expectation of passing the State Licensing Examination when it is given in November, after which I shall be officially qualified as an LPN.

I have enjoyed every aspect of the medical work that I have been exposed to this past year, but as I also enjoy meeting people, I feel that I shall be more effective in a large medical office such as yours than in private duty.

In addition to the usual minor medical skills included in my recent training, I type well, having taken a business course in high school; and as I worked as a receptionist at the Latrobe Clinic for a year before I took my training, I am experienced at answering telephones, making appointments, keeping records, and filling out claim forms.

As to my personal qualifications, feel free to consult the following:

Miss Amy Beutell, R. N.
Beaufort Hospital
Danvers, Virginia 24329

Mrs. Elaine Burgess, Director
Health Department
Murdock, N.C. 27851

Dr. James Morgan, M.D.
Latrobe Clinic
Murdock, N.C. 27851

I shall be very happy to come to your office for an interview at your convenience.

Sample Letter C: In Hope of an Opening (to an Editor)

If you have an opening on your editorial staff for a young reporter, or expect to have one shortly, I should be very happy to be considered. I enclose a data sheet detailing my qualifications.

As for my motivation, let me say that ever since I first worked on our high school paper at Evansburg and discovered my deep interest in people and events, I have wanted to make journalism my career. I did not choose a college where I could major in journalism, however, as I felt that it was more important to get the broadest possible background in nontechnical subjects. Therefore, I attended a liberal arts college where, as you will see from my data sheet, I took a broad assortment of work in various departments, in addition to my major (English) and my minor (history): courses such as political science, economics, and anthropology, for background. I am also an avid reader.

Throughout my four years at Higdon, I worked on the staff of the *Gimlet,* our college paper, becoming one of its co-editors during my senior year. I also reported college news for the nearby *Langsberg Post* for two years, and have been working for it full time since my graduation in June. I might add that I am an able typist, as I took a course in typing while I was still in high school and have used the skill steadily ever since.

My reason for applying to you (and to you alone, at this time) is that I have long admired the policies and the reputation of the *Journal,* and would like nothing better than an opportunity to make my real start in journalism as a "cub" on your staff. May I see you personally?

Data Sheet to Accompany Sample Letter C

PERSONAL
Name: James Prosser Waldron, Jr.
Present address: Julian Apartments, Langsberg, Pa. 19239
Home address: 206 S. Bogard St., Evansburg, N.J. 07729
Age: 22          Height: 6'1"
Sex: male        Weight: 160 lbs.
Health: excellent     Marital status: single

EDUCATION
Higdon College, Langsberg, Pa. Graduated June 1975 with
    honors
Major: English language and literature
Minor: history
Special courses: political science, economics, anthropology,
    sociology, philosophy, geography

Evansburg High School, Evansburg, N.J. Graduated vale-
dictorian June, 1971

ACTIVITIES
Higdon College debate team, 3 years
Ernie Pyle Club (journalism), 3 years (president, 3rd year)
Student Union, 3 years
American Civil Liberties Union, college branch, 3 years (sec-
retary, 2nd year)

EXPERIENCE
Reporter, full time, *Langsberg Post,* 2 months (and at pres-
ent)
Reporter, part time, *Langsberg Post,* 2 years (while in col-
lege)
Co-editor, Higdon College *Gimlet,* senior year
Reporter, Higdon College *Gimlet,* sophomore and junior
years
Reporter, Evansburg High School paper, 4 years

REFERENCES
Mr. Joseph Darnell, Editor
*Langsberg Post*
Langsberg, Pa. 19239

Professor Robert Meers, Head
English Department
Higdon College
Anvers, Pa. 15721

Dean J. J. Flowers
Higdon College
Anvers, Pa. 15721

**EXERCISES**

**1.** Identify the conventional parts of the letter form in
Model B on p. 273.

**2.** Is the choice of complimentary close in this letter
appropriate to its salutation? Explain.

**3.**  Address an envelope (any suitably sized rectangle will serve for practice) for Model C, following the letter pattern and including your return.

**4.**  Practice folding a standard sheet of typing paper and inserting it properly into a small business envelope; into a large business envelope. Repeat these operations until you can do them smoothly and correctly without pausing to think.

**5.**  Point out all the errors you can discover in this letter form.

June 17, 1975
145 Glassell Ave.
Syracuse, New York

Brandon Brothers,
  1818 Dover Street
    Pullman, Washington.


    Dear sir,


. . . . . . . . . . . . . . . . . . . . . . . .



Yours Truly

Mabel Saunders.

**6.**  The following requirements are stated generally, instead of being given in the form of specific problems, so that you can choose subjects you are really interested in, some real-life situations for which you are writing actual letters, instead of merely going through the motions of a classroom exercise.

1.  Write a letter inquiring about vacation tours, resort accommodations, services offered, goods for sale—to any actual business firm from whom you would really be interested in getting information. (Look through the current issue of a popular magazine for suggestions.)

2.  Write a letter ordering merchandise, repairs, tickets —anything that you would actually like to have from an actual firm with a real address.

3.  Write a letter complaining about any unsatisfactory goods or services (repairs, transportation, and the like) that you have recently had the misfortune to encounter.

4.  Write a letter replying to a classified ad in your local paper, in which you apply for a position that you are actually qualified to fill.

5.  Write a letter applying for part-time or summer work at some place where you know there is an opening in some line of work of which you are capable.

6.  Write a letter of application, accompanied by a data sheet, applying for the position that you think you would like when you get out of college. Direct it to an actual firm by whom you would like to be employed.

# APPENDIXES

# GLOSSARY OF GRAMMATICAL TERMS

Four types of cross-references are included in order to tie the material in this Glossary to the rest of the text:

1. References to the Chart of Pronouns, the Chart of Verb Forms, and Tenses are to tables in the appendixes following this Glossary.
2. References to words and phrases *(Voice, Adverb clause,* etc.) are to terms defined and illustrated elsewhere in this Glossary.
3. References to abbreviations followed by page numbers *V v* (p. 158), *A p* (p. 140), etc.—are to sections in the main body of the text that are labeled with these symbols.
4. References to page numbers alone (p. 123, etc.) are to other related areas in the text.

**Active voice.**   See *Voice, V v* (p. 158), and p. 111.

**Adjective.**   The part of speech that modifies a noun by limiting (*ten* cents, *several* people) or describing it (*green* book, *noisy* traffic). See *Demonstrative adjective, Possessive adjective, Predicate adjective, Degree, Com* (p. 167), and p. 112.

**Adjective clause.**   A group of words containing a subject and a predicate but used in the sentence as a dependent unit modifying a noun. Adjective clauses are usually introduced by relative pronouns (*who, which, that*), sometimes by subordinating conjunctions (*when, where*).

Those *who came to cheer* remained on the spot *where he disappeared.*

See *Dependent clause* and p. 113.

**Adjective phrase.** See *Prepositional phrase, Participial phrase, Infinitive phrase.*

**Adverb.** The part of speech that modifies a verb, adjective, or other adverb by telling how (look *carefully*), when (come *soon*), where (sit *down*), or to what degree (*exceptionally* strong, *very* capably). Adverbs are usually adjectives to which *ly* has been added (*quick* action, acted *quickly*) but not always (did *well,* ran *fast*), and not all words ending in *ly* are adverbs (*lonely* spot, *friendly* people). See *Degree, Com* (p. 167), and p. 112.

**Adverb clause.** A group of words containing a subject and a predicate but used in the sentence as a dependent unit modifying a verb, adjective, or adverb. Adverb clauses may be introduced by a great variety of subordinating conjunctions.

We hastily called a taxi *because the car wouldn't start.* (Tells why about *called.*)

See *Dependent clause, Subordinating conjunction,* and p. 113–114.

**Adverb phrase.** See *Prepositional phrase, Infinitive phrase.*

**Adverbial conjunction.** A word that has an adverbial idea but does not modify another word in the sentence as an adverb would. It has the value of a conjunction, rather, being used as a transitional connective between sentences or independent clauses; but being weaker, it requires stronger punctuation. See *Ps* (pp. 198–199).

His life at home was unhappy; *therefore* he decided to run away.
His life at home was unhappy. *Therefore* he decided to run away.

Like other adverbs and unlike other conjunctions, the conjunctive adverb may be moved around in the sentence:

His life at home was unhappy; he decided, *therefore,* to run away.

Other common adverbial conjunctions are *however, also, consequently, yet, then, moreover, thus, nevertheless.*

**Agreement.** Correspondence between a verb and its subject in number and person, and between a pronoun and its andecedent in number, person, and gender. See *A p* (p. 140), *A V* (p. 136).

*Jack has* an assistant; *we have* none. (Verb *has* is singular number, third person, to agree with subject *Jack;* verb *have* is plural number, first person, to agree with subject *we.*)

*Mary* lost *her* ring while *she* was swimming. (Pronouns *her* and *she* are third person, singular number, feminine gender, to agree with antecedent *Mary.*

**Antecedent.**   A noun or pronoun to which a pronoun that takes its place refers. See *A p* (p. 140).

Jim is wearing his parka, the one that he had in the Army. (*Jim* is the antecedent of *his* and *he, parka* of *one, one* of *that*).

**Appositive.**   A noun immediately following another noun to rename or explain it (the singer *Dylan;* "Greensleeves," a *ballad*). See *C* (p. 144) and p. 117.

**Article.**   One of three small words (*a, an, the*) used to announce nouns. The definite article *the* indicates one or more particular things (*the* briefcase, *the* papers). The indefinite articles indicate one of a class; *a* is used before the sound of a consonant (*a* book, *a* hand), *an* before the sound of a vowel (*an* article, *an* hour—the consonant *h* is silent). See p. 110.

**Auxiliary verb.**   See *Helping verb* and *V h* (p. 151).

**Case.**   The relationship of nouns, pronouns, and some adjectives to other words in the sentence, indicated by form and position. See *Nominative case, Objective case, Possessive case,* and *C* (p. 144).

**Clause.**   A group of words containing a subject and a predicate, used with one or more other clauses to make a compound or complex sentence. See *Independent clause, Dependent clause, Adjective clause, Adverb clause, Noun clause.*

**Collective noun.**   A noun that indicates a group (*crowd, family*). It is usually singular, requiring singular verbs and pronouns (Our *team wins* all *its* games), but it is considered plural if the individuals are implied rather than the group (The team *go* to take *their showers*). See *A v,* p. 138.

**Common noun.**   See *Noun.*

**Comparative degree.**   See *Degree* and *Com* (p. 167).

**Complement.**   A word that completes a predicate. See *Subject complement, Object complement.*

**Complete predicate.**   See *Predicate.*

**Complete subject.**   See *Subject.*

**Complex sentence.** A sentence made up of one independent clause and one or more dependent clauses. See *SV c* (p. 119) and p. 113.

Because I had lost my wallet, I had no way to pay my fare.

**Complex-complex sentence.** A sentence made up of an independent clause and one or more dependent clauses which in turn contain one or more dependent clauses. See p. 114.

[1] My wallet disappeared [2] because I had been careless [3] when I pocketed it. (Clause 2 is an adverb clause modifying the verb *disappeared* in clause 1, the independent clause; and its predicate adjective *careless* is in turn modified by clause 3, another adverb clause.)

**Compound.** A construction containing two or more grammatically equal parts, such as nouns (dogs and cats), verbs (read and think), and clauses. See *Compound sentence* and p. 113.

**Compound sentence.** A sentence made up of two or more independent clauses whose connection is indicated by a coordinating conjunction or by punctuation. See *SV c* (p. 119) and p. 113.

My wallet had disappeared, *and* I had no way to pay my fare.

My wallet had disappeared; I had no way to pay my fare. (See *P s* 1, p. 198.)

**Compound-complex sentence.** A sentence made up of two or more independent clauses and one or more dependent clauses. See p. 114.

Because I had been careless, my wallet had disappeared, and I had no way to pay my fare. (Dependent, independent, independent)

**Conjunction.** The part of speech that serves as a connecting word, indicating the relationship between two or more similar sentence elements. See *Coordinating conjunction, Subordinating conjunction, Adverbial conjunction, Correlative conjunction,* and p. 113.

**Conjunctive adverb.** See *Adverbial conjunction.*

**Coordinating conjunction.** A conjunction that connects two or more grammatically similar parts: words, phrases, or clauses. These conjunctions are *and, but, or, nor.*

The teacher *and* the students laughed, *but* I wept. (*And* connects two nouns; *but,* two independent clauses.)

Compare *Correlative conjunction* and *Subordinating conjunction,* and see p. 113.

**Correlative conjunction.** Coordinating conjunctions always used in pairs to connect equal grammatical parts: *either . . . or, neither . . . nor, not only . . . but also, both . . . and, whether . . . or.*

*Not only* children *but also* adults learned *both* to read *and* to write. (Two pairs of correlative conjunctions.)

**Declarative sentence.** See *Sentence.*

**Definite article.** See *Article.*

**Degree.** A property of adjectives and adverbs indicating different levels of the quality named:

1. *Positive* degree states the quality (*easy* problem).
2. *Comparative* degree compares one thing with another (an *easier* problem than this).
3. *Superlative* degree shows one thing to be superior in that quality to two or more (the *easiest* problem of the three, or of all.)

The comparative and superlative degrees are formed by adding *er* and *est,* respectively, to the positive, in words of one syllable (nice, nicer, nicest). For words of three or more syllables, the positive is preceded by *more* and *most* (beautiful, *more* beautiful, *most* beautiful). For words of two syllables, use the form that sounds the better (noble, nobler, noblest; languid, more languid, most languid). Adverbs show degree as adjectives do, save that they are more likely to require *more* and *most* because they so often end with an extra syllable (fast, faster, fastest; but rapidly, more rapidly, most rapidly). A few words are irregular (good, better, best; bad, worse, worst); consult your dictionary. See *Com* (p. 167).

**Demonstrative adjective.** The same form as a demonstrative pronoun (see *Demonstrative pronoun*), but the adjective modifies a noun or pronoun instead of taking its place. Compare:

*This* book is my Shakespeare; *that* is hers. (Adjective, pronoun)

**Demonstrative pronoun.** A pronoun that points out: *this* (singular), *these* (plural)—near; *that* and *those*—far. The antecedent may be expressed, or implied in the pointing.

*These* are my skis; *those* are yours.

Compare *Demonstrative adjective*.

**Dependent clause.** A group of words that contains a subject and a predicate but does not by itself make a complete statement. Joined with an independent clause, however, it becomes part of a complex sentence. See *Adjective clause, Adverb clause, Noun clause, Independent clause, Complex sentence,* and pp. 113–114.

**Descriptive adjective.** See *Adjective*.

**Direct object.** See *Object of verb, Indirect object*.

**Emphatic tense.** See *Tense* and the Chart of Verb Forms.

**Exclamatory sentence.** See *Sentence*.

**Feminine gender.** See *Gender*.

**First person.** See *Person*.

**Future tense.** See *Tense* and the Chart of Verb Forms.

**Future perfect tense.** See *Tense* and the Chart of Verb Forms.

**Gender.** A grammatical property of nouns and pronouns indicating sex. Unlike many other languages, in which sexless objects may be designated as grammatically masculine or feminine, English has *natural* gender, which causes relatively little trouble. *Masculine* gender denotes males (That *man,* an *actor,* is known for *his* character roles.); *feminine* gender denotes females (That *woman,* an *actress,* is known for *her* Broadway successes.); *neuter* gender denotes all things sexless (The *newspaper* was here; I must have mislaid *it*.); *Common* gender denotes unspecified sex (The *person* with the *child* and the *cat* is here.). This last gives the most difficulty, arising from the problem of what pronouns should follow. See *A p 3* (pp. 142–143).

**Gerund.** A verb form (usually ending in *-ing* or *-ed*) used as a noun. See *Verbal,* p. 116, and Tenses.

**Gerund phrase.** A gerund with its modifiers, object, or complement. See *Verbal* and p. 116.

**Helping verb.** An auxiliary verb form used with other verbs to effect their changes in tense (*have* gone), voice (*was* sent), and mode. Common helping verbs are *shall* (*should*), *will* (*would*), *may* (*might*), *can* (*could*), *must*. See *V t* (p. 155), *V v* (p. 158), *V m* (p. 159), *V h* (p. 151), *Tense,* and the Chart of Verb Forms.

**Imperative mood.** See *Mood* and *SV t* (p. 118).

**Imperative sentence.** See *Sentence*.

**Indefinite article.** See *Article*.

**Indefinite pronoun.** A pronoun that refers to someone or something not specified. See *Ap 1* (p. 141) and *R* (pp. 150–151).

*Something* is wrong; can't *anyone* explain?

**Independent clause.** A group of words containing a subject and a predicate and capable of standing alone, but acting as part of a compound or complex sentence.

I wanted to go. But I didn't. (Two sentences)
I wanted to go, but I didn't. (One compound sentence with two independent clauses)

Compare *Dependent clause, Adjective clause, Adverb clause, Noun clause,* and p. 113.

**Indicative mood.** See *Mood.*

**Indirect object.** A noun or pronoun that stands between the verb and the direct object (see *Object of verb*) and names what the action of the verb is being done to or for:

Do *me* a favor. (Compare "Do a favor *for* me," in which *me* is the object of a preposition.)
He gave the *stone* a kick.

See p. 111.

**Infinitive.** A verb form (usually preceded by *to*) used as an adjective, adverb, or noun. See *Verbal,* p. 116, and Tenses.

**Infinitive phrase.** An infinitive with its modifiers, complement, and even subject. See *Verbal* and pp. 116–117.

**Interjection.** The part of speech that is structurally independent of the sentence. It is exclamatory, ranging from a mild introductory word (*Oh,* I doubt it) to a strong exclamation (*Ugh!* how nasty it smells!). See p. 118.

**Interrogative pronoun.** A pronoun used to ask a question (*who, which, what*):

*Who* is there? *What* do you want?

These pronouns may also be used interrogatively as adjectives:

*Whose* book is this? *What* number do you want?

See the Chart of Pronouns.

**Interrogative sentence.** See *Sentence.*

**Intransititve verb.** See *Verb.*

**Irregular adjective, adverb.** One whose degrees are not formed according to the normal patterns of *-er, -est,* and *more, most* (*bad, worse, worst; well, better, best*). See *Degree,* and consult your dictionary.

**Irregular verb.** One whose past and past participle are not formed according to the normal pattern of adding *-ed* (*see, saw,* *seen*).    See *Principal parts of verbs,* the Chart of Verb Forms, *V p* (p. 153), and consult your dictionary.

**Limiting adjective.**  See *Adjective.*

**Linking verb.**  See *Verb.*

**Main clause.**  See *Independent clause.*

**Masculine gender.**  See *Gender.*

**Mode.**  See *Mood.*

**Modifier.**  See *Adjective, Adjective clause, Adverb, Adverb clause, Prepositional phrase, Participial phrase, Infinitive phrase,* and p. 112–114.

**Mood (mode).**  One of the several attitudes expressed by verbs. The *indicative* mood expresses a statement or a question:

I *was* in Florida. *Were* you there?

The *subjunctive* mood expresses a wish or a condition contrary to fact.

I wish I *were* in Florida; if I *were* you, I should go.
I move that the nominations *be* closed.

The *imperative* mood expresses a command:

*Come* with me. *Step* lively.

See *V m* (p. 159).

**Neuter gender.**  See *Gender.*

**Nominative absolute.**  A phrase consisting of a noun or pronoun modified by a participle and grammatically independent of the rest of the sentence, although adding to its meaning. See p. 117.

My *work being done,* I took a shower and changed my clothes.

**Nominative case.**  The case of a noun or pronoun used as the subject of a sentence or in related positions.

*Subject:* The *bus* came, and *we* boarded quickly.
*Subject complement* (predicate nominative): My brother is an *aviator;* this is *he.*
*Nominative absolute: Bill* having left and *I* now working alone, production fell off sharply.
*Nominative of address. Jimmy*—hey, *you*—come here!
*Appositive* following nominative case: The arrested suspect was Gordon, my *companion;* the real culprit—*I*—went unnoticed.

See *Objective case, Possessive case,* and *C* (p. 144).

**Nominative of address.**   A word that indicates the person being spoken to. It may appear anywhere in the sentence. See p. 117.

The question is, *Ronald,* whether you believe him or not.
*Waiter!* bring me another cup of coffee.

**Noun.**   The part of speech that names a person (policeman), place (street), object (motorcycle), concept (speed). These examples are all common nouns, which name one or more of a group, and are not capitalized. Proper nouns, which name a particular, are always capitalized (Officer Osborne, Main Street, Honda). See *Sp c* (p. 92).

**Noun clause.**   A group of words containing a subject and a predicate but used in the sentence as a single unit in some noun position. It is easily identified as a noun use by substituting the words *somebody* or *something.*

*Whoever wants a ticket* should apply early. (*Somebody* should—subject)
They told me *what I wanted to know.* (Told me *something*—direct object)

See *Dependent clause* and *Pc 4* (p. 193).

**Noun phrase.**   A group of proper nouns having a single meaning and used as a single noun.

*George Washington Carver* worked at *Tuskegee Institute.*

(Other words accompanying common nouns are modifying adjectives, not part of a noun phrase—*bush* pilot, *gentleman* farmer.) See *Gerund phrase, Infinitive phrase.*

**Number.**   A grammatical property of nouns, pronouns, and verbs, the singular number indicating one, the plural indicating any number beyond one. See *A v* (p. 136) and *A p* (p. 140).

*He carries his coat* in front of *him.*
*They carry their coats* in front of *them.*

**Object complement.**   A noun or adjective that follows a direct object and renames it or modifies it to complete its meaning. See p. 111.

We chose Mr. Grant our *director.*
The Winthrops have painted their house *gray.*

**Object of preposition.**   A noun or pronoun that follows a preposition and is related by it to some other word in the sentence. See *Preposition* and p. 113.

He gave me the news *of* the day. (*Day* is related by *of* to noun *news.*)
Sit down *on* this *chair*. (*Chair* is related by *on* to verb *sit.*)

**Object of verb** (direct object).   A noun or pronoun that receives the action of the predicate.

My father built our *house;* a tornado destroyed it. (*House* received the action of building; *it,* of destroying.

**Objective case.**   The case of a noun or pronoun used as an object word or in related positions, or as the subject of an infinitive (this last is the only subject in the objective case; see *Verbal* 3).

*Direct object of verb:* I dropped my *glasses* as a thought suddenly struck *me.*
*Indirect object:* Give *yourself* a swift kick and do *us* a favor.
*Object complement:* The class chose Susan *queen* of the carnival.
*Object of preposition:* The card is on the *table;* give it to *her.*
*Appositive* following objective case: They called my uncle, a *doctor*, who came to revive the unconscious man—*me.*

See *Nominative case, Possessive case,* and *C* (p. 144).
**Part of speech.**   Any of the eight groups into which all our words are traditionally classified according to their grammatical functions in the sentence. These groups consist of three statement words, two modifiers, two connectives, and one exclamation. See *Noun, Pronoun, Verb; Adjective, Adverb; Preposition, Conjunction; Interjection.* See also pp. 109–118. Many words may function as more than one part of speech, but we can readily tell which by the use in the sentence. Take the word *down,* for example:

*Noun:* The team has made a first *down.*
*Verb:* I usually *down* my opponent within three minutes.
*Adjective:* I prefer a *down* sleeping bag.
*Adverb:* I can't get him to come *down.*
*Preposition:* He swaggered *down* the street.

**Participial phrase.**   A participle with its modifiers, object, or complement, used in the sentence as a single adjective. See *Verbal* and p. 116.

**Participle.**   A verb form (usually ending in *-ing* or *-ed*) used as an adjective. See *Verbal,* p. 116, the Chart of Verb Forms, and Tenses.

**Passive voice.**   See *Voice, V v* (p. 158), and p. 111.

**Past principal part.**   See *Principal part of verb* and the Chart of Verb Forms.

**Past perfect tense.**   See *Tense* and the Chart of Verb Forms.

**Past tense.**   See *Tense* and the Chart of Verb Forms.

**Person.**   A grammatical property of pronouns and verbs indicating one of the three roles in the process of communication.

*First person* denotes those speaking:

*I* did the work; *we* all got the credit.

*Second person* denotes those spoken to:

*You* did the work; *you* should get the credit.

*Third person* denotes those spoken of:

*He* did the work; *they* shouldn't get the credit.

Nouns do not, strictly speaking, have person in English, since they do not change form, but being spoken of, they are commonly regarded as third person for purposes of agreement. A verb changes only in the third person singular, where it regularly adds *s*:

I speak, you speak, he speaks; we speak, you speak, they speak.

See the Chart of Pronouns, *A v* (p. 136), and *A p* (p. 140).

**Personal pronoun.**   A pronoun that indicates one of the three grammatical *persons,* in all genders, numbers, and cases (she, they, me, etc.) See the Chart of Pronouns and *R* (p. 148).

**Phrase.**   A group of related words without subject or predicate, used as a single grammatical unit. There are several kinds, known by their distinguishing words. See *Prepositional phrase, Participial phrase, Gerund phrase, Infinitive phrase, Noun phrase, Verb phrase,* and pp. 112–113, 116–117.

**Plural.**   See *Number, A v* (p. 136), and *A p* (p. 140).

**Positive degree.**   See *Degree.*

**Possessive adjective.**   A special form of a noun or pronoun used in the possessive case (see *Possessive case*) as a modifier of a noun to show possession. Nouns add *'s* to the singular, the apostrophe alone to the plural (the *company's* profit, the *companies'* profits. Personal pronouns, having special possessive forms (see the Chart of Pronouns) never take the apostrophe (*his* weight, *their* excuse). See *Sp a* (p. 96).

**Possessive case.** The case of a noun or pronoun used as an adjective to show possession (*Harry's* car, *their* street, *my friend's* house). Personal pronouns have special possessive forms not used as adjectives (see the last column in the Chart of Pronouns) but as pronouns in their own right; therefore they are not in possessive but in nominative or objective positions:

The fault is *mine.* (Compare "It is *my* fault.")

An appositive following the possessive case must also be possessive:

I am taking care of the Dexters' our *neighbors',* dog.
That is the boss's—*my*—responsibility.

See *Nominative case, Objective case,* and *C* (pp. 145–147).

**Possessive pronoun.** A pronoun that shows possession but appears in a nominative or objective position.

*Mine* is the one on the left of *yours.* (Subject, object of preposition)

See the Chart of Pronouns.

**Predicate.** A verb or verb phrase that makes a statement about the noun or pronoun that is its subject. See p. 110.

The baby *cried.*
The grass *has been growing* fast.

The verbs above are *simple predicates,* as in "The wind *blew.*" The simple predicate with any modifiers, objects, or complements is the *complete predicate.*

The wind *blew furiously from the north across the open space in front of our house trailer.*

**Predicate adjective.** An adjective that follows the predicate (a linking verb) as a subject complement but modifies the preceding subject. See p. 112.

The Townsends are *healthy.* (Healthy Townsends; compare "The Townsends are a *healthy family.*")
The weather is becoming very *pleasant.* (Pleasant weather)

**Predicate noun** (predicate nominative). A noun or pronoun that follows the predicate (a linking verb) as a subject complement and means the same as the subject. See p. 112.

Our biology instructor is a *woman;* that is *she.*

**Preposition.** The part of speech that shows the relationship between a following noun or pronoun (its object) and some other word in the sentence. Note the different relationships between the noun *desk* and the verb *will find* in the following:

You will find my dictionary (on, in, under, above, beside) my desk.

Prepositions are sometimes compound:

He went *out of* the house.

Do not confuse a preposition, which must stay put in its phrase, with an adverb, which can be moved around:

I put *down* the book = I put the book *down.* (Adverb, not preposition. *Book* remains the object of the verb *put* in both arrangements.)

Distinguish also between the preposition *to,* whose object will be a noun, and the sign of the infinitive *to,* which will be followed by a verb:

I went *to* town *to* shop. (First *to,* preposition; second, sign of infinitive.)

See *Prepositional phrase* and p. 113.
**Prepositional phrase.** A preposition with its object and any modifiers, forming a single unit and used as an adjective or an adverb. See *Preposition* and p. 113.

I like the picture *on the wall.* (Adjective—which picture)
I hung the picture *on the wall.* (Adverb—where hung)

**Present perfect tense.** See *Tense* and the Chart of Verb Forms.
**Present principal part.** See *Principal part of verb* and the Chart of Verb Forms.
**Present tense.** See *Tense* and the Chart of Verb Forms.
**Principal clause.** See *Independent clause.*
**Principal part of verb.** One of the four forms from which all tenses (see *Tense*) are formed.

| Present | Present Participle | Past | Past Participle |
|---------|--------------------|------|-----------------|
| look | looking | looked | looked |
| fall | falling | fell | fallen |

All verbs form the present participle with *ing* added to the present. Regular verbs like *look* form the past and the past participle by adding *ed*. *Fall* is only one of a number of irregular verbs, whose parts a dictionary will supply. See the Chart of Verb Forms.

**Progressive tense.**   See *Tense* and the Chart of Verb Forms.

**Pronoun.**   The part of speech that takes the place of a noun, avoiding its repetition.

The sheriff put *his* gun in *its* holster and *he* set out.

See *Personal pronoun, Reflexive pronoun, Interrogative pronoun, Demonstrative pronoun, Indefinite pronoun, Possessive pronoun*, and the Chart of Pronouns.

**Proper noun.**   See *Noun*.

**Reflexive pronoun.**   A combination of certain personal pronouns with the word *self* (singular) or *selves* (plural). It has two uses:

1. To repeat after a verb the idea of the subject.

I hurt *myself.* (Object)
He is *himself* again. (Predicate nominative)
The Harveys have bought *themselves* a new car. (Indirect object)

2. To intensify the idea of a preceding noun or pronoun.

I *myself* wrote the letter. (Appositive)
I admire my father for having built our house by *himself.* (Object of preposition)

The reflexive is popularly but not yet preferably used without a preceding personal pronoun:

He is going with John and *myself.* (Preferably "John and *me*")

See the Chart of Pronouns and *R 7* (p. 151).

**Regular adjective, adverb.**   One that forms its degrees according to the conventional patterns. See *Degree*.

**Regular verb.**   One whose past and past participle end in *ed,* the usual pattern. See *Principal part of verbs* and the Chart of Verb Forms.

**Relative clause.**   See *Adjective clause.*

**Relative pronoun.**   A pronoun that relates to the rest of the sentence the dependent clause (adjective or noun) that it introduces, and that has a use (subject, object, or complement) within its own clause. *Who, which,* and *that* usually have antecedents that they should follow as directly as possible. *What* and the compound forms *whatever, whoever,* and *whichever* are indefinite relative pronouns and have no antecedents. See the Chart of Pronouns, *Subordinating conjunctions,* and p. 114.

> It was a mystery *that* puzzled us all. (Adjective clause; antecedent of *that,* the subject of *puzzled,* is *mystery.*)
> I don't care *what he* says about it. (Noun clause; *what* has no antecedent, but is the object of *says,* placed at the beginning of the clause so that it can "relate.")

**Second person.**   See *Person.*

**Sentence.**   A group of words containing as a minimum a subject (even if only understood) and a predicate, and making an intelligible statement. The sentence always begins with a capital letter; terminal punctuation depends on its kind, of which there are four:

> *Declarative*—makes a statement: Time is running short.
> *Interrogative*—asks a question: Can you get away today?
> *Imperative*—gives a command: Don't shout at me.
> *Exclamatory*—shows strong feeling: How I wish I could go!

An interrogative or an exclamatory sentence may be declarative in form, the purpose of questioning or exclaiming being indicated by punctuation only:

> I must go tomorrow. (Declarative)
> I must go tomorrow? (Interrogative)
> I must go tomorrow! (Exclamatory)

See *SV t* (p. 118). For kinds of sentences according to structure, see *Simple sentence, Compound sentence, Complex sentence, Compound-complex sentence, Complex-complex sentence,* and *SV c* (p. 119).

**Simple predicate.**   See Predicate.

**Simple sentence.**   A sentence containing only one subject and one predicate, no matter how many other words may attend them.

> *Oil lubricates.*
> *One* of his worst problems *has* always *been* heavy drinking.

Either the subject or the predicate or both may be compound, however:

> *Candy* and *flowers* are traditional gifts. (Compound subject)
> Candy *is* fattening and *costs a lot.* (Compound predicate)
> *Candy* and *flowers are* expensive but *give* pleasure. (Compound subject and predicate, but still a simple sentence. Compare *Compound sentence.*)

**Simple subject.**   See *Subject.*
**Simple tense.**   One of the six regular tenses. See *Tense,* the Chart of Verb Forms, and *V t* (p. 155).
**Singular.**   See *Number, A v* (p. 136), and *A p* (p. 140).
**Statement word.**   A noun or pronoun about which a statement is made (this is the subject of the sentence), or a verb, which makes the statement (this is the predicate). See p. 110.

> The *clerk argued,* but *I won.* (Noun, verb, pronoun, verb)

**Subject.**   The noun or pronoun about which a verb makes a statement, together with any modifiers. The noun or pronoun alone is the *simple subject;* the simple subject with its modifiers, if any, is the *complete subject.* See pp. 110, 115.

> The books needed for my current courses are expensive. (*Books* is the simple subject. *The books needed for my current courses* is the complete subject. In the sentence "Books are expensive," *books* is both the simple and the complete subject.)

**Subject complement.**   A word that follows a predicate (a linking verb) and refers to the subject. If a noun, it is a *predicate noun* (*predicate nominative*), meaning the same as the subject. See p. 112.

> My sister is a *nurse.*

If an adjective, it is a *predicate adjective,* modifying the subject.

> My sister is *beautiful.*

**Subjunctive mood.**   See *Mood.*
**Subordinate clause.**   See *Dependent clause.*
**Subordinating conjunction.**   A conjunction that connects a dependent (subordinate) clause to an independent one. These conjunctions may be recognized by the fact that the clauses they introduce do not read as complete statements, but act as nouns, adjectives, or adverbs. Noun clauses may be introduced by relative

pronouns as well; these not only connect but have a place in the structure of the clause.

> I am surprised *that* he is willing to go. (Subordinating conjunction)
> I wonder *who* will be elected. (Relative pronoun, subject of the dependent clause as well as serving as a connective)

Adjective clauses are usually introduced by relative pronouns, but occasionally by the subordinating conjunctions *when* and *where*.

> This is a celebrity *whom* I have met. (Relative pronoun, direct object in the dependent clause)
> This is the place *where* I met him. (Subordinating conjunction)

Adverb clauses are always introduced by subordinating conjunctions, of which there are a large number indicating various relationships. Some are compound.

> *Time:* I came *after* he had gone. (Also *when, whenever, while, before, since, as, as . . . as, until*)
> *Place:* I went *where* he told me to. (Also *wherever*)
> *Manner:* I jumped *as if* I had been shot. (Also *as, as . . . as, as though*)
> *Reason:* I went *because* it was my duty. (Also *as, since, for, why, in that, inasmuch as*)
> *Evidence:* He is here, *for* I hear his whistle.
> *Condition:* I will go *if* you will pay my way. (Also *unless, provided that*)
> *Concession:* I started out, *although* I didn't want to. (Also *though, whether, even if*)
> *Comparison:* He is *as* strong *as* an ox [is strong]. (Also *as, so . . . as*)
> *Purpose:* They died *so that* we might live. (Also *that, in order that*)
> *Result:* He was *so* popular *that* he was elected president. (Also *so, that, so that, such . . . that*)

Familiarize yourself with these possibilities for varying your sentence structure. See *Relative pronoun, Adverb clause, Noun clause, Adjective clause,* and p. 113.

**Superlative degree.**   See *Degree* and *Com* (pp. 167–168).

**Tense.**   The indication of time through changes in verb forms. There are six simple tenses in English, all formed from the four principal parts of verbs. See *Principal part of verb, V t* (p. 155), and for the parts of irregular verbs, your dictionary.

*Present* (happens at present)—use the present part:

I *go* immediately.

*Past* (happened in the past)—use the past part:

I *went* yesterday.

*Future* (will happen in the future)—use the helping verb *shall* or *will* with the present part:

I *shall* go tomorrow.

*Present perfect* (begun in the past but not perfected—finished— until the present)—use the present tense of the helping verb *have* with the past participle:

I *have gone* every Sunday for ten years.

*Past perfect* (perfected—finished—before a certain time in the past) —use the past tense of the helping verb *have* with the past participle:

I *had gone* before he came.

*Future perfect* (to be perfected—finished—before a certain time in the future)—use the helping verbs *shall* or *will* and *have* with the past participle:

I *shall have gone* before the letter will reach him.

There is a comparable set of six progressive tenses. These indicate a continuing rather than a limited verb statement. They are formed with the appropriate tense of the helping verb *be* and the present participle: I *am going,* I *was going,* I *shall be going,* I *have been going,* I *had been going,* I *shall have been going,* etc. In addition, to stress the statement of the verb, there are emphatic tenses, but only two of them, present and past. These are formed with the helping verbs *do* and *did* and the present principal part: I *do wish* to go, for he *did promise* that he would be there. For a full run of all tenses, see the Chart of Verb Forms, Tenses, and *V t* (p. 155).

**Third person.**   See *Person.*

**Transitive verb.**   See *Verb.*

**Verb.**   The part of speech that makes a statement about the noun or pronoun that is its subject by expressing various kinds and degrees of action and various states of being.

1. Action verbs (see p. 110)

*Transitive:* I *opened* the door. (*Opened* has an object, *door.*)
*Intransitive:* The diamonds *sparkled* on the tray. (*Sparkled* has no object.)

The same verb may be transitive or intransitive depending on whether or not it has an object. See *V ti* (p. 154).

The chauffeur *drove* a limousine. (Transitive—object is *limousine.*)
The chauffeur *drove* carefully. (Intransitive—no object.)

2. Linking verbs (see p. 112)

My father *is* an electrician. (*Is* indicates state of being, not action, and links the subject complement—a predicate nominative—*electrician* with the subject *father*, which means the same person.)
The music *sounds* cheerful. (*Sounds* links the subject complement —a predicate adjective—with the subject *music*, which it describes.)

Other common linking verbs are *become, grow, appear, look, smell, taste, feel.* These must be followed by adjectives (but not adverbs, which follow action verbs).

He *seemed thoughtful.* (Adjective after linking verb).
He *strolled thoughtfully.* (Adverb after action verb)

3. Some verbs can be used as either linking or action verbs, but with different meanings.

He *looked neat.* (State of looking—appearing; adjective needed.)
He *looked searchingly* at the map. (Action of looking—gazing; adverb needed.)

See *Helping verb, Mood, Principal part of verb, Tense, Voice.*
   **Verb phrase.**   A main verb with its helping verbs, used as a predicate. See *V h* (p. 151) and the Chart of Verb Forms.

I *shall be leaving* soon.

   **Verbal.**   A verb form used as another part of speech. Verbals do not make statements, as predicates do, but they do have limited tense changes and may be modified by adverbs and take objects like verbs. They are used, however, singly and in phrases, as adjectives, adverbs, and nouns. There are three kinds. See p. 116.

1. *Participles:* The present, past, and perfect participles (see Tenses) may be used as adjectives, either to modify a noun directly (*running* water) or from other positions in the sentence (most often at the beginning, from which it must modify the following subject—see *DM,* p. 160).

   *Running* down the stairs, the boy fell. (Modifies *boy*)
   The cattle, *having been run* by the dogs, stampeded. (Modifies cattle)

2. *Gerunds:* The present and past participles, used as nouns.

   *Running* is good exercise. (Subject of *is*)
   The ambulance was sent for the *injured.* (Object of preposition)

3. *Infinitives:* Verb forms (the present and perfect) usually introduced by *to,* and used as adjectives, adverbs, and nouns.

   I have an errand *to run.* (Adjective modifying noun *errand*)
   He went *to bargain.* (Adverb modifying verb *went*)
   *To have hesitated* would have been *to be lost.* (Nouns as subject and subject complement)
   He let me go. (The usual to is omitted but understood, following certain verbs.)

   **Verbal phrase.** A verbal (participle, gerund, or noun) with any modifiers, objects, or complements. The infinitive can even have a subject. See pp. 116–117.

   *Participial phrase: Driving his jalopy proudly down the street,* Jim waved to us all. (Adjective modifying *Jim. Driving,* the participle, has an object, *jalopy,* and is modified by the adverb *proudly* and the prepositional phrase *down the street* used as an adverb.)
   *Gerund phrase: Driving that truck over such rough roads* was a back-breaking job. (Subject of *was. Driving,* the gerund, has an object, *truck,* and is modified by the prepositional phrase *over such rough roads* used as an adverb.)
   *Infinitive phrase:* I don't want *him to drive his program roughshod over our hopes.* (Direct object of verb *do want. To drive,* the infiinitive, has a subject *him,* an object *program,* and is modified by the adverb *roughshod* and the prepositional phrase *over our hopes,* used as an adverb.)

   **Voice.** A property of transitive verbs only, indicating whether the subject is the doer of the action stated by the predicate or is the recipient of it. The passive is formed with the appropriate tense of the helping verb *be* and the past participle.

*Active voice:* I *paid* the bill.
*Passive voice:* The bill *was paid.*

See the Chart of Verb Forms, *V v* (p. 158), and p. 111.

## CHART OF PRONOUNS

| Kinds | Number | Person | Gender | NOMINA-TIVE | OBJEC-TIVE | POSSESSIVE Adjective | POSSESSIVE Pronoun |
|---|---|---|---|---|---|---|---|
| Personal | Singular | 1st | | I | me | my | mine |
| | | 2nd | | you | you | your | yours |
| | | 3rd | M | he | him | his | his |
| | | | F | she | her | her | hers |
| | | | N | it | it | its | its |
| | Plural | 1st | | we | us | our | ours |
| | | 2nd | | you | you | your | yours |
| | | 3rd | | they | them | their | theirs |
| Reflexive | Singular | 1st | | myself | | | |
| | | 2nd | | yourself | | | |
| | | 3rd | M | himself | | | |
| | | | F | herself | } No case change | | |
| | | | N | itself | | | |
| | | | | oneself | | | |
| | Plural | 1st | | ourselves | | | |
| | | 2nd | | yourselves | | | |
| | | 3rd | | themselves | | | |
| Relative Compound | Singular or plural | | | who | whom | whose | |
| | | | | whoever | whomever | whosever | |
| | | | | which | | | |
| | | | | whichever | | | |
| | | | | that | } No case change | | |
| | | | | what | | | |
| | | | | whatever | | | |
| Interrogative | Singular or plural | | | who | whom | whose | |
| | | | | whoever | whomever | whosever | |
| | | | | which | | | |
| | | | | whichever | } No case change | | |
| | | | | what | | | |
| | | | | whatever | | | |
| Demonstrative | Singular | | | this | | | |
| | | | | that | } No case change | | |
| | Plural | | | these | | | |
| | | | | those | | | |
| Indefinite | Singular | | | *one | | | |
| | | | | none | | | |
| | | | | *nobody | | | |
| | | | | nothing | | | |
| | | | | any | | | |
| | | | | *anyone | | | |
| | | | | *anybody | | | |
| | | | | anything | No case change except for those starred, which form possessives with 's, as singular nouns do. | | |
| | | | | *everyone | | | |
| | | | | *everybody | | | |
| | | | | everything | | | |
| | | | | some | | | |
| | | | | *someone | | | |
| | | | | *somebody | | | |
| | | | | something | | | |
| | | | | each | | | |
| | | | | either | | | |
| | | | | neither | | | |
| | Plural | | | all | | | |

## CHART OF VERB FORMS

### PRINCIPLE PARTS

| | PRESENT | PRESENT PARTICIPLE | PAST | PAST PARTICIPLE |
|---|---|---|---|---|
| **Regular Verb** | see | calling | called | called |
| **Irregular Verb** | call | seeing | saw | seen |

| Tense | Number | Person | Active Voice | Passive Voice |
|---|---|---|---|---|
| | | | SIMPLE | |
| Present | Singular | 1st | I call, see | am called, seen |
| | | 2nd | you call, see | are called, seen |
| | | 3rd | he calls, sees | is called, seen |
| | Plural | 1st | we call, see | are called, seen |
| | | 2nd | you call, see | are called, seen |
| | | 3rd | they call, see | are called, seen |
| Past | | | I called, saw | was called, seen |
| | | | you called, saw | were called, seen |
| | | | he called, saw | was called, seen |
| | | | we called, saw | were called, seen |
| | | | you called, saw | were called, seen |
| | | | they called, saw | were called, seen |
| Future | | | I shall call, see | shall be called, seen |
| | | | you will call, see | will be called, seen |
| | | | he will call, see | will be called, seen |
| | | | we shall call, see | shall be called, seen |
| | | | you will call, see | will be called, seen |
| | | | they will call, see | will be called, seen |
| Present Perfect | | | I have called, seen | have been called, seen |
| | | | you have called, seen | have been called, seen |
| | | | he has called, seen | has been called, seen |
| | | | we have called, seen | have been called, seen |
| | | | you have called, seen | have been called, seen |
| | | | they have called, seen | have been called, seen |
| Past Perfect | | | I had called, seen | had been called, seen |
| | | | You had called, seen | had been called, seen |
| | | | He had called, seen | had been called, seen |
| | | | We had called, seen | had been called, seen |
| | | | You had called, seen | had been called, seen |
| | | | They had called, seen | had been called, seen |
| Future Perfect | | | I shall have called, seen | shall have been called, seen |
| | | | You will have called, seen | will have been called, seen |
| | | | He will have called, seen | will have been called, seen |
| | | | We shall have called, seen | shall have been called, seen |
| | | | You will have called, seen | will have been called, seen |
| | | | They will have called, seen | will have been called, seen |
| | | | PROGRESSIVE (SUMMARY) | |
| Present | | | I am calling, seeing | am being called, seen |
| Past | | | I was calling, seeing | was being called, seen |
| Future | | | I shall be calling, seeing | |
| Present Perfect | | | I have been calling, seeing | |
| Past Perfect | | | I had been calling, seeing | |
| Future Perfect | | | I shall have been calling, seeing | |

## CHART OF VERB FORMS (Continued)

| Tense | Number | Person | Active Voice | Passive Voice |
|-------|--------|--------|--------------|---------------|

### EMPHATIC (SUMMARY)

| Tense | Active Voice |
|-------|--------------|
| Present | I do call, see |
| Past | I did call, see |

### VERBALS

| | Active Voice | Passive Voice |
|--|--------------|---------------|
| **Infinitives** | | |
| Present | to call, see | to be called, seen |
| Progressive | to be calling, seeing | — |
| Perfect | to have called, seen | to have been called, seen |
| Progressive | to have been calling, seeing | — |
| **Participles** | | |
| Present | calling, seeing | being called, seen |
| Past | — | called, seen |
| Perfect | having called, seen | having been called, seen |
| Progressive | having been calling, seeing | — |
| **Gerunds** | | |
| Present | calling, seeing | — |
| Past | — | called, seen |

### TENSES

| | Past Perfect | Past | Present Perfect | Present | Future Perfect | Future |
|--|--------------|------|-----------------|---------|----------------|--------|
| **SIMPLE** | had seen | saw | have seen | see | shall have seen | shall see |
| **PROGRESSIVE** | had been seeing | was seeing | have been seeing | am seeing | shall have been seeing | shall be seeing |
| **EMPHATIC** | — | did see | — | do see | — | — |

| | Simple | Progressive | Emphatic |
|--|--------|-------------|----------|
| **PRESENT** | I see him now. | I am seeing him daily. | I do see him, really. |
| **PAST** | I saw him yesterday. | I was seeing him regularly then. | I did see him, actually. |
| **FUTURE** | I shall see him tomorrow. | I shall be seeing him occasionally. | — |
| **PRESENT PERFECT** | I have seen him frequently. | I have been seeing him intermittently. | — |
| **PAST PERFECT** | I had seen him before you did. | I had been seeing him occasionally before he left. | — |
| **FUTURE PERFECT** | I shall have seen him before you will. | I shall have been seeing him often before you will. | — |

# AUTHORIZED TWO-LETTER ABBREVIATIONS FOR USE WITH ZIP CODE

| | | | | |
|---|---|---|---|---|
| Alaska | AK | Montana | MT |
| Alabama | AL | Nebraska | NB |
| Arizona | AZ | Nevada | NV |
| Arkansas | AR | New Hampshire | NH |
| California | CA | New Jersey | NJ |
| Canal Zone | CZ | New Mexico | NM |
| Colorado | CO | New York | NY |
| Connecticut | CT | North Carolina | NC |
| Delaware | DE | North Dakota | ND |
| District of Columbia | DC | Ohio | OH |
| Florida | FL | Oklahoma | OK |
| Georgia | GA | Oregon | OR |
| Guam | GU | Pennsylvania | PA |
| Hawaii | HI | Puerto Rico | PR |
| Idaho | ID | Rhode Island | RI |
| Illinois | IL | South Carolina | SC |
| Indiana | IN | South Dakota | SD |
| Iowa | IA | Tennessee | TN |
| Kansas | KS | Texas | TX |
| Kentucky | KY | Utah | UT |
| Louisiana | LA | Vermont | VT |
| Maine | ME | Virginia | VA |
| Maryland | MD | Virgin Islands | VI |
| Massachusetts | MA | Washington | WA |
| Michigan | MI | West Virginia | WV |
| Minnesota | MN | Wisconsin | WI |
| Mississippi | MS | Wyoming | WY |
| Missouri | MO | | |

# INDEX

This index locates terms appearing in the text. Grammatical terms appearing here, and others, are alphabetized, with definitions and illustrations, in the Glossary of Grammatical Terms, pp. 293–313.

76 77 78 7 6 5 4 3 2

JOURNAS

# SECTION SYMBOLS LISTED IN ORDER OF APPEARANCE